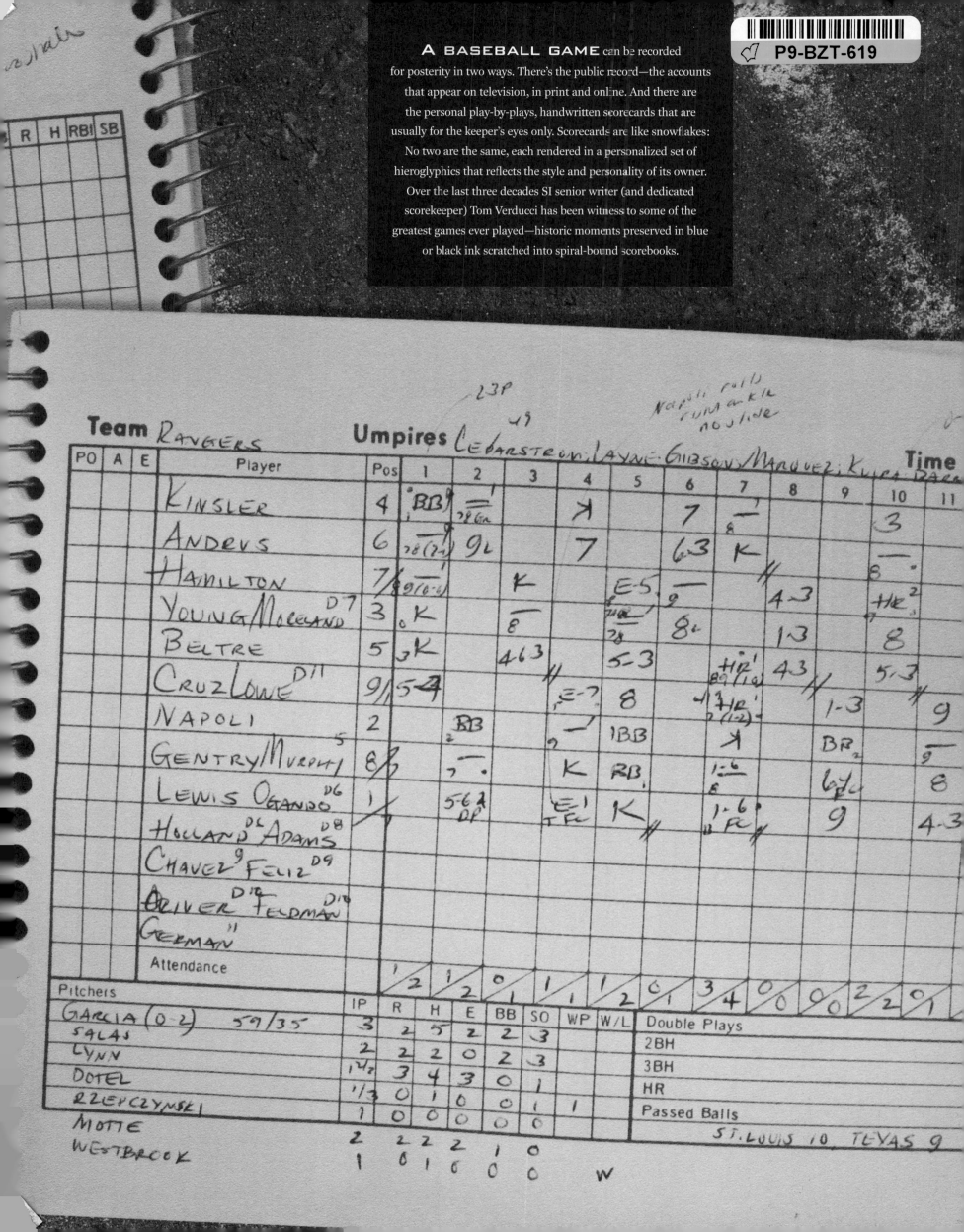

A BASEBALL GAME can be recorded for posterity in two ways. There's the public record—the accounts that appear on television, in print and online. And there are the personal play-by-plays, handwritten scorecards that are usually for the keeper's eyes only. Scorecards are like snowflakes: No two are the same, each rendered in a personalized set of hieroglyphics that reflects the style and personality of its owner. Over the last three decades SI senior writer (and dedicated scorekeeper) Tom Verducci has been witness to some of the greatest games ever played—historic moments preserved in blue or black ink scratched into spiral-bound scorebooks.

2001 World Series, Game 7

Few World Series have ended in such shocking fashion: Yankees closer Mariano Rivera, previously all but invincible in his postseason career, let a 2–1 lead slip away in the bottom of the ninth, and the Diamondbacks won their first world championship when Luis Gonzalez knocked in Jay Bell with a bloop base hit to center.

Nov. 4 D (N) 5:57 80° Team DIAMONDBACKS City PHOENIX

Attendance 49,589

Pitchers	IP	R	H	E	BB	SO	WP	W/L
CLEMENS	6⅓	1	7	1	1	10		
STANTON	⅔	0	0	0	0	0		L
RIVERA	1⅓	2	3	2	0	3		

Team YANKEES   Game 7

Umpires RIPPLEY, HIRSCHBECK, SCOTT, RAPUANO, JOYCE, DeMUTH

Time of Game 3:2

Pitchers	IP	R	H	E	BB	SO	WP	W/L
SCHILLING	7⅓	2	6	2	0	9		
BATISTA	⅓	0	0	0	0	0		
JOHNSON	1⅓	0	0	0	0	1		W

ARIZONA 3 NEW YORK 2

Sports Illustrated

BASEBALL'S GREATEST

BASE

GREA

BALL'S
TEST

NO.
4

RIGHTFIELDER

PHOTOGRAPH BY OZZIE SWEET

CONTENTS

BILL SYKEN *Editor* / STEVEN HOFFMAN *Creative Director*

CRISTINA SCALET *Photo Editor* / KEVIN KERR *Copy Editor* / JOSH DENKIN *Designer*

STEFANIE KAUFMAN *Project Manager*

SEEING THE BIGGER PICTURE

IF YOU THINK THE STARS OF YESTERYEAR DON'T LOOK LIKE THEY COULD COMPETE WITH TODAY'S ATHLETES, GAZE MORE DEEPLY INTO THEIR PHOTOS

BY STEVE RUSHIN

AYBE IT'S ALL THOSE WHISKEY BOTTLES, or the neat comb-over cresting across his scalp, or the way his necktie stops halfway down the front of his shirt—like an arrow pointing to his modest paunch—but the man behind the counter looks older than 52. His right hand rests atop a cash register, on which he has just rung up a customer for the sad sum of 40 cents. That sadness is reflected in the cashier's face. He is not happy in the least to have his picture taken.

But here he is, posing. It's October 2, 1939 at 2:14 in the afternoon—the clock is the only nonalcoholic appurtenance on the wall behind him—and the World Series will in a couple days be under way in Yankee Stadium. All of which serves as a reminder to the man behind the counter that he is 19 years removed—literally removed—from the game he once dominated. He knows this is the reason he's being photographed: because he used to be one thing and now he is another.

The man leaves little physical trace (as his eyes urge the photographer to take the damn picture already) that he was once the preeminent athlete in baseball, or that he will still be considered, 75 years hence, among the very best in the game's history. No—to get any hint of that, you have to step outside, onto the sidewalk, and look again at the sign painted in the window of this shop at 1262 Pendleton Street in Greenville, S.C.

It says, simply, JOE JACKSON'S LIQUOR STORE, and the man behind the counter is Shoeless Joe himself.

This liquor store owner is our No. 7 leftfielder.

7

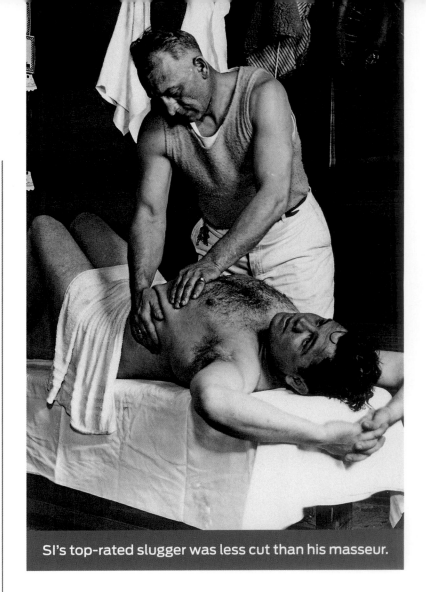

SI's top-rated slugger was less cut than his masseur.

THAT PHOTO ILLUSTRATES A DIFFICULTY at the heart of this book: comparing athletes across eras. Bygone players exist less vividly to us than contemporary ones, surviving only in their statistics or in well-worn anecdotes or in photos such as Jackson's, a bewitching vignette that tells its own stories, not all of them true.

It's true that Jackson is working a real job for modest compensation, as ballplayers did for the first 100 years of professional baseball. (The winter following his first season in the big leagues, Nolan Ryan pumped gas from 3 p.m. to 9 p.m.) Off-season workouts were minimal or nonexistent, in part because there was no off-season. Today, of course, Justin Verlander is pumping iron, not Unleaded.

But even conceding that Joe Jackson, at 52, was well past his physical prime, it is hard to look at the picture and conjure a man who was ever among the very best in the world at hitting a baseball, perhaps the most difficult discipline in all of sports.

It doesn't help that Jackson is entirely surrounded in this picture by alcoholic beverages, as baseball players still are on occasion, though not as an occupational necessity.

Jackson had previously owned a dry cleaning business and his clothes, it must be said, look neatly pressed and mildly starched. But does he resemble, by contemporary standards, the seventh best leftfielder in the history of baseball? For that is where our panel of experts have placed him: Three spots behind Barry Bonds and three spots ahead of Manny Ramirez, two other players touched by scandals of their own.

Bonds and Ramirez—their careers unspooling on videotape, their laboratory-aided bodies still fresh in our minds—appear to belong to a higher species, and a different game, from Jackson, who has a latent power in his 6' 1" frame. But that power is the same, unspoken Don't-Even-Think-About-Robbing-Me posture required of any liquor-store clerk.

There is nothing to suggest, beyond the borehole intensity of his gaze, that the Jackson in this photo could have hit .356 over 13 major league seasons and been the envy of every hitter from Ty Cobb to Ted Williams.

Indeed, little more than 12 years after the picture was taken, Jackson would be dead of a heart attack and consigned to an afterlife of ignominy, accused—though never convicted—of conspiring to throw the 1919 World Series. In the series he was alleged to have thrown, Jackson batted .375 for the White Sox. He was, for his or any other time, exceptionally proficient at hitting a baseball. That much is beyond debate, even if our eyes tell us otherwise in the 21st century.

GIVEN VERY LITTLE TIME AND THE SAME amount of dignity, one can turn up photos of a nearly naked Babe Ruth on the Internet. Explaining their presence on one's computer search history is more challenging, but these pictures illustrate another point.

If not for the small blessing of an even smaller towel, the Bambino would be disporting in the altogether in these photographs, throwing into sharp relief just how different the superstars of another epoch look from the frailest slap-hitters of the modern era.

This photo also shows a baseball great surrounded by bottles, though these are for various unguents, ointments and liniments. Beneath them, Babe Ruth is supine on a table in the Yankee Stadium clubhouse. Yankees trainer Doc Wood is giving him a rubdown, working out the knots in one of Ruth's incipient love handles as the Babe airs out his armpits, hands clasped behind his head, biceps flat-lining even in their flexed state. Doc Wood, who possesses a genuinely impressive pair

Our ninth-rated slugger showed a powerful physique.

IT DOESN'T SEEM POSSIBLE, MUCH LESS PLAUSIBLE, THAT BABE RUTH TRUMPS ALBERT PUJOLS IN A FEAT OF PHYSICAL PROWESS. YET WE KNOW IT TO BE TRUE.

5' 5". Miller Huggins, Phil Rizzuto and Hack Wilson were each 5' 6". In the 21st century, we have Astros second baseman Jose Altuve, who is 5' 5", though he's unlikely to drive in 191 runs in a season, as Wilson did.

That's why these photos are so deceptive. It doesn't seem possible, much less plausible, that Babe Ruth trumps Albert Pujols in a feat of physical prowess. But we know it to be true, even if it doesn't pass the eye test.

And boy, does it not pass the eye test. There is another photograph of Ruth, from another day, sitting up, naked, in the clubhouse, again covered by a small towel, again his slightly gelatinous body getting a somewhat jiggly rubdown while this time seated on a newspaper (in what might pass for a withering commentary on the fourth estate).

In this photo, too, Ruth looks perfectly at ease, unmistakably comfortable being klieg-lit in this milieu. His is the nudity of an old man at the gym, entirely devoid of self-consciousness.

And by today's standard, that's what Ruth is, there in the clubhouse at Yankee Stadium: an old man at the gym. It's what he looks like to us, though not to his contemporaries, to whom he was a man of uncommon strength, capable of whipping a 42-ounce Louisville Slugger through the strike zone. He is a power hitter whose source of power, like a vampire's face, cannot be captured by photography.

On the other hand, here is where photographs tell the unambiguous truth: This is how these men looked. The camera might add 10 pounds, but it does not add lines to the face, erase muscle definition, insert cigarettes in mouths or age people beyond their years. Life does that, and it did so at an accelerated pace 50 or 75 or 100 years ago.

People got older younger. To paraphrase Yogi, it got late early. Only three players 35 or older appeared in 100 or more games during the 1950 season. In 2012, the New York Yankees alone had that many. And one of them—Alex Rodriguez—has been

of guns, is the far more fearsome physical specimen here.

It's a poignant tableau—tender even—a baseball version of Michelangelo's *Pietà*.

But the picture lies, for Ruth is the greatest slugger of his day, and of any other day, for that matter. That opinion is asserted and defended in this book, whose ranking of players from every era in countless categories forms a complete taxonomy of the game, with Ruth at its apex.

As the No. 1 power hitter of all time, he is eight spots ahead of Albert Pujols, though all physical evidence would suggest a reversal of that order. Indeed, if someone were to manufacture, mascot-style, an exact-scale costume of Albert Pujols, Ruth would fit comfortably inside its fiberglass body, like a Russian nesting doll. And yet it is Ruth—in the mind's eye—who cuts a far bigger figure. It is Ruth who gave us the adjective Ruthian to describe anything outsized or larger-than-life.

Of course human beings are larger than they once were, and growing larger at an alarming rate. The average size of men 20 and older in the U.S. in 2002 was 5' 9½" and 190 pounds, more than a full inch taller and 25 pounds heavier than in 1960, according to the Centers for Disease Control and Prevention. Stars of a previous age were smaller in part because everyone was smaller. Willie Keeler was 5' 4", Rabbit Maranville was linked through a representative to a Miami "anti-aging clinic," for our culture now thinks it can hedge against mortality. Sixty is the new 40, 40 is the new 20, 20 is the new six.

Ted Williams's desire to live forever took hold late in life—and continues now, in his cryonically frozen afterlife. But a half century ago, through exceptional ability and sheer bloody-mindedness, he defied age without the aid of chemists or the physical bulk that armors today's players against an endless season. He famously played to age 42, homering in his final at bat.

But when he sat there shirtless in the Red Sox clubhouse, the farmer-tanned Williams—his neck and arms a chocolate brown, his torso inducing snowblindness—was skinny even by the standards of his day: The Splendid Splinter. Baseball has always reserved a prominent place for the superskinny. Ewell (The Whip) Blackwell was 6' 6" and indeed whip-thin while throwing sidearm in the 1940s and '50s. Thirty years later, Kent Tekulve was 6' 4" and 170 pounds throwing sidearm for the Pirates. Before the 2012 season, Giants ace Tim Lincecum clocked in at 160 pounds. In street clothes, none of them looked like an athlete.

Williams looked frailer still when photographed next to teammate Jimmie Foxx, whose "muscled physique" in the parlance of the day was remarkable then and remains impressive, though it would serve only as a baseline for today's star athlete.

Williams and Foxx are at opposite ends of a wide spectrum. Physically, neither represents the players of their era. But then old photos are seldom representative of the world as it really was. That world was never black and white, though the photos always are. It was not a world bereft of smiles, though nobody smiles in old photos, mimicking—as they were—painted portraits throughout human history.

Look at all those wax-mustached players in pointed collars and pillbox-style caps posing for their tobacco cards. They'd have thought our undignified penchant for grinning in all snapshots—and what we say while posing for them—to be one and the same thing: Cheese.

Which brings us back to the grim-faced Joe Jackson. George Orwell wrote: "At 50, everyone has the face he deserves." But Jackson didn't deserve that face. Nobody does. To paraphrase a movie that came out that year: Pay no attention to the man behind the counter. It doesn't reveal who he was—among the greatest baseball players of all time—or who he is again, in these pages, for posterity. ∎

HOW WE RANKED THEM

These Top 10 lists bring together the expert opinions of seven writers and editors whose knowledge of the game runs deep

FOR THIS BOOK SI WRITERS AND EDITORS were polled before the 2013 season and asked to submit their Top 10 lists in 19 categories. Votes were tallied with 10 points awarded for a first-place vote, nine points for a second-place vote and so on. Voters were also asked to justify their selections, and those comments appear with each Top 10 player. In most cases, if a panelist had a player ranked higher than others, he was asked to speak on that player's behalf.

We defined many of our player categories by defensive position. In regard to players who changed positions during their careers, panelists were free to place players wherever they saw them as one of the 10 best, and could even vote for players in more then one category if they so chose. This happened with Pete Rose, who played at least 589 games at five positions, and he received votes here at four of them. He makes our Top 10 list at two positions, which makes the Hit King the only player to collect that double.

THE PANELISTS

DAVID BAUER *SI Senior Contributing Editor*

STEPHEN CANNELLA *SI Assistant Managing Editor*

ALBERT CHEN *SI Staff Writer*

DICK FRIEDMAN *former SI Senior Editor*

KOSTYA KENNEDY *SI Senior Editor*

DAVID SABINO *former SI Associate Editor*

TOM VERDUCCI *SI Senior Writer*

DENNIS ECKERSLEY

NO. 2
RELIEF PITCHER

PHOTOGRAPH BY V.J. LOVERO

376 FT.

For a Winning DEAL on the 1955 Motoramic CHEVROLET
Say Benjamin Before You Buy!
BENJAMIN CHEVROLET INC.
2025 ATLANTIC AVE. F
EVergreen 5-340

the soft collars on
Van Heusen
CENTURY Shirts
won't wrinkle...ever !

Official Timepiece
Brooklyn Dodgers

BULOVA
AMERICA RUNS ON BULOVA TIME

Top Octane
Proved Mi
Econom
Mo
SPE

Disosway & Fisher

AUTO SUPPLY CO.
AUTO ACCESSORIE
RADIO
AUTO GLASS-LOCKS & KEYS
1410

EBBETS FIELD

NO.
4

BALLPARK

PHOTOGRAPH BY HY PESKIN

DEREK JETER

NO.
3

SHORTSTOP

PHOTOGRAPH BY CHUCK SOLOMON

Sports Illustrated

BASE
GREA

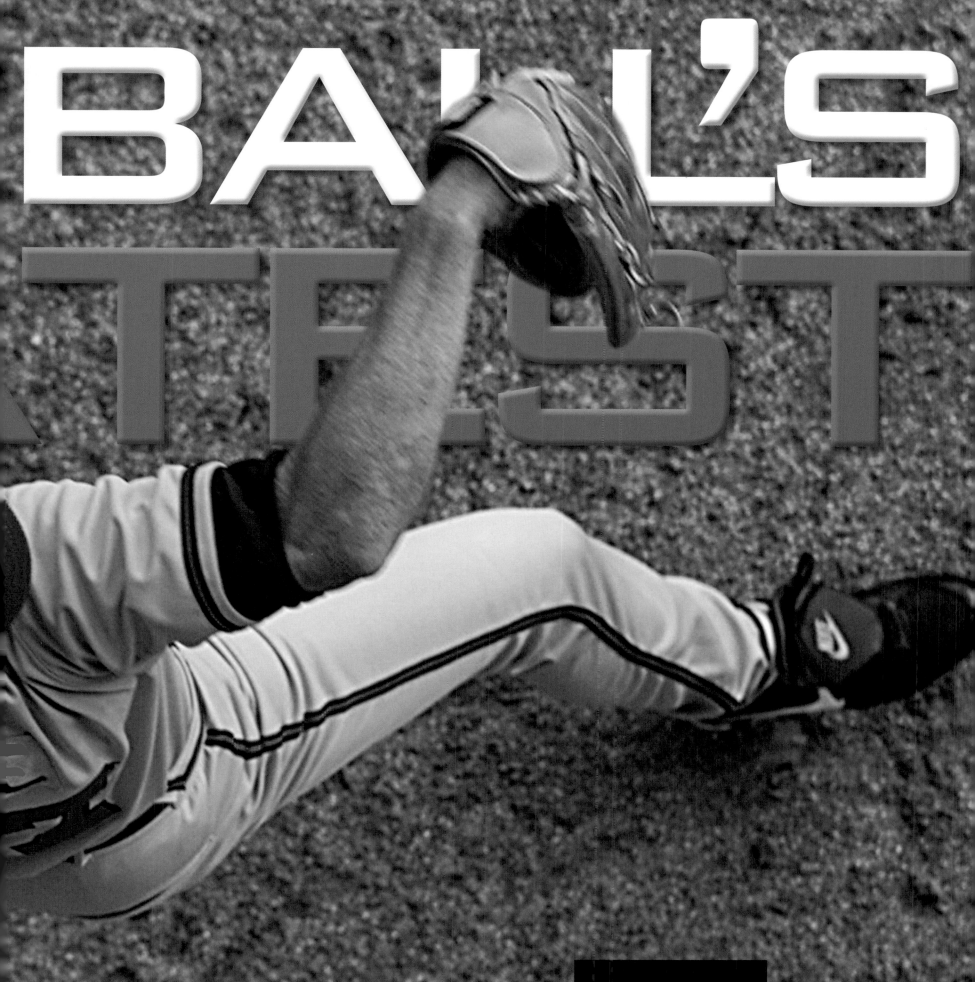

BALL'S
TEST

Tom Glavine

NO.
9

LEFTHANDED
PITCHER

10 THE

BEST FIRST BASEMEN

JOHNNY MIZE WAS NICKNAMED THE BIG CAT, AND, WHILE THE NICKNAME MAY CONJURE THOUGHTS OF QUICK REFLEXES AND NIMBLE LANDINGS ON ONE'S FEET, UNDERSTAND THAT IN MIZE'S CASE, THE EMPHASIS WAS MORE ON THE "BIG" THAN THE "CAT." HE REPORTEDLY EARNED THE NICKNAME WHEN GIANTS TEAMMATE BILL RIGNEY SAW MIZE SUNNING HIMSELF ON THE POLO GROUNDS BENCH AND SAID "NOTHING BOTHERS HIM. HE LOOKS LIKE A BIG CAT SLEEPING IN THE SUN."

AND YET THE BIG CAT IS HERE, IN THE REAR GUARD OF A PARADE THAT IS LED BY NO LESS THAN AN IRON HORSE. SUCH IS THE NATURE OF FIRST BASE, WHERE THE SKILLS THAT MIZE DID POSSESS—A KEEN EYE AND GREAT POWER—MORE THAN COMPENSATED FOR ATHLETIC SHORTCOMINGS THAT WOULD HAVE BEEN LESS CONCEALABLE IF HE HAD BEEN ASKED TO CHASE DEEP FLY BALLS IN CENTERFIELD.

SUFFICE TO SAY THAT, WHILE OUR LIST INCLUDES SOME FINE GLOVEMEN, THIS POSITION IS MORE ABOUT MEN WHO ADD TO THEIR TEAM'S RUN TOTAL RATHER THAN THOSE WHO SPECIALIZE IN KEEPING THE OTHER GUYS OFF THE BOARD. HERE IS WHERE YOU'LL FIND THE BIGGEST BATS IN THE INFIELD. IN FACT, LATER IN THIS BOOK WE CHOOSE BASEBALL'S TOP SLUGGERS, AND FOUR OF THE 10 ARE FIRST BASEMEN. THE GRAND TOTAL OF THE OTHER INFIELD POSITIONS COMBINED? THAT WOULD BE ZERO.

1

LOU GEHRIG

YANKEES 1923–1939

" He's famed for his 2,130 consecutive games, but perhaps a more astounding number is this: Over one 11-season span Gehrig averaged 153 RBIs. " —DAVID BAUER

1934 AL TRIPLE CROWN WINNER ▸ HIT .361 IN SEVEN WORLD SERIES APPEARANCES

I CAN truthfully say that I did not want to play that day. I wanted my boyhood hero to go on with his streak. Lou slapped me on the back and said, "Go on, get out there and knock in some runs." Up the dugout steps he went with the lineup, and my eyes followed him to the plate where he handed the card to umpire Steve Basil. A moment later it was announced over the public address system that Lou was stopping his consecutive game streak, and as he turned from the plate to return to the dugout the fans stood up and cheered. When he reached the dugout, Lou headed for the drinking fountain. It was a long time before he looked up, with watery eyes, and the players looked away to yell at the Tigers in this awkward moment. I guess they were all glassy-eyed. Lou wiped his eyes with one of the big fluffy towels while nobody looked, and the game was on.

—Babe Dahlgren, SI, June 18, 1956

Gehrig hit 493 home runs, including 23 grand slams.

2

ALBERT PUJOLS

CARDINALS 2001–2011
ANGELS 2012–PRESENT

"A 13th-round draft pick in 1999, Pujols is the rare modern-day superstar who arrived without notice or expectations. He was Rookie of the Year at 21, MVP at 25, and by 30 already owned 10 seasons with 30 homers, 100 RBI and a .300 batting average, a collection of superlative seasons exceeded in entire baseball lifetimes only by Babe Ruth." —TOM VERDUCCI

▸ THREE-TIME NL MVP
▸ ACTIVE LEADER IN BATTING AVERAGE, SLUGGING PERCENTAGE

QUIET. Albert Pujols's swing is quiet. It begins with a slow waggle of the right elbow—the promise of contact, the imminence of eruption. Then there is the quick whip of the bat, the instant of impact and the follow-through. The beauty of Pujols's swing resides in the powerful grace of its unfurling. But quiet. Yadier Molina, the Cardinals' catcher, and Pujols's hitting protégé, does not easily articulate what Pujols has taught him, but he works around to this: "Just try to be quiet. Don't mess, don't get pulled around moving your head, don't go like this"— Molina shuffles his hands on the handle of an imaginary bat, jerks his shoulders, wriggles in discomfort—"just, quiet."

—Daniel G. Habib, SI, May 22, 2006

Pujols led the NL in Wins Above Replacement five times.
PHOTOGRAPH BY DAVID E. KLUTHO

3
JIMMIE FOXX

A'S 1925–1935
RED SOX 1936–1942
TWO TEAMS 1942, 1944, 1945

"He powered the A's to three straight championships and was the most dominant hitter of the 1930s. His '32 season (58 home runs and 169 RBI) is on the short list for greatest of all time." —ALBERT CHEN

▸ THREE-TIME AL MVP
▸ 534 CAREER HOME RUNS

LEFTY GOMEZ threw the ball that Foxx drove into the upper deck in Yankee Stadium. Years later Gomez was watching an astronaut on TV pick up what appeared to be a white object [on the surface of the moon]. "I wonder what that is," said Gomez's wife. "That's the ball Foxx hit off me in New York," Gomez replied.

—William Nack, SI, August 19, 1996

Foxx hit for power and average, batting .325 for his career.

TIGERS 1930, 1933–1941,
1945–1946
PIRATES 1947

Greenberg had 170 RBI in 1935 and 183 RBI in '37.

PHOTOGRAPH BY SPORTING NEWS/GETTY IMAGES

4

" The first great Jewish player, he answered the anti-Semitic slurs with colossal clouts. Greenberg would lose seasons to military service but burnish his aura as a man and a symbol. " —DICK FRIEDMAN

GREENBERG WAS at his peak when he became the first baseball star to enter the service. Greenberg missed three full seasons and a major portion of two others, returning in time to hit the grand slam home run in the final game of 1945 that gave Detroit one more pennant.

—*Sports Illustrated, September 15, 1986*

‣ 58 HOME RUNS IN 1938
‣ 1935 AL MVP

HANK
GREENBERG

5

HARMON KILLEBREW

SENATORS/TWINS, 1954–1974
ROYALS 1975

❝ When Killebrew retired only two players—Babe Ruth and Ralph Kiner—had hit home runs at a higher career rate than his of one in every 14.2 at bats. ❞ —DAVID SABINO

▸ 1969 AL MVP
▸ 573 CAREER HOME RUNS

IN 1959 Killebrew was nicknamed "Killer" by desperate sportswriters. The term Killer eventually died of its own silliness, and from being good-naturedly abused by Harmon's teammates. You can't look an abstraction of amiability in the eye and call it Killer, day after day, no matter how hard it hits. But the name persists in some newspapers, and this may be because reporters trying to make colorful and intimate copy out of Harmon have discovered that he is a killer indeed. What makes a reporter happy is someone with a facial tic, conversational peculiarities, a hobby involving off-season archaeology or perhaps an acquittal in the dim past for the murder of an aunt. And Harmon Killebrew is a sensible, good-tempered man who loves his wife and children and has no curious hobbies. ("Come on, Harm. You must have some unusual hobby." "Just washing the dishes, I guess," says Harmon, trying to help.)

—*Barbara Heilman, SI, April 8, 1963*

The sharp-eyed Killebrew led the AL in walks four times.

PHOTOGRAPH BY FRED KAPLAN

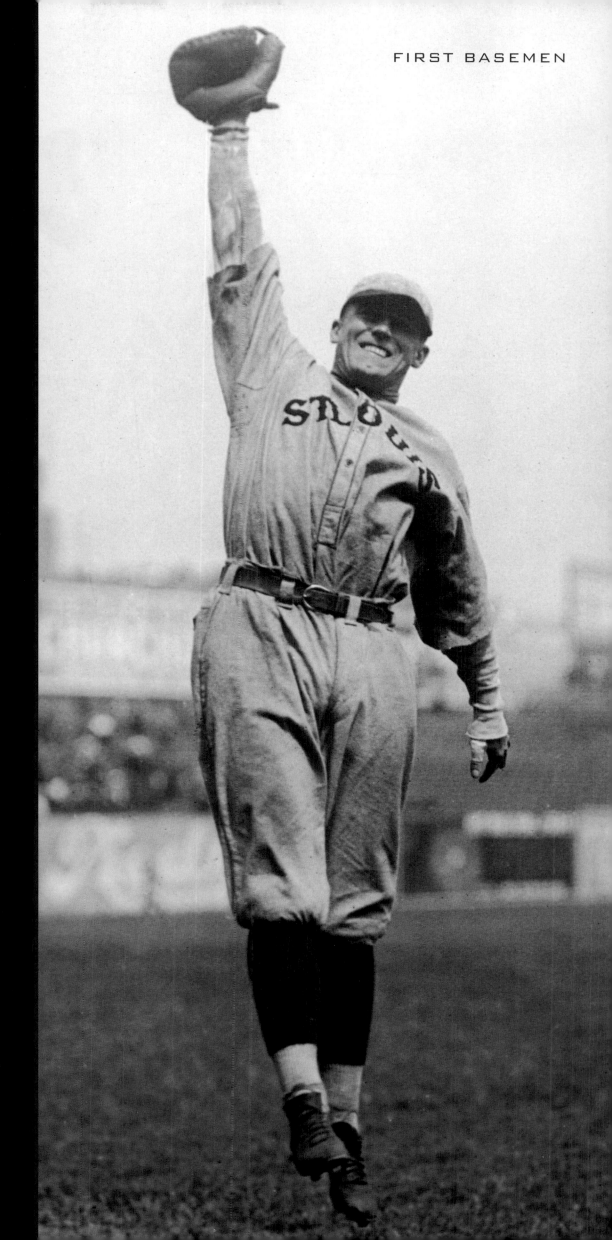

6
GEORGE SISLER

" His 257 hits in a 154-game season is his enduring signature, but Sisler could dominate games defensively too. His 1922 MVP season (.420, 51 steals, 134 runs, 105 RBI) was arguably baseball's finest to that point—and his last truly great one before sinusitis diminished his eyesight at age 30. " —KOSTYA KENNEDY

▸ .340 CAREER AVERAGE
▸ TWO .400 SEASONS

THE INEPT hitting was particularly distressing to the Pirates' special batting coach, George Sisler. Sisler, 64, sits quietly in the Pirates clubhouse before the game and answers questions put to him by the Pirates players. Johnny O'Brien, his baby face trying to look tough behind a two-day growth of beard and a stub of a cigar, asks, "Mr. Sisler, how did you hit the change?" Sisler, sitting in a chair, grabs an imaginary bat, unconsciously sets his feet in a semblance of a batting stance, and explains about waiting until the last minute, and pushing the ball or pulling it. O'Brien puffs on the cigar and nods, asks another question, nods again. "You have to wait," Sisler says, "and. . . " He flicks the imaginary bat, and for the briefest part of a second it is Sportsman's Park in 1922.

—Robert W. Creamer, SI, May 6, 1957

Sisler had a 41-game hitting streak in 1922.

McCovey led the NL in slugging percentage three times.

GIANTS 1959–1973, 1977–1980
PADRES 1974–1976
A'S 1976

" He won Rookie of the Year in 1959, MVP in 1969 and Comeback Player of the Year in 1977. It's ironic that many home runs hit by Barry Bonds—the lone lefthanded NL batter with more home runs—landed in McCovey Cove. " —DAVID SABINO

IN SAN Francisco conversation tends to narrow down to two topics: the weather and Willie McCovey. No wind in the history of the world is so analytically dissected as the wind at Candlestick Park. If Willie McCovey wasn't around to hit home runs off Don Drysdale, the wind is all that San Francisco would ever talk about.

—Robert W. Creamer, SI, July 1, 1963

▸ 521 CAREER HOME RUNS
▸ 2,211 CAREER HITS

WILLIE McCOVEY

THE HEART OF A GIANT

When a player and a city have a relationship like Willie McCovey did with San Francisco, it's easy to see why they decided to name a cove after him

BY RON FIMRITE

S WILLIE MCCOVEY SAT in the San Francisco Giants' clubhouse at Candlestick Park, blissfully contemplating the start of his 20th major league season, he was approached by a curious figure attired entirely in red. A mechanical monkey clutching cymbals hung from the intruder's neck, and in his right hand the man held a kazoo. "I have a telegram for Willie McCovey," he announced, heralding his arrival with a kazoo chorus. "Are you that gentleman?" McCovey identified himself, and the stranger, from Grams-n-Gags Singing Telegram Service, began to warble, with simian accompaniment and more or less to the tune of *Seventy-Six Trombones*, "How d'ya do, Willie McCovey/The Riviera Rats have asked me here/To express best wishes to you. . . ."

McCovey exploded with laughter. "That's from my fan club in San Diego," he told his teammates. "I used to live on Riviera Drive when I was playing down there. The Riviera Rats were my neighbors." Because the Padres were the Giants' Opening Day opponents, was it not odd that he should be celebrated in song by San Diegans? "Oh, no, they're just good friends. They root for me wherever I am," McCovey said. "I have fans down there. Nothing like here, though. This is something special. There's nothing really like it." True. Remarkably true.

Not many professional baseball players today are actually loved by their fans. Admired, certainly; encouraged, naturally; respected, possibly. But loved? Not on your life.

What truly sets McCovey apart from the run of modern athletes, then, is that in a time when cynicism is rampant in the clubhouses he embodies the ancient virtues of love and loyalty. He recalls simpler times, older sentiments. During spring training last month McCovey was having dinner in a Phoenix restaurant with two fans, one nearly 70, the other in his teens. Both the man and the boy were wrestling with the anomaly of McCovey's wondrous popularity in a city, San Francisco, that has hardly clasped its baseball team to its communal bosom in recent years. "Maybe it's because you're such a nice guy, Willie," said the older fan. "I think people sense that."

McCovey is not one for hasty responses. Among his good qualities is a penchant for thinking before speaking. And his speech itself is distinctive; though there can be no questioning his impressive masculinity, he has the vocal mannerisms of an elderly Southern black woman. Speaking softly, employing homespun phrases, he is reminiscent of Ethel Waters in *The Member of the Wedding*. He considered the older man's compliment for a moment, set his napkin aside and said, quietly,

"I would rather be remembered as a decent human being than as a guy who hit a lot of home runs. I love San Francisco and the people of the Bay Area. I think people there consider me a part of the city. San Francisco is identified with certain things—the bridges, the fog, the cable cars. Without bragging, I feel I've gotten to the place where people are thinking of me along those lines. I'd like to think that when people think of San Francisco they also think of Willie McCovey. It's where I want to be, where I belong. I hope the people there love me a little in return."

Do they ever! Traded to San Diego in 1974, McCovey returned home in triumph last season. When he was introduced with the starting lineup on Opening Day of 1977, he was cheered for a solid five minutes. When he stepped to the plate for the first time, there was another standing ovation. The applause continued all year long. It was an outpouring of affection unparalleled in the city's athletic history. And on Willie McCovey Day last Sept. 18, it achieved idolatrous dimensions. If McCovey harbored even the faintest doubt about his place in the community, it was quickly dispelled by this love feast. Newspaper editorials extolled him, television news programs recapitulated his life story. Even academe joined the celebration with a paean composed for the *San Francisco Examiner* by San Francisco State University English professor Eric Solomon. "He has always been one of ours, as boy and man," the professor wrote of the player, "and he typifies San Francisco's ambiguous relationship to youth and age. . . . We all want to come to the edge of the Pacific, find success when young, and discover success again, gain another chance before it's too late. . . . In an era of hard, financially aggressive, contract-minded athletes, Willie McCovey seems free, kind, warm, the way we like to think of San Francisco itself, a bit laid-back, no New York or Chicago, cities always on the make. . . . Let New York have the brawling power of Babe Ruth, let Boston have the arrogant force of Ted Williams. Let us have the warm strength of Willie McCovey."

Few love affairs have been as satisfactorily consummated as the one between McCovey and his fans on his "Day." Smiling back tears before the microphone, McCovey seemed to be trying to thank everyone in the stands individually—master of ceremonies Lon Simmons feared he might actually succeed—but in the end it was, fittingly, his bat that did the talking. Struggling all afternoon to reward his followers with a home run, he was hitless when he came to bat in the ninth inning with two outs, the score tied and the winning run on third. He hit the first pitch thrown by Cincinnati's Pedro Borbon on a line to left center for a clean single that won the game for the Giants 3-2.

"I think Willie showed everyone today what kind of an individual he is," said manager Joe Altobelli. It was hardly necessary, because everyone there already knew.

∎

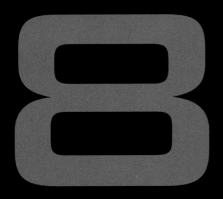

8

EDDIE
MURRAY

ORIOLES 1977–1988, 1996
DODGERS 1989–1991, 1997
THREE OTHER TEAMS

" He wasn't flashy or a media darling, which is partly why he was one of his generation's most underrated players. He is one of only three players with 500 home runs and 3,000 hits. Steady Eddie was a true model of consistency, averaging .297 with 28 home runs over his first nine seasons. " —ALBERT CHEN

> 3,255 CAREER HITS,
504 CAREER HOME RUNS
> MLB RECORD 128 CAREER
SACRIFICE FLIES

THE BEAUTY of Murray's career is its unspectacular consistency. He is, as Indians general manager John Hart says in homage to Murray's spray hits, "still the master of the flare"—a sobriquet that doesn't conjure the majesty of, say, Sultan of Swat. But that's Murray: an intelligent hitter whose knack for getting hits is heightened in clutch situations. This is Murray too: a beloved teammate, and a charitable and intensely private person. In 1992, when the Mets wanted to nominate Murray for the Roberto Clemente Award, Murray politely declined to provide the club with his charitable involvements. When the Mets then obtained the list—it ran several pages—Murray became upset. He wanted no recognition for those efforts.

—*Tom Verducci, SI, May 22, 1995*

Murray has the most RBI (1,917) of any switch-hitter.

FIRST BASEMEN

9

CARDINALS 1936–1941
GIANTS 1942, 1946–1949
YANKEES 1949–1953

" How disciplined was slugger Johnny Mize? In 1947, the Big Cat slammed 51 homers and struck out 42 times, making him the only player with more than 50 dingers and fewer than 50 whiffs in a season. " —DICK FRIEDMAN

▸ 359 CAREER HOME RUNS
▸ .312 CAREER AVERAGE

JOHNNY MIZE

Mize led the NL in RBIs three times.

PHOTOGRAPH BY AP

MIZE WAS not much of a fielder. When Ralph Houk, who played with Mize on the Yankees, was asked to name the ideal designated hitter, he replied, "Johnny Mize." Late in his career his hitting inspired these famous lines from sportswriter Dan Parker: "Your arm is gone, your legs likewise. But not your eyes, Mize, not your eyes."

—*Sports Illustrated, June 14, 1993*

10

MARK McGWIRE

A'S 1986–1997
CARDINALS 1997–2001

" He's one of the torchbearers for a tainted era, but even if judged only against his flawed peers, McGwire belongs on the list of alltime greats. He was one of the most fearsome pure power hitters the game has seen. And if you look hard enough on that résumé you'll see a Gold Glove. " —STEPHEN CANNELLA

▸ 583 CAREER HOME RUNS
▸ 70 HOME RUNS IN 1998

IN OCTOBER McGwire went to Las Vegas, where [pro golfer] friend Billy Andrade was in the Las Vegas Invitational. As Andrade recalls, "We were staying at Caesars Palace, and we'd just finished working out and were sitting in a Jacuzzi at the health club. There was a TV in the corner, and one of the World Series games was on. Mark was watching the game, and I could see that it was getting to him. He didn't come right out and say it, but I knew what he was thinking: I don't want to be sitting here in a hot tub. I want to be playing in the Series." McGwire agrees that he experienced an epiphany of sorts in Vegas. "I realized what it meant to play in the Series. I also realized that unless I did something about it. I might never get another chance. So right then and there, I rededicated myself to baseball."

—Steve Wulf, SI, June 1, 1992

In 2010 McGwire admitted to steroid use.

10 THE

BEST SECOND BASEMEN

AT BASEBALL'S DAWN, SECOND BASEMEN TENDED TO BE BIGGER POWER HITTERS WHILE THE GUYS AT THE CORNERS WERE QUICKER AND MORE NIMBLE. THIS REFLECTED THE DIAMOND STRATEGIES OF THE DAY, WHICH WERE MORE ABOUT GETTING DOWN BUNTS AND MOVING RUNNERS OVER. TEAMS NEEDED THEIR THIRD BASEMEN TO BE READY TO CHARGE.

BUT WHEN BABE RUTH CAME ALONG AND POINTED TO THE FENCES, HE CHANGED THE VERY NATURE OF BASEBALL OFFENSE—AND, CORRESPONDINGLY, THE WAY TEAMS ORCHESTATED THEIR DEFENSE. AS JOE SHEEHAN EXPLAINED, WRITING IN SI IN 2008, "OVER TIME TEAMS LEARNED TO PUT LUMBERING POWER HITTERS AT THIRD BASE AND NIMBLE, SLAP-HITTING GLOVE MEN AT SECOND." THIS ONLY BEGAN TO CHANGE, HE WROTE, IN THE '70S AND '80S WITH THE EMERGENCE OF SLICK-FIELDING SECOND BASEMEN WHO ALSO HAD POP AT THE PLATE—GUYS LIKE JOE MORGAN AND RYNE SANDBERG WHO REMINDED MANAGERS THAT SECOND-SACKERS ARE CAPABLE OF DOING IT ALL.

OUR RANKINGS REFLECT THESE TRENDS. NEARLY ALL SELECTIONS PLAYED EITHER WITH RUTH AND BEFORE HIM, OR FROM MORGAN'S TIME FORWARD. FROM PLAYERS WHOSE PRIMES WERE FROM THE IN-BETWEEN DECADES, WE HAVE ONLY ONE REPRESENTATIVE: THE TRULY EXCEPTIONAL JACKIE ROBINSON.

1

ROGERS HORNSBY

CARDINALS 1915–1926, 1933
THREE TEAMS 1927–1932
BROWNS 1933–1937

" Hornsby may be the greatest righthanded hitter ever, especially when measured by an unmatched six-year peak (1920 through '25) in which he hit .397 and led the league in batting, on-base percentage and slugging percentage every year. Hornsby managed six teams, including the 1926 Cardinals, who followed their player/manager to the franchise's first World Series title. " —TOM VERDUCCI

▸ TRIPLE CROWNS IN 1922, 1925
▸ .358 CAREER AVERAGE

MANY OF the good hitters in the game today pay homage to Ted Williams. But who today pays his respects to Hornsby, the Splinter's hitting forebear, the Newton to his Einstein? Who talks about the father of the father of modern hitting? Only old-timers. Bob Feller's first two years as a big league pitcher, 1936 and '37, were Hornsby's final two as a player. "In '37 Hornsby was 41 years old and still the best hitter on the St. Louis Browns," says Feller. "He was very difficult to strike out. He had his theories about hitting. He didn't try to pull the ball; he hit everything right through the box. He wasn't the talker Ted was, but then again a lot of what Ted said was horsefeathers. Hornsby didn't need a lot of words."

—*Michael Bamberger, SI, June 24, 2002*

Hornsby hit above .400 three times.

Morgan had nine 40-steal seasons.

PHOTOGRAPH BY JOHN IACONO

2

ASTROS 1963–1971, 1980
REDS 1972–1979
THREE TEAMS THROUGH 1984

" For pitchers, few things were more frightening than the sight of Morgan's left arm flapping as he waited in the batter's box. And he was one of the best defensive second basemen ever. " —STEPHEN CANNELLA

"I'VE ALWAYS BELIEVED that a .320 hitter is not an asset unless he contributes in other areas," Morgan said. "To me, my greatest moments are when I walk, steal second and third, then score on a sacrifice fly. Think what it does to a pitcher's mind when he hasn't given up a hit but he's gotten one run behind."

—Mark Mulvoy, SI, April 12, 1976

JOE MORGAN

▸ TWO-TIME NL MVP
▸ LED NL IN WALKS FOUR TIMES

3

EDDIE COLLINS

A'S 1906–1914, 1927–1930
WHITE SOX 1915–1926

❝ He was a brilliant base stealer, an exceptional defensive player, and he finished his career with 3,315 hits. Even acknowledging the vagaries of comparison over different eras, it wouldn't be wrong to call Collins the best second baseman ever. ❞ —DAVID BAUER

▸ .333 CAREER AVERAGE
▸ 1914 AL MVP

FOR ALL THEIR skill, the White Sox in 1919 weren't a harmonious club. Baseball players in my day had a lot more cutthroat toughness anyway, and we had our share of personal feuds, but there was a common bond among most of us—our dislike for [owner Charles] Comiskey. I would like to blame the trouble we got into on Comiskey's cheapness, but my conscience won't let me. We had no one to blame except ourselves. Most of the griping on the club centered around salaries, which were much lower than any other club in the league. Only one man on the club was drawing what I'd call a decent salary, Eddie Collins. He was making about $14,000 a year. Naturally, Collins was happier with Comiskey than we were. So when the opportunity came in 1919 to pick up some easy change on the World Series, Collins wasn't included in our plans.

—*Arnold (Chick) Gandil as told to Melvin Durslag, SI, September 17, 1956*

Collins, a pro at 19, played 25 major league seasons.

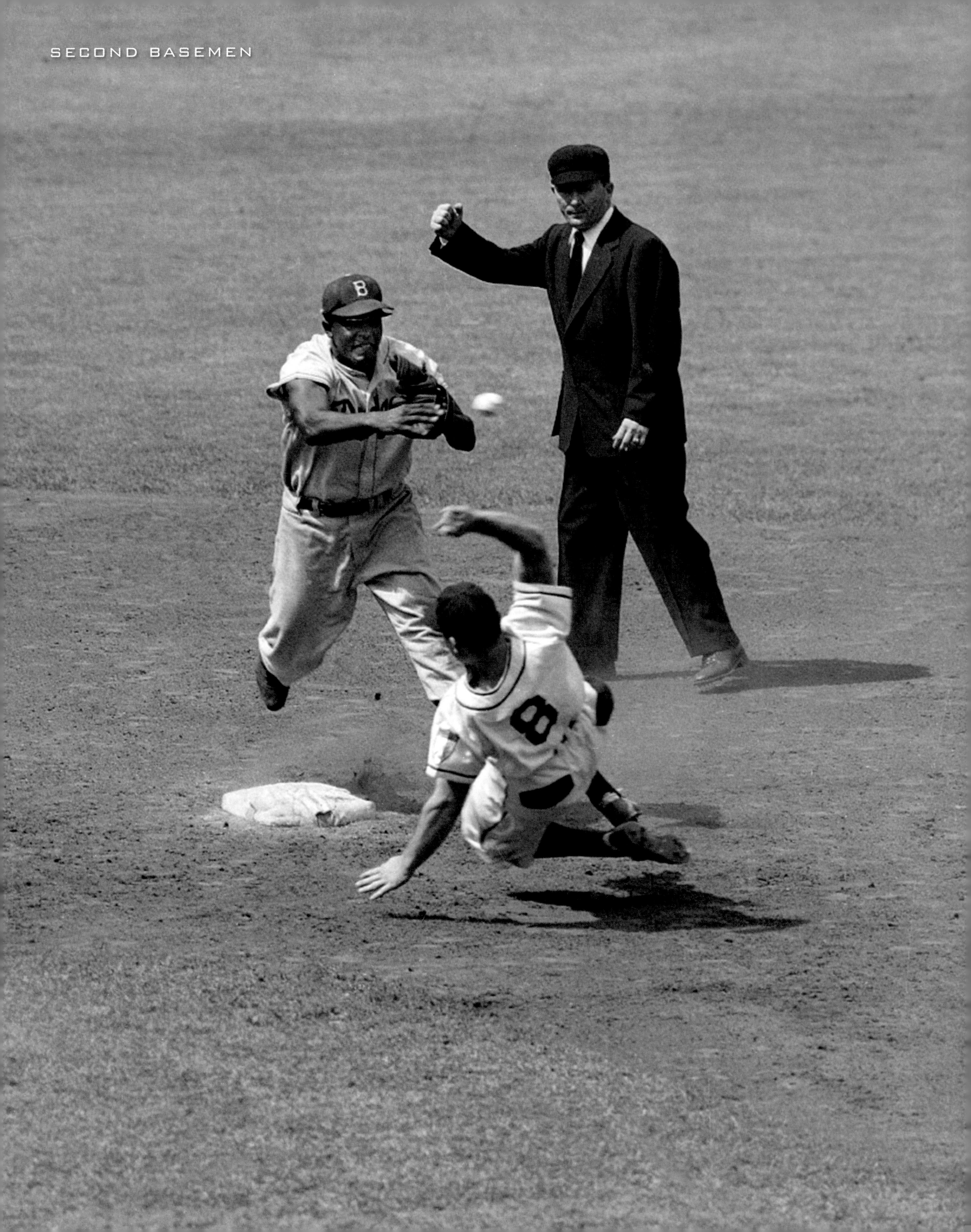
B
8

4

JACKIE ROBINSON

DODGERS 1947–1956

❝ The player who would break baseball's color barrier needed to have thick skin— but he also needed to be able to play. And Robinson certainly could, transforming the Dodgers into perennial contenders with his bat (.311 average, .409 on-base percentage) and his aggressiveness on the bases. On the short list of Hall of Famers who truly inspired America, Jackie is alone at the top. ❞ —KOSTYA KENNEDY

▸ 1949 NL MVP
▸ STOLE HOME 19 TIMES

AFTER JACKIE ROBINSON'S death, one of our baseball writers was moved to observe: "He had a passion for truth, for what he felt was the truth, and he could be a bit frightening at times. But he was always impressive. And refreshing. I don't remember ever talking to anyone else quite like him. . . . He was unique on the ball field too. He was the most aggressively exciting player of my experience. Ty Cobb was before my time, but I saw Babe Ruth and DiMaggio, Musial and Willie Mays, Aaron and Ted Williams. Robinson's statistical record seems meager compared with theirs, but if all of them were somehow playing on the same team I have no doubt that Robinson would be the dominating figure. He made things happen. He was an extraordinary man."

—*Sports Illustrated, SI, November 6, 1972*

Robinson excelled amid unprecedented scrutiny.

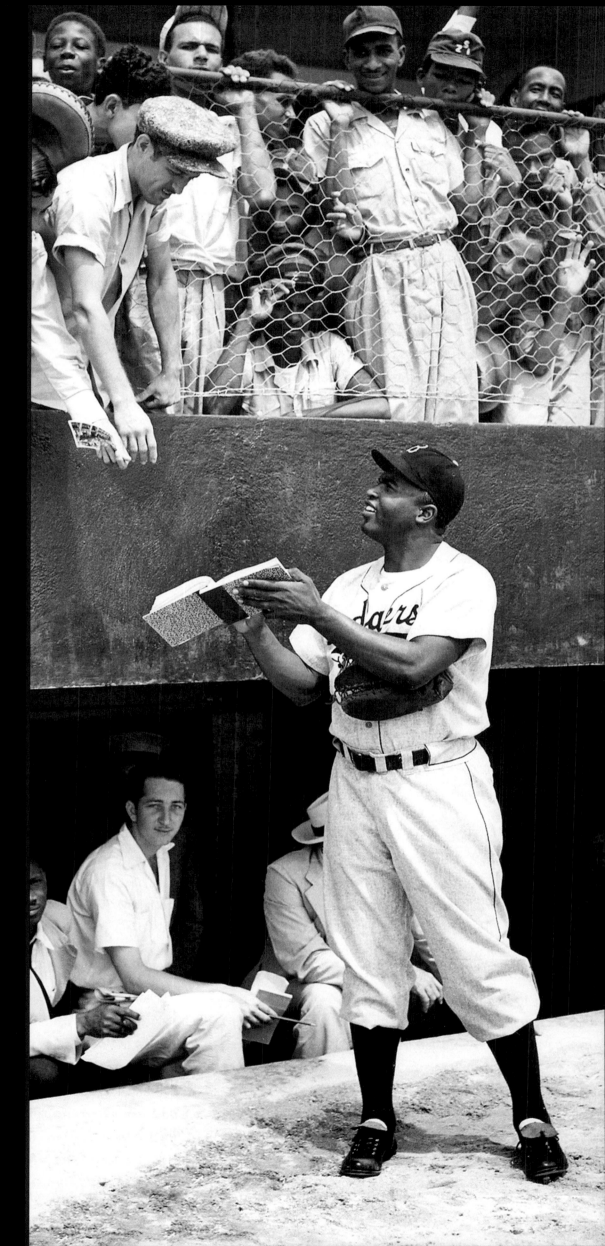

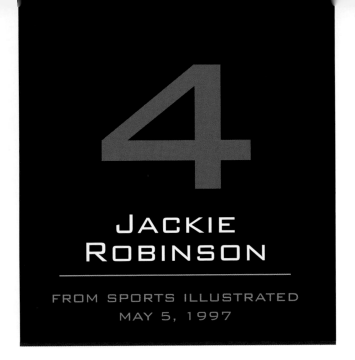

JACKIE ROBINSON

FROM SPORTS ILLUSTRATED
MAY 5, 1997

MAJOR LEAGUE HOT STREAK

Jackie Robinson's roll in May 1947 silenced critics who had been calling for the Dodgers rookie to be benched

BY WILLIAM NACK

N THE MIDDLE OF THE COOL, DRIZZLY afternoon of Sunday, May 25, 1947, as the Brooklyn Dodgers led the Philadelphia Phillies 4–3 in the eighth inning, Jackie Robinson ground his spikes into the rain-softened dirt of the batter's box at Ebbets Field, turned to face Phillies reliever Tommy Hughes and waited for Hughes's 3-and-1 cripple.

Forty days had passed since Robinson donned a Dodgers uniform and became the first black man in this century to play in the majors, going 0 for 3 in his debut at Ebbets on April 15. In recent games the 28-year-old rookie had begun to evince signs of settling down and playing the crisp, commanding brand of ball that Branch Rickey, the Dodgers' president, had predicted of him. "You haven't seen the real Robinson yet," Rickey had been telling writers all spring. "Just wait."

Through his first 30 big league games, played in six National League cities, the rookie had alternately struggled and soared, at times performing brilliantly at first base (a position new to him that year) but often pressing at the plate. Of course, Robinson had also been the target of racial epithets and flying cleats, of hate letters and death threats, of pitchers throwing at his head and legs, and catchers spitting on his shoes. In the midst of all this bristling animus, there was a circuslike quality to Dodgers games, with Robinson on display like a freak; with large crowds, including many blacks, lustily cheering even his dinkiest pop-ups; and with the daily papers singling him out as the "black meteor," the "sepia speedster," the "stellar Negro," the "muscular Negro," the "lithe Negro" and "dusky Robbie."

"More eyes were on Jackie than on any rookie who ever played," recalls Rex Barney, a Brooklyn reliever that year. It was a wonder, as he endured the mounting pressure of his first weeks in the bigs, that Robinson could perform at all. Yet perform he did, putting together a 14-game hitting streak in the first 2½ weeks of May. By May 25, with the first extended road trip behind him and the novelty of his presence on the wane, Robinson was sensing what he later called a "new confidence" in his game. As he took the field that day against the Phillies—who, led by their Southern-born manager, Ben Chapman, had lacerated him with taunts of "nigger" and "black boy" from the dugout during their first series in April—Robinson had begun to feel, as he would put it, "some of the old power returning."

In the fourth inning, with the Dodgers down 2–0 and their shortstop, Pee Wee Reese, on first, Robinson lashed a single to right center off Phillies starter Dick Mauney. Moments later Reese and Robinson raced home when Dodgers centerfielder "Pistol" Pete Reiser crashed a double off the left-centerfield wall. Two innings after that, with Reese again on first and Hughes now pitching, Robinson reached for a fastball and lined a single to left. Reese later scored when Hughes balked him home from third.

Having been at the center of the rallies that gave Brooklyn that tenuous one-run lead in the eighth, Robinson now dug in against Hughes and worked the count to 3 and 1. Hughes delivered a fastball high in the strike zone, fat as a melon, and Robinson turned all his 195 pounds into it, striking the ball harder than he had struck one all spring. Dick Young, the Dodgers' beat reporter for the New York *Daily News* mixed jazz with golf in search of a simile to describe the blast, rhapsodizing that the ball left home plate "like something out of Louis Armstrong's trumpet."

The Dodgers won 5–3, and contemporary accounts viewed the game as Robinson's breakthrough in that young season, fulfilling Rickey's prophesy that when the real Robinson at last arrived, he would be worth all the waiting. No one on that afternoon in May appeared more relieved than Burt Shotton, the Dodgers' manager. "He has finally become relaxed and is playing the kind of ball that earned him his major league chance," Shotton said. "Until today we just couldn't get him to take a normal cut at the cripples they were getting him out on. Time after time we gave him signals to hit the 3-and-1 pitch, but very often he didn't even swing. Guess he had too much on his mind."

Despite all he had on his mind, despite all he had endured during the early days of that long season, it had grown clear by mid-May that Robinson, even a struggling Robinson, was in the Brooklyn lineup to stay. "The guy just had too much talent," says Reese, "and too much guts." Indeed, Robinson had won over teammates and opponents alike during his 14-game hitting streak, which was all the more impressive because it was a direct response to a horrible slump that would have finished lesser men in his situation.

As Robinson nursed an old college football injury to his right shoulder, he went 0 for 20 between April 23 and April 30, which dropped his average from .444 to .225 and prompted talk that he ought to be benched. "He should be given a rest in view of his ailing right arm and slump-pressing at the plate," Young wrote in the May 1 *Daily News*, "but the Dodger powers appear reluctant to bench him for attendance and possible public relations reasons." Young was not sympathetic to Robinson in those days, and he wasn't the only doubter among baseball writers.

"Right now Jackie Robinson doesn't shape up as a first baseman," wrote Pat Lynch of the New York *Journal American*. "His weak hitting is something the shrewd assayers of baseball talent have been on to all along."

The more sympathetic writers offered an alternative solution to Robinson's problems at the plate: bunt. In *The New York Sun* of May 1, under the headline ROBINSON'S JOB IN JEOPARDY, Herbert Goren urged the rookie to start laying the ball down: "In Robinson's case, a deep sense of pride is getting the call over common sense. Jack wants to prove in the big leagues that he is not a leg hitter. . . . Yet he is one of the best bunters in baseball."

In fact, as Robinson would soon admit, Rickey had been pushing him to bunt the ball as a way of restoring his confidence at the plate, but Robinson did not want to give his many detractors further cause for disparaging his play and spreading doubt about him as a major leaguer. "Mr. Rickey wants me to lay it down more," Robinson told Harold Burr of the *Brooklyn Eagle*, "but I don't want to bunt my way through the National League. That's what they said about me at Montreal last year, and I want to live that reputation down."

The chief cause for hope that Robinson would break out of his slump was that he was hitting the ball hard—though mostly at someone. On April 30, after the 3–1 loss to the Cubs at Ebbets Field, Shotton said he had thought about benching Robinson but then decided to let him work out of his difficulties at the plate. "There's no reason to get all excited," Shotton said, "no reason to panic."

Jackie Robinson would hit .311 for his career.

Those late April days in '47 would remain the most trying in Robinson's professional life, and the deepening pain was evident on the man's face. "You'd look at him and you knew he was pressing and pushing," Barney, the former reliever, recalls. "He had all that other stuff on his mind. He worked hard to break out of that slump."

No sooner had the alarms been set off by suggestions that the rookie be benched than Robinson was standing in the batter's box at Ebbets Field in the first inning on May 1, facing Bob Chipman of the Cubs. With one slash of the bat, on a pitch hard and in, Robinson made his way into the next day's headline in the New York *Herald Tribune*: ROBINSON SNAPS HIS BATTING SLUMP WITH TWO-BAGGER. The collar was off, at last.

It was in Pittsburgh, recalls Barney, that pitcher Ralph Branca tried to rally the team around Robinson. For weeks Reese had been quietly urging his teammates to get behind the rookie, but it was Branca who called the first meeting for that purpose. Robinson was not present. "We have to get behind Jackie to help him," Branca said. "They're all on him. He's gonna be here. He's here to stay. And he's gonna help us win the pennant."

That was prophetic. On May 18, before 46,572 people, the largest paying crowd ever to see a baseball game in Chicago's Wrigley Field, Robinson went hitless in four at bats, ending his streak, but the Dodgers rallied in the seventh inning to defeat the Cubs 4–2. Brooklyn was on its way to beating St. Louis in the race for the National League pennant, and Robinson, who would end his first season hitting .297, was on track to win the majors' first Rookie of the Year award. The crowds and Robinson's fellow big leaguers were beginning to learn what kind of player he could be. Certainly the Phillies were learning faster than any other team.

"Robinson was one ballplayer you didn't want to get riled up," recalls Andy Seminick, then the Phillies' catcher. "Something about certain players: Get 'em mad and they'd hurt you. Jackie Robinson was definitely one of 'em. He rose to the occasion and clobbered the tar out of us. He beat us everywhere—at bat, on the bases, in the field. Finally Ben Chapman said, 'Let's lay off him. It's not doing any good.' " By the end of May, during that series at Ebbets Field, the Phillies were poking fun at Chapman, who hailed from Alabama, on the subject of Robinson. Philadelphia outfielder Del Ennis had singled and was standing on first base when he heard Robinson singing and humming to himself.

"What was he singing?" Chapman asked Ennis when he returned to the bench.

Ennis did not miss a beat or crack a smile. "*Alabama Lullaby*," he said.

It was during that series, of course, that Robinson climbed on Hughes's cripple and drove it into the seats for his second big league home run. As Robinson started toward first, Hughes angrily threw his glove in the air. And third baseman Lee Handley, taking a new ball from Seminick, wound up and threw the ball and his mitt to the ground. The 18,016 customers at Ebbets Field roared as Robinson crossed home plate and headed for the bench.

There, on the dugout steps, the white hands reached for the black. ∎

Lajoie's defense was once described as "living poetry."

5

NAP LAJOIE

PHILLIES 1896–1900
A'S 1901–1902, 1915–1916
INDIANS 1902–1914

" He was so popular that the Cleveland franchise, before it adopted the Indians nickname, was known as the Naps. In the AL's first year, 1901, Lajoie won the Triple Crown and put up a .426 average. " —TOM VERDUCCI

▸ 3,242 CAREER HITS
▸ .338 CAREER AVERAGE

HE WAS SO feared by opponents that he was once walked intentionally with the bases loaded. In the field he played every position except pitcher before settling on second base. The sportswriter Fred Lieb called him "the most important personage in American history [from] Rhode Island since the Revolution."

—L. Jon Wertheim, SI, September 20, 2010

Alomar won two World Series in Toronto.

PHOTOGRAPH BY CHUCK SOLOMON

6

PADRES 1988–1990
BLUE JAYS 1991–1995
ORIOLES 1996–1998
THREE TEAMS THROUGH 2004

" There's never been a smoother second baseman. One of the most complete players of his generation, he was a brainy, switch-hitting, basestealing force. "—STEPHEN CANNELLA

▸ 10 GOLD GLOVES
▸ .300 CAREER AVERAGE

ROBERTO
ALOMAR

WHEN THE Padres traded Roberto Alomar, 22, to Toronto in 1990, then commissioner Fay Vincent remarked, "They traded a future Hall of Famer." Last Friday, Alomar, now 37, made two errors in one inning for the Devil Rays and walked off the diamond for good. "I said I would never embarrass myself on the field," he said.

—Tom Verducci, SI, March 28, 2005

7

CHARLIE GEHRINGER

TIGERS 1924–1942

" He was called the Mechanical Man for his consistency and durability. "You wind him up Opening Day and forget him," Tigers teammate Doc Cramer said. He was regarded the best fielder of his day and was the cornerstone of Tigers teams that won three pennants. " —ALBERT CHEN

▸ 1937 AL MVP
▸ SEVEN 200-HIT SEASONS

"I SAW Ty Cobb when I was a kid," 86-year-old Arthur Brooks says. "My grandfather had a deal with the Tigers: Whenever it snowed he would hitch up the horses and plow all around the stadium. The Tigers gave him four tickets to every game for that. The best player I ever saw was Charlie Gehringer, second base. He was just smooth. He made everything look easy. At the plate— this was before all of this home run stuff, all these lunkheads with all their money—he was a place hitter. Is that a term you know? Nobody does it now. He was a place hitter. All line drives." The lumberyard is still in business beyond rightfield: Brooks Lumber, run by Arthur Brooks's descendants. Baseball has been played at the corner of Michigan and Trumbull avenues since 1896. The lumberyard has been the Tigers' neighbor almost from the beginning.

—Leigh Montville, SI, July 12, 1999

Gehringer had 14 seasons hitting .300 or better.

8

RYNE SANDBERG

PHILLIES 1981
CUBS 1982–1994, 1996–1997

" In 1984 Ryne Sandberg helped lead the
Cubs to the postseason after a four-decade
absence. For 15 seasons he patrolled
Wrigley Field's friendly confines as the
NL's greatest hitter (282 home runs) and
fielder (nine consecutive Gold Gloves) at
his position. " —DAVID SABINO

▸ 1984 NL MVP
▸ 40 HOME RUNS IN 1990

HE PLAYS second base like Yo-Yo
Ma plays cello. He once played in
123 straight games without an error.
But he still carries a trace of the boy
from Spokane, the North Central
shortstop who made four errors
against Western Valley the day
scout Bill Harper told Sandberg that
Philadelphia would draft him. He has
hit 40 home runs in a season, stolen
50 bases in another, and no one else
in major league history can say that.
He has played in nine All-Star Games.
He was the leading vote-getter in '91.
There is growing sentiment that he is
the best second baseman ever to play
the game. In March '92 he signed a
contract, the richest in history, that will
pay him $7.1 million a year for the next
four seasons. But he still carries just a
hint of the boy who, when told that he
might get a signing bonus of $50,000,
turned to his high school coach with
bug eyes and said, "Oh . . . *really*?"

—*Steve Rushin, SI, July 27, 1992*

Sandberg was near perfect in the field.

9

ROD CAREW

" He held his narrow bat with the delicacy of an expert fisherman holding a fly reel, and he wielded it with similar precision. Carew did not just win batting titles he ran off with them, three times winning by at least 44 points. " —KOSTYA KENNEDY

▸ 3,053 CAREER HITS
▸ SEVEN BATTING TITLES

FOR CAREW it was starting again. His early-season hitting had thrust him once more into the glare of publicity. There was talk of his becoming the first .400 hitter since Ted Williams. "I've never seen anybody hit like that for so long," said Reggie Jackson. "I was like that in the '77 World Series, but that was only six games."

—Ron Fimrite, SI, June 13, 1983

Carew made 18 consecutive All-Star teams.

PHOTOGRAPH BY V.J. LOVERO

10

FRANKIE FRISCH

GIANTS 1919–1926
CARDINALS 1927–1937

" Lynchpin and leader, the switch-hitting Frisch had three 100-plus RBI seasons and was also distinguished enough as a second baseman to start in the first All-Star Game, in 1933. The next year, as a player-manager, he masterminded St. Louis's Gas House Gang to a World Series win. " —DICK FRIEDMAN

▸ .316 CAREER AVERAGE
▸ LED NL IN STEALS THREE TIMES

IF A SUPERIOR player continues to play superior ball and does not let discouragement or ennui set in, the chances are good that the franchise as a whole will begin to pick itself up and edge toward the pennant. Then, the addition of only one or two catalytic ballplayers, and suddenly there's a pennant. [For example] Frankie Frisch was second baseman on eight pennant winners. His teams won four of their World Series. Frisch was even manager of the 1934 Cardinals and, in the seventh game of their World Series with Detroit that year, it was Frisch who broke the back of his opponents. It was the third inning and the game was scoreless when the Cardinals loaded the bases, manager Frisch at bat. He cleaned the bases with a double. The Cardinals swept on to a seven-run inning and the world championship.

—*Jim Murray, SI, April 15, 1957*

Frisch hit above .300 in 11 consecutive seasons.

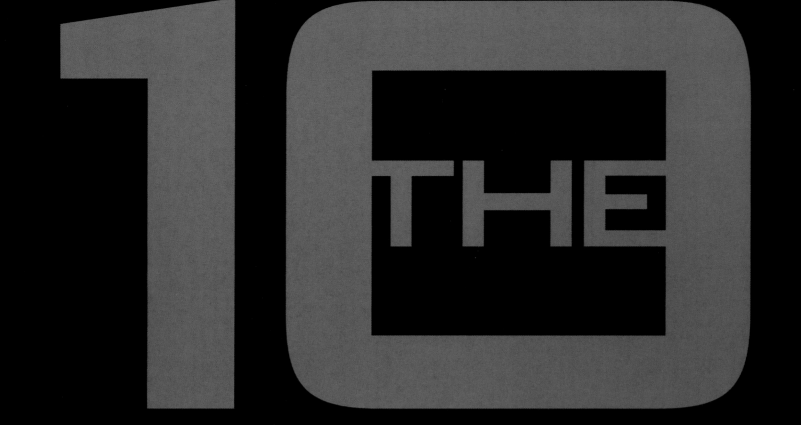

10

THE

BEST THIRD BASEMEN

THE SHOTS THAT THIRD BASEMEN MUST DEAL WITH DON'T ALWAYS COME FROM THE BATTER'S BOX. ONE EMANATED FROM THE MOUTH OF FRANKIE FRISCH, ONE OF OUR TOP 10 SECOND BASEMEN, WHO FAMOUSLY DECLARED, "THERE'S NOTHING TOUGH ABOUT PLAYING THIRD. ALL A GUY NEEDS IS A STRONG ARM AND A STRONG CHEST."

WHAT REALLY HURT ABOUT FRISCH'S ZINGER, THOUGH, WAS THAT IT SEEMED TO BE BACKED UP BY INSTITUTIONAL DISDAIN. ONLY 16 THIRD BASEMEN HAVE BEEN VOTED INTO THE HALL OF FAME, WHICH TIES THEM WITH CATCHERS FOR FEWEST INDUCTEES IN THE INFIELD. (THE NEXT FEWEST IS FRISCH'S SPOT, SECOND BASE, WITH 20.) THE NUMBERS AT THIRD ARE ACTUALLY AN IMPROVEMENT FROM 1981, WHEN ONLY SIX THIRD BASEMEN HAD BEEN VOTED IN, ALTHOUGH IT WAS CLEAR AT THAT TIME THAT CHANGE WAS COMING. BROOKS ROBINSON, TWO YEARS AWAY FROM INDUCTION, TOLD SI "THERE ARE MORE GOOD THIRD BASEMEN TODAY THAN AT ANY OTHER TIME IN HISTORY."

ROBINSON DECLARED THIS IN SI'S 1981 BASEBALL PREVIEW, WHICH FEATURED ON ITS COVER MIKE SCHMIDT AND GEORGE BRETT. BOTH OF THOSE MEN ARE NOW IN THE HALL OF FAME, AND THEY ARE ALSO NUMBERS 1 AND 2 ON OUR THIRD BASEMAN'S LIST. BROOKS WAS RIGHT: THE HOT CORNER WAS JUST HEATING UP.

1

MIKE SCHMIDT

PHILLIES 1972–1989

" Sure, he was prone to the big whiff, but his hard hitting and soft hands make him the greatest all-around third baseman. His ultimate credential? Schmitty was the engine of the Phillies' rise from laughingstock to world champion, in 1980. " —DICK FRIEDMAN

▸ THREE-TIME NL MVP
▸ 548 CAREER HOME RUNS

THE DEFENSIVE Schmidt and the offensive Schmidt appear to be opposing individuals. The offensive Schmidt is a calculating technician; the defensive Schmidt is the man on the flying trapeze. His face clouds over when he expounds on the intricacies of contending with the inside pitch; he usually breaks up when talking about his fielding adventures. "I love fielding," he says. "You know how it is when you're a kid. You always like to be tossing a ball around. You like to do things with it—catch it between your legs, behind your back. It's fun. I'm good at fielding because I take it lightly. I don't even do things fundamentally right, and I hate infield practice. But I have a lot more range than anyone else and I'm good at anticipating. I win Gold Gloves because I can kill a rally with a great play, make a barehanded stop, do something that really stands out. I have some charisma out there."

—*Ron Fimrite, SI, May 31, 1982*

The 12-time All-Star won 10 Gold Gloves.

PHOTOGRAPHS BY TOM DIPACE (LEFT) AND MANNY MILLAN

GEORGE BRETT

ROYALS 1973–1993

❝ One of four players in history with 3,000 hits, 300 home runs and a .300 average, Mr. Royal seemed to dominate every game with the way he beat out ground balls and made impossible plays with his glove. ❞ —ALBERT CHEN

▸ THREE BATTING TITLES
▸ HIT .390 IN 1980

JIM PALMER spied the Orioles' rookie leftfielder, Andres Mora, playing shallow and well toward center as if George Brett were the usual sort of lefthanded pull hitter. Waving his arms like a signal corpsman, Palmer directed Mora to a position closer to the foul line and considerably deeper. It was the first inning, the Royals' Tom Poquette was on third base, there was no score and one out. Palmer delivered a fast ball for strike one. Then, reasoning that Brett enjoyed crossing up the opposition by hitting inside pitches to left, he threw a hard slider in on the wrists. Brett pulled it neatly to rightfield and Poquette scored. For all of his accumulated knowledge, Palmer had committed the blunder of trying to outsmart George Brett. Before his career has ended, Brett, who is just 23, will have sent many such deep thinkers to the showers. Pitchers do not get rich matching wits with George Brett.

—Ron Fimrite, SI, June 21, 1976

Brett was the 1980 AL MVP.

PHOTOGRAPH BY STEVEN GOLDSTEIN

3

Mathews was SI's first-ever cover boy.

PHOTOGRAPH BY RICHARD MEEK

❝ He was the Steady Eddie of power hitters: nine straight 30-plus homer seasons, including four of 40 or more. Mathews also was the only player to suit up for the Braves in Boston, Milwaukee and Atlanta. ❞ —DICK FRIEDMAN

"[MY FATHER] played catch with me every day," Mathews recalled. "My mother would pitch and I'd hit and my father would shag the balls in the outfield. But then I clipped my mother with a couple of line drives, so my father had to pitch and my mother shagged balls."

—*Robert W. Creamer, SI, June 2, 1958*

EDDIE
MATHEWS

▸ 512 CAREER HOME RLNS

Boggs had seven consecutive 200-hit seasons.

PHOTOGRAPH BY JOHN D. HANLON

4

WADE BOGGS

RED SOX 1982–1992
YANKEES 1993–1997
RAYS 1998–1999

" He won five batting titles with a stroke perfectly suited to tattooing Fenway Park's Green Monster with line drives. As a pure hitter and a student of the craft, Boggs was his generation's Ted Williams. " —STEPHEN CANNELLA

▸ .328 CAREER AVERAGE
▸ 3,010 CAREER HITS

"THE SCOUTING bureau rep came down, watched one game and graded him a 25, which is about 13 points below the minimal level to be drafted," says Red Sox scout George Digby. "I just kept telling [Boston scouting director] Haywood Sullivan, 'Draft Boggs somewhere. Hitters like him don't come along often.'"

—Peter Gammons, SI, April 14, 1986

5

BROOKS ROBINSON

" His defensive skill was so transcendent it overrides the fact that other third basemen swung a better bat. Good field, no hit? Hardly. Robinson hit 20 or more home runs in six seasons and had 80 or more RBIs eight times. " —DAVID BAUER

▸ MLB RECORD HOLDER FOR CAREER PUTOUTS, ASSISTS AND DOUBLE PLAYS AT 3B

ROBINSON MADE a spectacular play on Lee May [in the World Series]. Harry Dalton, Baltimore's GM, told manager Earl Weaver after the game, "That's got to be one of the 10 best plays Brooks ever made, Earl." Weaver disagreed. "I'd put it in his top 100 plays." Then he corrected himself. "Those hundred," he said, "are only since I've been here."
—*William Leggett, SI, October 19, 1970*

Robinson was nicknamed the Human Vacuum Cleaner.

PHOTOGRAPH BY WALTER IOOSS JR.

6

CHIPPER JONES

BRAVES 1993, 1995–2012

" When the Braves, put off by contract demands of high school pitcher Todd Van Poppel, took Jones with the first pick of the 1990 draft, they wound up with a franchise icon who won a World Series (in 1995) and never played a day for another franchise. " —TOM VERDUCCI

▸ SWITCH-HITTER AVERAGED .303 FROM LEFT SIDE OF THE PLATE, .304 FROM THE RIGHT

PEOPLE TELL Chip he makes it look easy. He knows better. He knows the parts you don't see: the pregame trip to the trainer's room to return life to his cement-stiff right leg, the mid-game trip to the video room to scout a newly arrived reliever, the postseason trip to Japan to inspect raw wood for potential bats. It helps that he has some ridiculous gifts. He was in a visiting clubhouse a while back, reading the crawl on a cable channel from about 30 feet away. A teammate said, "You can read that?" Jones thought, You can't? He can remember hundreds, maybe thousands of at bats. One night last week, after a game in which he saw two dozen pitches, he could remember in detail all but two or three of them: count, pitch, location, result. He watches game tape like a detective, and if a pitcher tends to slightly open his glove before throwing a curve, Jones knows it.

—*Michael Bamberger, SI, June 16, 2008*

Jones won the NL MVP in 1999.

7

A'S 1908–1914
YANKEES 1916–1919, 1921–1922

Baker slugged with a 52-ounce bat held at the handle.

" Owner of one of the greatest nicknames in baseball history, Baker earned such fame with two clutch clouts in the 1911 World Series against two future Hall of Famers of the Giants, Rube Marquard and Christy Mathewson. " —TOM VERDUCCI

SPORTS WAS standard movie material. Thomas Edison put the first baseball game on film as early as 1898 and made the first comedy, *Casey at the Bat*, the following year. "Home Run" Baker became the first famous athlete to turn movie actor when he starred in *The Short Stop's Double* in 1913.

—*Robert Cantwell, SI, September 15, 1969*

HOME RUN
BAKER

▸ LED AL IN HOMERS FOUR TIMES
▸ HIT .363 IN SIX WORLD SERIES

RON SANTO

CUBS 1960–1973
WHITE SOX 1974

" Before becoming an adored Cubs broadcaster, he was a beloved Cubs player. A perfect blend of defensive excellence and power, he wore his love for the game on his sleeve. " —DAVID BAUER

▸ 342 CAREER HOME RUNS
▸ FIVE GOLD GLOVES

THE CUBS look like a winner. They bunt, they take the extra base, they hit home runs. The Cubs have a truly exciting team. . . . Ernie Banks and Ron Santo give the Cubs solid anchorage. In the words of [catcher] Gene Oliver, Santo is "the team leader. I used to hear that he was a red-neck, that he'd break bats, but this guy here is the greatest, and I've played with the Boyers and Hank Aaron and Dick Groat. He's the man, he's the finest leader I've seen." This season the Cubs infield is probably the best in baseball, both hitting and fielding. Dodgers manager Walter Alston says that the infield, including catcher Randy Hundley, should make the All-Star team. When a Chicago paper recently ran a photo of what was captioned as the Cubs' Million-Dollar Infield, Glenn Beckert showed it to Don Kessinger and was heard to say, pointing to Banks and Santo, "There's $990,000."

—Robert H. Boyle, SI, June 30, 1969

Santo led the NL in walks four times.

PHOTOGRAPH BY TONY TRIOLO

HAPPINESS AND HEARTBREAK

Ron Santo didn't live to see his election to the Hall of Fame—which seemed typical of a career in which blessings often came with an accompanying curse

BY PHIL TAYLOR

MY FIRST MEMORY OF RON Santo, the longtime Cubs third baseman, is from the summer of 1969. He was in the on-deck circle at Shea Stadium when a black cat crossed his path on its way toward the Chicago dugout. The photo of Santo looking over his shoulder as the cat scampered past him would become an enduring symbol of the buzzard's luck that has forever plagued the Cubs; they would famously fall out of first place later that season, a collapse that allowed the Miracle Mets to pass them on the way to a World Series championship. I was watching on TV in Brooklyn, an eight-year-old kid and budding Mets fan, hoping that the cat really *had* hexed the Cubs.

I felt guilty about that in later years, because for the rest of his life the curse of the Cubbies seemed to have an unusually strong hold on Santo. It doomed him to waiting, working and praying for things that never came, from the franchise's first World Series title since 1908 to a cure for the diabetes that eventually took both his legs. Even when the third of his greatest longings—election to the Hall of Fame—finally became a reality last week, as 15 of the 16 members of the new Golden Era Committee voted Santo in after years of his being denied, it was a blessing with a touch of the curse: The good news arrived nearly a year to the day after his death, at age 70, from bladder cancer.

No one would have blamed members of Santo's family if their appreciation of the honor was tainted by irritation at how it had come too late for him to enjoy it. But for the people who loved him, there was hardly a trace of bitterness to mix with the sweet. "It would be great if he could have been here to see it," says his son Jeff, 48, the second of Santo's four children. "But out of all the emotions I'm feeling, it's mostly joy, for my dad and all the people who wanted this for him. I'm not saying my dad wouldn't get disappointed over the years when he wouldn't get enough votes, but he always bounced back. He felt like a very lucky guy."

That's because for Ron Santo there was a happy side to every heartbreak. The Cubs brought him misery by never reaching the Series in his lifetime, but that misery also brought him love—from fellow Chicago fans who listened to him when he became a radio analyst for the team in 1990 and felt his emotions rise and fall with every win or loss just as theirs did. He was one of them, so true to the team that his ashes were scattered around third base at Wrigley Field. The despair in his voice when things went badly for the Cubs, as when Brant Brown dropped a ninth-inning fly ball that cost them a game in 1998 ("Ohhh, no! *Nooo!*") was classic, tragicomic Santo. "That was one of his gifts as a broadcaster and as a person," said former teammate Billy Williams, who was a member of the Hall of Fame committee that finally voted Santo in. "He could make you smile even when you felt bad for him."

The diabetes, which was discovered early in his 15-year career, didn't keep Santo from hitting 342 home runs, winning five Gold Gloves and making nine All-Star Game appearances during a time when it was much more difficult to monitor the disease than it is today. The positive side of his condition wasn't only that it spurred him to help raise millions of dollars for juvenile diabetes research but also that it brought him closer to Jeff, a filmmaker whose 2004 documentary on his father, *This Old Cub*, still does a brisk DVD business on his website, santofilms.com.

Jeff approached his father for permission to follow him with a video camera when Santo was facing his second leg amputation. "He immediately said, 'Aw, son, I don't think so,'" Jeff says. "He was a very humble guy. He finally said he'd give me two weeks, and if he didn't like how it was going, he'd pull the plug on the project, just like he was some studio head." But he didn't pull the plug, in part because of the time he got to spend with his youngest son. "To see his determination up close, and to see the way people felt about him was invaluable to both of us," Jeff says. "Without the disease, we wouldn't have had that opportunity."

For the first 15 years of Santo's eligibility, the Hall of Fame vote became an annual source of frustration; he never drew more than 43.1% of the vote, well shy of the 75% needed.

"When he fell short, he would get not so much angry but disappointed," Jeff says. "He'd say that this was it, that he wasn't going to be so serious about [getting into the Hall]. Then the next time would come around, and he'd say he really thought this was going to be the year." But if he hadn't been snubbed by the voters so many times, Santo might never have known how much he was appreciated by everyone else, including the Cubs franchise, which retired his number 10 in 2003, an honor the team previously reserved for Hall of Famers.

Now Santo is finally a member of that exclusive group, and though his family, friends and former teammates have made their peace with the honor coming posthumously, the eight-year-old version of me always will regret rooting against a man who so clearly deserved better. I'd like to think he would have appreciated that, even though it would have reminded him of the collapse of the '69 Cubs. He'd probably say, *Just my luck* ∎

Cabrera has twice led the league in home runs.

PHOTOGRAPH BY DEANNE FITZMAURICE

9

MIGUEL CABRERA

MARLINS 2003-2007
TIGERS 2008-PRESENT

66 There's simply no way to consistently get him out. Since becoming an every-day major leaguer in 2004 he has driven in more runs (1,061) than any other player and ranks in the top five of nearly every other major hitting category. 99 —DAVID SABINO

▸ 2012 AL TRIPLE CROWN WINNER
▸ TWO AL BATTING TITLES

"HE'S THE best hitter I've played with," says Tigers teammate Johnny Damon. "Manny [Ramirez] was the best two-out hitter and Alex [Rodriguez] has the perfect swing. But nobody hits like [Cabrera]. I think he realizes that five years from now people could be talking about him among the best hitters ever."

—Tom Verducci, SI, July 19, 2010

10
PETE ROSE

REDS 1963–1978, 1984–1986
PHILLIES 1979–1983
EXPOS 1984

" He barreled headfirst into baseball as a
Rookie of the Year at age 22 in 1963, hit
in 44 straight at age 37 and became
baseball's Hit King at age 44. He had a
poor arm, average speed and just a dollop
of power. But no one has ever given more
on the field. " —KOSTYA KENNEDY

▸ ALL-STAR AT FIVE POSITIONS
▸ ONLY PLAYER TO APPEAR IN
THIS BOOK AT TWO POSITIONS

ROSE'S HITTING STREAK [which
reached 44 games] provided plenty
of drama. And he kept it going
without any assistance from kindly
official scorers or bonus turns at
the plate in extra-inning games. Six
times he saved himself with hits in
his last at bat; four times his only hit
was a bunt. Almost all of his closest
calls came against Philadelphia:
in Games 32 and 41 he dropped
perfect bunts in front of Phillies
third baseman Mike Schmidt. "Pete
gave me two chances to stop the
streak, and I didn't do it either time,"
says Schmidt, a Gold Glove fielder.
"He'd never bunted on me before,
and then he laid down two perfect
ones that I couldn't come up with.
I've really got to respect him. He's
the epitome of concentration.
He's turned into my idol."
—Larry Keith, SI, August 7, 1978

Rose never feared getting the uniform dirty.

PHOTOGRAPH BY RONALD C. MODRA

10

THE

BEST SHORTSTOPS

THE SHORTSTOP IS "THE MOST IMPORTANT PART OF THE DEFENSE EXCEPT FOR THE PITCHING," ROBERT W. CREAMER WROTE IN SI IN 1982. "DEFENSIVE SKILL IS SO IMPORTANT THERE THAT CLUBS HAVE GONE LONG PERIODS WITH NONHITTERS AT THE POSITION. MARK BELANGER, A .227 BATTER WHO WAS THE ORIOLES SHORTSTOP FOR 17 SEASONS, IS A CASE IN POINT. SO WAS DETROIT'S RAY OYLER; IN 1968 HE BATTED ONLY .135, BUT HIS FIELDING HELPED WIN THE AMERICAN LEAGUE PENNANT."

THE LIGHT-HITTING MR. OYLER DID NOT MAKE OUR TOP 10, BUT IT DOES GIVE A WINDOW INTO HOW A CAREER .262 HITTER WHO NUDGED OUT A MERE 28 HOME RUNS IN 19 SEASONS WAS ABLE TO SOMERSAULT HIS WAY TO THE NUMBER FOUR SPOT. OZZIE SMITH DID SO ON THE STRENGTH OF BEING, IN THE EYES OF OUR PANELISTS, THE BEST DEFENSIVE PLAYER IN BASEBALL HISTORY AT ANY POSITION.

ONE SUBPLOT OF THE SHORTSTOPS LIST IS THAT IT INCLUDES A PAIR OF MEN WHO, SINCE 2004, HAVE BEEN TEAMMATES, WITH ONE ABANDONING HIS NATURAL POSITION OF SHORTSTOP TO AC-COMODATE THE PRESENSCE OF THE OTHER. OUR PANEL RANKING AFFIRMS THAT, DESPITE THE PRODIGIOUS TALENTS OF ALEX RODRI-GUEZ, IT WOULD HAVE BEEN A SUBVERSION OF PROPER ORDER TO HAVE DEREK JETER BE THE ONE TO SLIDE OVER TO THIRD.

1

HONUS WAGNER

LOUISVILLE COLONELS 1897–1899
PIRATES 1900–1917

" Wagner, an icon of the Dead Ball Era, is on the short list of the greatest players ever. The Flying Dutchman hit for power, won batting titles and stole bases with ease. " —STEPHEN CANNELLA

- EIGHT NL BATTING TITLES
- 723 CAREER STOLEN BASES

WAGNER WAS so popular that he aroused the jealous ire of Pittsburgh's great philanthropist Andrew Carnegie. Smarting over a banner that proclaimed the shortstop the GREATEST MAN IN OUR TOWN, Carnegie threatened in 1909 to discontinue his contributions to the city's social and cultural causes. This prompted a young sportswriter, Grantland Rice, to compose the verse. *Oh, Andy, Andy, Andy—though you stand upon the street /And shovel out a million unto every guy you meet; Though you blow a half a billion, you will never have the call, As the greatest man in Pittsburgh while H. Wagner hits the ball. . . .* At 5' 11" and 200-plus pounds, with legs so bowed that, according to one writer, they "take off at the ankles in an outward and upward direction and join his torso at the belt with some element of surprise," Wagner looked more like a catcher—which was the only position he did not play.

—Ron Fimrite, SI, June 10, 1996

Wagner was one of five charter Hall of Fame inductees.

PHOTOGRAPH BY NATIONAL BASEBALL HALL OF FAME

ORIOLES 1981–2001

Ripken celebrated setting the consecutive games mark.

PHOTOGRAPH BY WALTER IOOSS JR.

2

CAL RIPKEN JR.

" His Ironman streak has always obscured just how great he was as a player. He is just one of seven players with 3,000 hits and 400 home runs and, in 1990, he set a mark for single-season fielding percentage by a shortstop. " —ALBERT CHEN

▸ 3,184 CAREER HITS,
431 CAREER HOME RUNS
▸ TWO-TIME AL MVP

"I GREW UP in a family where everything was a competition," says Ripken. "If you didn't [try hard], it wasn't fun. My dream was to make it in baseball, then go to the Superstars competition. When my chance came, I had no time to prepare, so I didn't go. I wasn't going to go down there and just go through the motions."

—Tim Kurkjian, SI, July 29, 1991

FROM SPORTS ILLUSTRATED
DECEMBER 18,1995

HAND IT TO CAL

*Cal Ripken was named SI's Sportsman of the Year
after he broke baseball's consecutive games record and
gave even the most jaded fans a reason to cheer*

BY RICHARD HOFFER

THIS HAS BEEN AN ERA OF diminished expectations, of lowered standards in sports. Today's fan, disappointed by his heroes and his pastimes, watches his games with more resignation than anticipation. It's entertainment, all right, but it's not what the fan remembers as sport. And there's hardly anything to root for anymore. He settles for the sullen competence that is allowed to qualify as stardom these days.

Then there comes a year like this.

There's a man, close-cropped gray hair, looks older than 35, standing in the partial glow of stadium lights, standing along the railing of an empty field, signing autographs hours after a game. He doesn't really have any place to go, his family is asleep, so it's no big deal. He signs away, not to rekindle a country's love affair with its national pastime (that kind of calculation is beyond him) but because somebody wants something and it's easy to give. A teammate offers him a big leaguer's diagnosis: "You're sick."

The man shrugs. He has played in more games consecutively than any other man, dead or alive. Punched in, punched out. It's not so much a record, not a reward for greatness, as it is a by-product of sustained adolescence and, of course, unusual good health. A milestone is all it is. He knows it too. The man shrugs, signing away beneath the stadium lights. "If you could play baseball every day," he says, "wouldn't you?"

Cal Ripken Jr. is not the greatest baseball player ever, or even of his day. But how could he not be our Sportsman of the Year? He's like the rest in our little galaxy—but more so. He's dedicated to his craft, respectful of his game and proud enough of his abilities to continue their refinement well into his 30s.

His "assault" on Lou Gehrig's record of 2,130 consecutive games played was surely the least dramatic record run of all time. We knew for years that, barring an injury, Gehrig's record was going to fall. Nobody had to wonder whether some Orioles manager was going to yank Ripken from the lineup to rest him, or whether Ripken himself was going to beg out of the second half of a doubleheader to nurture some mysterious ache. And assuming the fan could read a baseball schedule, he knew months in advance exactly when (Sept. 6) and where (Camden Yards) the record-breaking would happen. There was nothing conditional about this record except Ripken's attendance. He didn't have to hit in his 57th straight game, pitch a seventh no-hitter, clout his 62nd home run. No record, before or since, has been set with less pressure. All Ripken had to do to set it was be there.

Yet it turned out to be one of the great feel-good events in sports—ever—and if there wasn't a lump in your throat when Ripken circled the field in a reluctant kind of victory lap, you weren't paying attention. It released a pent-up emotion after two strike-shortened seasons, a missed World Series and a general surliness had destroyed a hundred-plus years' worth of fan loyalty. The fan had long ago learned to cope with the huge salaries and the sordid commerce that had infected his game. But the owners' and players' indifference to tradition was stunning. They would sacrifice a World Series for . . . what? Can anybody remember? A fan who was no stranger to nostalgia was used to wondering, Can't anybody play this game? It was an old argument, an inviting complaint, harmless. But now he had to ask the far more discouraging question, Won't anybody play this game?

Ripken would. He would play all the games he could, as hard as he could. In a sport accustomed to celebrating freaks of different and unique abilities, Ripken was instead a freak of disposition. He just liked to play baseball. You can't play 14 seasons through and through if you don't like it. Why Ripken liked baseball this much is anyone's guess, though there surely is a genetic component to it.

For him, family life was the residue of baseball; it was whatever was left over from the game. Cal Sr. was a longtime manager and coach in the Orioles' organization, making stops in places like Elmira and Rochester, dragging the family along. And Cal Jr. took to the game, understanding his childhood to be privileged—taking infield practice with future major leaguers or just listening to his father detail the Orioles' cutoff play. As a 12-year-old he was developing resource material.

Still, heredity doesn't account for the sense of obligation and appreciation he has for baseball. Nor does his entry into pro ball, when scouts placed him on the slow track, to the extent they put him on any track at all. Remember that Ripken was not encouraged to believe he had any special talents back in 1978, when eight shortstops were picked ahead of him in the baseball draft.

Sixteen years later he has outlasted those eight and plenty more. His endurance has become the new standard of sport, and his run for the record couldn't have been more timely. In an era of slouching gods, this devotion to duty was a curative. Here was Ripken, looking somewhat old in his gray-stubble buzz cut, coming to the park every day. It helped that he didn't bounce around, didn't exaggerate his love of the game, didn't act like some caricatured goof from a Norman Rockwell painting. He just kept coming to work because . . . why wouldn't you? "Look," he says, wholly ignorant of the heavenly glow he might attach to his myth with this statement, "the season's long, 162 games, and a pennant could be decided in any one of them. You never know which one. But do you want to take a chance? Is that the game you'd want to sit out?" ∎

3

DEREK JETER

YANKEES 1995–PRESENT

The 13-time All-Star has won five Gold Gloves.

PHOTOGRAPH BY TOM DIPACE

" Judging Derek Jeter's value by his numbers alone does him a disservice. For a true appreciation you must examine the intangibles, as seen in his backhanded relay to nab Jeremy Giambi at the plate against Oakland during the 2001 ALDS. " —DAVID SABINO

▸ MOST HITS BY A YANKEE
▸ .308 POSTSEASON AVERAGE

"EVERYTHING HE does has such a grace about it," A's general manager Billy Beane says. "Even now, people say to me, 'You must be rooting against the Yankees.' But you know, maybe because of Jeter, the Yankees know how to win. It's not an act. The Yankees' brand name in this era is that it is Jeter's era.

—*Tom Verducci, SI, December 7, 2009*

OZZIE
SMITH

PADRES 1978–1981
CARDINALS 1982–1996

" As statistical measures for defense grow
more sophisticated, the numbers only
confirm what we saw with our own eyes:
Ozzie is baseball's best defender ever, at
any position. But 2,460 hits, 580 stolen
bases and uncounted backflips should be
remembered too. " —DAVID BAUER

▸ 13 GOLD GLOVES
▸ MLB RECORD HOLDER FOR
ASSISTS AT SS

"I MAY BE his teammate, but I'm
also his fan," says Cardinals second
baseman Tommy Herr. "So many
times I'll see the ball leave the bat
and say, 'O.K., that's a base hit.' And
then somehow Ozzie will come up
with it. A lot of the time I feel like
standing out there and applauding."
Andy MacPhail, the Twins executive
vice president who is the son of
former American League president
Lee MacPhail and the grandson of
baseball executive Larry MacPhail,
has been hearing about the old days
longer than he cares to recall. "I've
heard scouts talking about modern
players, and they'll always say, 'Yeah,
but Mickey Mantle could do this,' or
'Willie Mays could do that.' There was
always a player in the past who was
better. But with Ozzie Smith they
always acknowledge that he's the best
defensive shortstop they've ever seen.

—Ron Fimrite, SI, September 28, 1987

Smith's backflips showcased his great athleticism.

PHOTOGRAPH BY RICHARD PILLING

5

ERNIE BANKS

CUBS 1953–1971

" Mr. Cub was a freak—a slugging shortstop when there were none. No shortstop had ever hit 40 home runs in a season, or come close, before Banks, who did it five times in six years. And no shortstop has ever fielded a ground ball with more grace. " —DAVID BAUER

▸ TWO-TIME NL MVP
▸ 512 CAREER HOME RUNS

HIS PERFORMANCE aside, the impressive facet of Banks has been his implacability, his unruffled calm in the face of utter futility and embarrassment. Playing for the Cubs was like doing 10 to 20 at Folsom; a fine season for them was one in which they flirted with mediocrity. In an atmosphere such as this it is hard for a player—even if he is Ernie Banks—to retain his identity. An abacus is necessary to tabulate the number of people Banks played under. Confronted by a parade of emotions, personalities, techniques and desperation, Banks remained Banks. His deportment never tottered amid the chaos. He veered away from club politics, and he seemed to play a private game in his own little corner, never stopping to ponder how insignificant he might be or becoming sullen over the fact that all he could look toward each season was a lonely war with those dreadful figures.

—Mark Kram, SI, September 29, 1969

Banks was as skilled as his disposition was sunny.

PHOTOGRAPH BY NEIL LEIFER

6

ARKY VAUGHAN

PIRATES 1932–1941
DODGERS 1942–1943, 1947–1948

" In Pitt did Arky Vaughan hit, and how, particularly in 1935, when the Pirates' shortstop won the batting crown with a .385 average—best-ever at the time for a modern-era shortstop—and led the NL in on-base (.491) and slugging percentage (.607). " —DICK FRIEDMAN

▸ .318 CAREER AVERAGE
▸ LED NL IN RUNS THREE TIMES

IN A DECADE of great shortstops, Vaughan was the best, a high-average line-drive hitter and a steady, dependable fielder who was also much better than his reputation would seem to indicate. (There's a definite syndrome in baseball thinking that goes: If a shortstop is a good hitter, then he mustn't be able to field.)

—*Robert W. Creamer, SI, September 27, 1982*

Vaughan hit above .300 every season he was in Pittsburgh.

**MARINERS 1994–2000,
RANGERS 2001–2003,
YANKEES 2004–PRESENT**

> "The latter part of his career is marked by controversy, but before he was a cartoonish slugger he was a graceful shortstop who blended power and speed like few righthanded hitters ever have." —STEPHEN CANNELLA

▸ THREE-TIME AL MVP
▸ EIGHT 40-HOMER SEASONS

Rodriguez arrived in the majors with all the tools.

PHOTOGRAPH BY ROBERT BECK

AS A BALLPLAYER he's almost too good to be true. He is 195 pounds of pure skill and grace, an immensely gifted shortstop who routinely leaves baseball people drooling over their clipboards. He's the youngest position player in the American League, but already he has turned his potential into performance.

—*Gerry Callahan, SI, July 8, 1996*

ALEX RODRIGUEZ

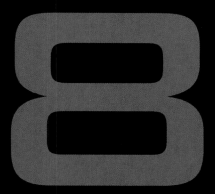

8

BARRY
LARKIN

REDS 1986–2004

" Cincinnati kid Barry Larkin spent all 19 years of his career as the beating heart of his hometown Reds. He showcased his all-around skills in the 1990 World Series, in which he batted .353 as his club swept the favored A's. " —DICK FRIEDMAN

> NINE .300 SEASONS
> 1995 NL MVP

AFTER THE Reds selected him fourth overall in the 1985 amateur draft, Larkin burst through the bushes despite the prognostication of a Cincinnati executive who told Larkin he would never make it to the majors as a shortstop. As if to prove him wrong, Larkin was named the Triple A American Association's MVP in 1986 and was summoned to the majors late that season. Arriving before his equipment did, Larkin had to outfit himself in other players' gear. As he crouched in the on-deck circle before his first big league at bat, wearing Dave Concepcion's shorts, a batboy handed him a note: "Look back, Honey. Your mom and dad are sitting with me in the owner's box—Marge Schott." Larkin turned, waved one of Eric Davis's batting gloves to his folks and strode to the plate in Pete Rose's spikes. He swung Buddy Bell's bat and drove in a run. "Wearing everyone else's stuff," he says, "made me feel like I was part of the team."

—Franz Lidz, SI, June 12, 1995

Larkin brought defense in addition to power and speed.

PHOTOGRAPH BY CHUCK SOLOMON

Yount's long career had an early start, at age 18.

PHOTOGRAPH BY JERRY WACHTER

" An All-Star and an MVP-winner during his decade as a shortstop, he became an All-Star and an MVP-winner during his decade as a centerfielder too. He had a long and robust prime—call it 14 seasons—over which he batted a hard .299. " —KOSTYA KENNEDY

"HE'S AS complete a ballplayer as there is in the game," says Frank Howard, who coached Yount. "Plus, he's a super person. He has the respect of everybody in baseball. Let me put it this way: If your daughter came home with a Robin Yount, you'd be so grateful you'd light candles for the rest of your life."

—*Robert W. Creamer, SI, September 27, 1982*

ROBIN YOUNT

▸ 3,142 CAREER HITS
▸ TWO-TIME AL MVP

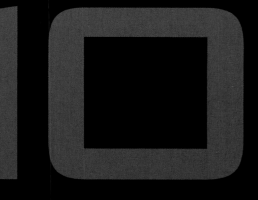

JOE CRONIN

PIRATES 1926–1927
SENATORS 1928–1934
RED SOX 1935–1945

" His Hall of Fame plaque makes note of his extraordinary value: After the shortstop's fifth straight 100-RBI season for Washington, the Senators traded Cronin, then 28, to the Red Sox in 1934 "for reported record price of $250,000." Cronin earned high praise from Connie Mack, who once said, 'With a man on third and one out, I'd rather have Cronin hitting for me than anybody I've ever seen.' " —TOM VERDUCCI

▸ .301 CAREER AVERAGE
▸ EIGHT 100-RBI SEASONS

TOM YAWKEY seems to haunt Fenway Park like a castle ghost. When he walks the corridors and tunnels of Fenway Park, this lank man with a squint and the creased leather face of a Brooks Brothers frontiersman, what does he see? Other ghosts, perhaps. Look. Jim Piersall is climbing the right-centerfield wall to make one of those catches old Casey Stengel said he never seen the likes of. Joe Cronin, the "Boy Manager" for whom the Red Sox paid top dollar, is describing mincing little circles at shortstop, all worried jaw and hunched shoulders. Joe is trying to decide whether to yank Wes Ferrell, who is scratching up furious clouds of dust around the rubber.

—*Melvin Maddocks, SI, September 15, 1975*

Cronin was a player-manager for the Senators and Red Sox.

PHOTOGRAPH BY BETTMANN/CORBIS

10 THE

BEST CATCHERS

HOLD OUT TWO FINGERS AND YOU COULD BE CALLING FOR THE CURVE, OR YOU COULD BE IDENTIFYING THE NUMBER OF CATCHERS WHO WON A BATTING TITLE IN THE 20TH CENTURY. THOSE MEN, LITTLE NOTED NOR LONG REMEMBERED, WOULD BE ERNIE LOMBARDI IN 1938 AND '42 AND BUBBLES HARGRAVE IN 1926. JOE MAUER HAS PULLED OFF THE FEAT THREE TIMES IN THE 21ST CENTURY, BUT IT UNDERLINES HOW RARE IT IS FOR A PLAYER TO STAND OUT WHEN HE SPENDS SO MUCH TIME CROUCHING.

BUT, "IF PITCHING IS THE HEART OF BASEBALL, CATCHING IS ITS MIND AND SOUL." SO WROTE SI'S RON FIMRITE IN A PAEAN TO THE NOBLE BACKSTOP IN JUNE 1972. "STILL, BRAINS ARE NOT ENOUGH. HE MUST ALSO BE BIG, STRONG, AGILE, DURABLE, AGGRESSIVE, CONGENIAL, INTUITIVE, COURAGEOUS AND, WITH REGARD TO PHYSICAL SUFFERING, STOICAL. SMALL WONDER, THEN, THAT THERE ARE SO FEW WHO MERIT IMMORTALITY."

FOUR DECADES LATER, OUR PANEL AGREES WITH FIMRITE THAT FEW CATCHERS MERIT IMMORTALITY: THE VOTE FOR THIS POSITION DREW BY FAR THE NARROWEST GROUP OF NOMINEES. USUALLY THE NUMBER OF PLAYERS CONSIDERED REACHED THE HIGH TEENS. BUT AT CATCHER ONLY 11 MEN WERE NOMINATED TO FILL 10 SLOTS. IT'S A TOUGH JOB TO DO; EVEN TOUGHER, IT SEEMS, TO STAKE A CLAIM AS ONE OF THE BEST EVER.

1

JOHNNY BENCH

REDS 1967–1983

" They talked about his arm ever since he threw out 28 straight base runners in the minor leagues, and they will talk about his bat forever. The anchor of the great Big Red Machine teams of the 1970s, Bench won 10 straight Gold Gloves and led the league in RBI three times— which no other catcher did more than once. " —KOSTYA KENNEDY

▸ TWO-TIME NL MVP
▸ 389 CAREER HOME RUNS

TO APPRECIATE Johnny Bench fully, one must first watch him throw. Jimmy Durante is more than merely a superb nose, and Bench is more than merely a great arm, but he is unimaginable without it. It works like a recoilless rifle. It even awes pitchers. George Culver, who threw well enough for the Reds himself last year to win 11 games, one a no-hitter, says, "I wish I had his arm." Or his hand, even. It is big enough, according to Bench's own assertion, to hold seven balls at once—and to grip one ball way out on the end of his fingers so that he gets a lot of whip. Sandy Koufax did not have such a meaty hand, but he had those long fingers. Dizzy and Paul Dean used to pull on young Paul's fingers when he was growing up, but as good as that boy's genes were his fingers would not stretch enough.

—Roy Blount Jr., SI, March 31, 1969

Bench played in four World Series, winning two.

PHOTOGRAPH BY WALTER IOOSS JR.

2
YOGI BERRA

YANKEES 1946–1963
METS 1965

" Berra seems sprung more from folklore than the sandlots of St. Louis. He fought at D-Day, played in 14 World Series (winning 10 of them), and became beloved in retirement as an affable pitchman and master of spot-on if oddly phrased wisdom. Berra's vast cultural renown may have left his baseball career underappreciated. " —TOM VERDUCCI

▸ THREE-TIME AL MVP
▸ FIVE 100-RBI SEASONS

TWO YEARS AGO Casey Stengel was asked who he thought was the best natural ballplayer in the American League. Stengel thought the question over carefully, his facile tongue temporarily stilled, and then replied: "[Ted] Williams is the best natural hitter, but Berra is the best natural ballplayer." It seemed an odd choice— the chunky, awkward-looking Berra over some graceful athlete like, say, Mickey Mantle or Al Kaline, but Stengel has a deep admiration for the man whose instincts and reflexes are perfectly geared to the environment of 98-mph pitches, 200-pound base runners with spikes high, sudden variations in the age-old theme of bat, ball and glove. No one feels baseball better than Yogi Berra, no one relishes the excitement of its competition more, no one reacts more quickly to its constant challenge.

—Robert W. Creamer, SI, October 22, 1956

Berra played in 17 consecutive All-Star Games.

3
ROY
CAMPANELLA

DODGERS 1948–1957

" He played only 10 seasons in the majors, but was an eight-time All-Star. Still, according to anyone who watched him, no catcher has ever been better at throwing out base runners. " —DAVID BAUER

‣ THREE-TIME NL MVP
‣ 41 HOME RUNS, 142 RBIS
IN 1953

THE SON of an Italian father and a black mother, he was 26 and had already played nine years in the Negro leagues when he finally made it to the majors with the Brooklyn Dodgers in 1948. Campy was a finished product by then, crafty and powerful, a brilliant catcher who had benefited from the tutelage of his manager with the Baltimore Elite Giants, Biz Mackey. Given his chance he quickly made up for lost time. In 1953 he became the first catcher to hit more than 40 homers in a season. And then, with terrible finality, it was all over. On a January night in 1958, Campy was driving from his liquor store in Harlem to his house on the North Shore of Long Island when his car hit an icy patch, spun out of control and, after glancing off a telephone pole, rolled over. Campy suffered spinal injuries that left him paralyzed— except for minimal movement of his hands—from the shoulders down.

—Ron Fimrite, SI, July 5, 1993

Campanella's defensive prowess matched his plate skills.

PHOTOGRAPH BY FRANK HURLEY/NEW YORK DAILY NEWS ARCHIVE/GETTY IMAGES

TRIUMPH OF THE SPIRIT

After a car crash left the catcher paralyzed at 36, Roy Campanella personified will and grace as he lived longer than his doctors believed he could

BY RON FIMRITE

THE CAMPANELLAS LIVE IN A FOUR-bedroom stucco house in the Los Angeles suburb of Woodland Hills. The children are all gone. The house is on one level, and the street outside is straight and flat. "Roy can go out and drive his wheelchair all the way around the block," says his wife, Roxie. "All the neighborhood children come out to see him. They all love him, and he loves them. It's important for Roy to stay active, to feel independent. I've always kept him busy, because as long as he's with people, he doesn't have time to think about himself. And, you know, he helps other people who've been paralyzed. They come from all over to see him. We get calls and letters. When we were still living in New York, we took in a paralyzed boy who wouldn't take his therapy. Roy got him going, and in no time he'd learned how to feed himself."

Campanella is in his trophy room. On the wall above him are his three Most Valuable Player plaques, as well as countless other trophies and citations. "At first, I didn't even play high school baseball," he says. "I loved the game, but I was playing football and basketball and running track at Simon Gratz High in the Nicetown section of Philadelphia, where I grew up. Then one day the physical education teacher and baseball coach, George Patchen, asked me to go out for the team. When I reported to him, I noticed there were four circles drawn down on the field—one each for pitchers, catchers, infielders and outfielders. The other circles were all full of boys. Nobody was standing in the catchers' circle. I figured that was my best chance of making the team, so I stepped into it. I was only in the ninth grade."

Roxie leans forward, clasps Campy under the arms and pulls him halfway out of his chair. He is as helpless as a baby in her grasp. But with his head facing straight-down, he says, "We have to do this. If I don't get off this chair from time to time, I get pressure and sores and bad blisters." Gently, she replaces him in his cushioned seat. His face is expressionless.

Campy motors into the dining room. He looks up at a photograph on the wall. Depicted kneeling on the grass at the perimeter of a diamond formed by four bats is one of the greatest—maybe the greatest—inner defenses in baseball history: Jackie Robinson, second base; Gil Hodges, first base; Campanella, catcher; Billy Cox, third base, and Pee Wee Reese, shortstop. Of that legendary quintet, only Reese and Campanella are still alive.

"When Roy got out of the hospital that first time," says Roxie, "the doctors gave him 10 years to live, 20 at the most. Roy has been in his wheelchair for 32 years. Dr. Rusk died last November." She looks away. "Roy has outlived all of his doctors."

Campy sits on the veranda of the lovely old Otesaga Hotel in Cooperstown, N.Y., at twilight. Below him on the patio, guests sip cocktails beneath green and white umbrellas. In the fading light the white wakes of speeding motorboats can be seen on the blue-gray surface of Lake Otsego. Campy, brilliant in a scarlet sport shirt, looks content. He is among old friends.

The Campanella party includes Campy's attendant, Richard Acosta; Roxie's daughter, Joni; Joni's son, Cary, 13, and her husband, Michael; and Roy and Roxie's old friends from New York City, Judy and Vincent Daquino. Campy is chatting with Vincent when a familiar figure appears on the veranda. "Roy," says Daquino, "there's somebody right behind you who I know you'll want to see."

"You know I can't see behind me."

"How're ya doin', Campy?" says Reese.

Campy laughs. "Well, I do believe I know that voice," he says. "That's my blue-eyed brother." Reese, a 1984 Hall of Fame inductee, pulls up a chair alongside his old teammate.

"You doin' O.K., pal?" Reese asks.

Campy says, "You know, if you haven't experienced it, you'll never know what it's like not being able to breathe. That's something you don't even think about. But a few weeks ago I couldn't do it right. What a feeling when you can't breathe."

Reese pats him on the shoulder and heads off for a television interview on the lawn below. "I'm just amazed he's here," Reese says.

There is quite a party at the Hall that night. Free food and drink. More than 30 Hall of Famers in one room: Ted Williams, Stan Musial, Enos Slaughter, Robin Roberts, Willie Stargell, Willie McCovey . . . and Campy, looking sharp in a checkered gray suit. About 11 o'clock, the celebrants adjourn to the bar at the Otesaga, where Musial entertains on the harmonica with rousing if repetitious choruses of "Wabash Cannonball" and "Oh! Dem Golden Slippers." The bar crowd and the noise swell as the partygoers return from the Hall. "Oh! dem golden slippers. . . . Oh! dem. . . ."

Outside in the cooling night air, where moonlight plays on the water and the shadowy evergreens whisper, the singing and the laughter are only a distant drumming. A limousine draws up to the old hotel's service entrance. Two men, Acosta and Daquino, step briskly out of it and begin unfolding a wheelchair. Campanella sits motionless in the backseat, staring dead ahead.

A shaft of moonlight illuminates that still face. There is a look there that one is not likely to forget. Of what? Resignation, perhaps. Patience, yes. Determination, certainly. Courage, to be sure. But there is something else there, something harder to define. Dignity, that's it. Immense, immeasurable dignity. For in that broken body, a man has prevailed. ∎

4

IVAN RODRIGUEZ

RANGERS 1991–2002, 2009
TIGERS 2004–2008
FOUR OTHER TEAMS

" True fans of greatness prayed that runners would try to steal on Rodriguez, because seeing him gun them down was like watching Hendrix solo or Picasso paint. " —STEPHEN CANNELLA

> 1999 AL MVP
> 13 GOLD GLOVES

NO ONE has to tell Johnny Oates he's got the most important position player in baseball on his team. The manager says that about four hours before every game he goes through the same angst-ridden ritual. "I know in my heart Pudge would put up better offensive numbers if he played fewer games," Oates says. "So every day I come to my office and I think, O.K., what I have to do now is tell Pudge he's getting the day off tomorrow." Sometimes Oates does just that. "But when I come in here the next day, I still write Pudge's name on the lineup card—I can't help it. I get in here and I say, 'Oh, this guy's hurt. That guy's slumping. I've got to play Pudge!'" On the field the temperature is 90°-plus, and Oates, his voice firm, says, "I'll tell you this: Tomorrow Pudge finally does get the day off." Then tomorrow's game comes—and the next and the next. Sheepishly, Oates says, "Looks like I lied again."

—Johnette Howard, SI, August 11, 1997

Pudge's 2,427 games catching are an MLB record.

NEGRO LEAGUES
TWO TEAMS FROM 1930 TO 1946

Gibson was admired for defense as well as hitting.

PHOTOGRAPH BY PERRY CRAGG

5

" His gargantuan clouts are the stuff of legend, and those who saw them swear that Josh Gibson was the greatest righthanded power hitter of all time. " —DICK FRIEDMAN

JOSH GIBSON

▶ .359 CAREER AVERAGE
▶ NINE HOME RUN TITLES

JOSH HIT a home run out of the ballpark, 470 feet if it was an inch. There were 500 people in the stands, but when they passed the hat, $66 was the best they could come up with. The umpires and ball chasers got paid first, and the two teams had to divvy up the $44 that remained. Josh's share was $1.67.

—*John Schulian, SI, June 26, 2000*

MICKEY COCHRANE

A'S 1925–1933
TIGERS 1934–1937

> " Had Cochrane's career not been cut short when he was nearly killed by a pitch to the head, his numbers would be even more impressive. " —DAVID BAUER

- ▸ TWO-TIME AL MVP
- ▸ .320 CAREER AVERAGE

MICKEY COCHRANE was by far the greatest catcher ever to play for the Philadelphia Athletics. He guarded the plate like a brick wall. His throw to second was a work of art. Eventually, Mickey left the A's to manage—and catch for—the Tigers. In 1934 the Tigers won the American League pennant. The next year the Tigers won the pennant *and* the World Series. Not bad for a young catcher-manager. And then Mickey Cochrane disappeared. Anyway, Cochrane was a friend of my father's. My father was a dentist. I think Cochrane liked my father a lot, which would explain why they let me sell something at Shibe Park. I was low man on the totem pole, so I sold the lowliest commodity, soda pop, in a section nicknamed Siberia. Still, I was going to a baseball game just about every day or night, and that's all that mattered. Besides, I didn't want to be a quitter and let Mr. Cochrane down.

—Chuck Barris, SI, October 1, 1984

Cochrane, a tough competitor, was nicknamed Black Mike.

7

CARLTON FISK

RED SOX 1969, 1971–1980
WHITE SOX 1981–1993

" He had his iconic moment—waving fair his home run in the 1975 World Series— but Fisk, beloved in two great baseball towns, was also astoundingly durable, with 24 seasons and 2,226 games behind the plate. " —ALBERT CHEN

▸ 11-TIME ALL-STAR
▸ 376 CAREER HOME RUNS

FISK IS a sophisticated country boy. He knows baseball is Only a Game. He knows there are More Important Things in Life. But, oh, how he wants to win! And to make everybody else want to win, too. "Show me a meek catcher," Campy liked to say, "and I'll show you a nuthin' catcher." Fisk is in no trouble here. He may begin by trotting out to the mound and doing a psych job. "If I can get a pitcher mad enough," he reasons with catcher logic, "he'll want to throw the ball right through me. He can't do that. But he might get a couple of batters out trying. Perfectionism is hard to contain, and once a perfectionist catcher gets going, he is carrying not only the pitching staff but a whole team of prodigal sons on his shoulders. His friends will call him a leader. His enemies will call him cocky. So be it. He wants to make things move, and for a man who really wants that, there are no off-hours.

—*Melvin Maddocks, SI, July 30, 1973*

Fisk had 2,356 career hits and 1,330 career RBIs.

PHOTOGRAPH BY WALTER IOOSS JR.

Dickey had dead aim for throwing out base runners.

" For the Yankees dynasty of the 1930s and '40s, long, lean Bill Dickey caught 100 or more games for 13 straight seasons, setting an AL record. His .362 average in '36 has, among catchers, been bettered only by Joe Mauer's .365 in 2009. " —DICK FRIEDMAN

I SUPPOSE I'd have to pick Bill Dickey as my All-Yankee catcher, but I'd sure like to have Yogi around. Berra had tremendous natural ability to start with and that great willingness to learn that made it almost easy for Dickey, the master, to teach him the finer points of catching.

—*Former Yankees G.M. George M. Weiss, with Robert Shaplen, SI, March 13, 1961*

BILL DICKEY

▸ .313 CAREER AVERAGE
▸ SEVEN WORLD SERIES RINGS

9

MIKE PIAZZA

DODGERS 1992–1998
METS 1998–2005
THREE TEAMS THROUGH 2007

" The Dodgers chose Piazza in the 62nd round of the 1988 draft, but not one of the 1,389 players taken before him enjoyed a better career. " —DAVID SABINO

- ▸ 427 CAREER HOME RUNS
- ▸ .308 CAREER AVERAGE

WHO COULD have known that this kid—the batboy who worked the Dodger games when the team played in Philly—would someday grow into a major league uniform of his own? Ted Williams, that's who. It just so happened that Williams was a friend of a friend of [Mike's dad] Vince Piazza's, and it just so happened that the Hall of Famer had a few hours to spare one Saturday morning in 1984 before making an appearance at a card show near the Piazzas' home. Breakfast that morning was followed by some cuts in the cage and a little batting instruction for 16-year-old Mike—an event the family videotaped. "Mike hits it harder than I did when I was 16," Williams says on the tape. "I guarantee you, this kid will hit the ball. I never saw anybody who looked better at his age." And no wonder. When Williams asked Mike, "Son, do you have my book on hitting?" the kid smiled. He had memorized it.

—*Kelly Whiteside, SI, July 5, 1993*

Piazza holds several slugging marks for catchers.

10
GARY CARTER

EXPOS 1974–1984, 1992
METS 1985–1989
TWO OTHER TEAMS

❝ That smile permanently plastered on the Kid's face? Don't let it fool you. Carter's Little Leaguer exuberance belied a fierce competitiveness that made him the heart and soul of an iconic world championship team. And oh yeah, he could hit a little bit too. ❞ —STEPHEN CANNELLA

▸ 324 CAREER HOME RUNS
▸ THREE GOLD GLOVES

HE IS still called The Kid by his teammates, even those who are years younger than he. His telephone answering service assures the caller, "The Kid'll get back to you," and he wears T-shirts labeled KID. The nickname dates to his rookie year, 1975, when indeed he was, at 21, a kid who was not afraid to act like one. There was no phony sophistication masking rookie terror for him. Carter came on to the older Expos as an Andy Hardy, effusing boyish ardor for everything from batting practice to calisthenics. Some found his gee-whiz manner grating. "I thought I was all grown-up," says pitcher Steve Rogers, who was then 25 and only a few years out of the University of Tulsa. "I was at the point where I considered all that youthful enthusiasm misguided. But with Gary, it was as genuine then as it is now."

—Ron Fimrite, SI, April 4, 1983

Carter's grin was a trademark of his career.

PHOTOGRAPH BY TOM DIPACE

10 THE

BEST LEFTFIELDERS

THE NATURE-OR-NURTURE DEBATE PROBES THE QUESTION OF WHAT INFLUENCES CHARACTER MORE—THE ENVIRONMENT INTO WHICH PEOPLE ARE BORN, OR SOMETHING INHERENT IN THEMSELVES. THE TOPIC POPS TO MIND BECAUSE THREE OF THE TOP 10 LEFTFIELDERS FOUND THEIR PROSPERITY AT FENWAY PARK. CONSIDER THAT AND IT RAISES THE QUESTION: DID THOSE TUSSLES WITH THE GREEN MONSTER SOMEHOW INSPIRE GREATNESS?

TED WILLIAMS AND CARL YASTRZEMSKI SPENT THEIR ENTIRE CAREERS WITH BOSTON. THE MORE PERIPATETIC MANNY RAMIREZ SPENT LESS THAN HALF HIS 19 SEASONS WITH THE RED SOX, BUT STILL, IT'S FOR HIS SLUGGING WITH THEIR TWO WORLD SERIES WINNERS THAT HE IS SO GREATLY REMEMBERED. WELL, THAT AND ALL "MANNY BEING MANNY" INCIDENTS—WHICH RANGE FROM THE GOOFY, LIKE GOING INSIDE THE MONSTER DURING A PITCHING CHANGE TO MAKE A CALL, TO THE SHAMEFUL, SUCH AS HIS SHOVING THE TEAM'S 64-YEAR-OLD TRAVELING SECRETARY TO THE GROUND.

COMPARE RAMIREZ'S EXAMPLE AGAINST THE MODESTY OF YAZ, OR BETTER YET TO THE FIERINESS OF TEDDY BALLGAME—THIS SECTION'S STORY EXCERPT ILLUSTRATES THAT HE WAS A MAN WHO SUFFERED NO FOOLS—AND IT UNDERLINES THAT THESE MEN RETAINED VERY DIFFERENT NATURES, NO MATTER WHAT WALL THEY HAPPENED TO BE PLAYING CAROMS OFF OF.

1

TED WILLIAMS

RED SOX 1939–1942, 1946–1960

" We can only imagine how much greater Ted Williams's career stats would have been under different circumstances. The owner of the last .400 season is still widely considered the greatest hitter ever despite missing most or all of five years in his prime while serving as a combat pilot in the U.S. Marines. " —DAVID SABINO

> .344 CAREER AVERAGE
> 521 CAREER HOME RUNS

"THEY SAY the secret of my hitting is natural ability and my good eyesight," Williams lashed out. "That's so easy to say and to give credit for. They never talk about the practice. Practice! Practice! Practice! Dammit, you gotta practice! . . . Ask anybody who had anything to do with T.S. Williams and they'll tell you he practiced more than anybody. Joe Cronin'll tell you that I hit before the games and after the games. There's never been a hitter who hit more baseballs than Williams. Hell, when I was a kid, I used to get to the schoolhouse before the janitor opened the doors. I'd get the balls and bat, and practice. Then at lunchtime, I'd run home and grab a bunch of fried potatoes and run back to school before anybody was through eating; and I was practicing again. Always practicing."

—Joan Flynn Dreyspool, SI, August 1, 1955

Williams won six AL batting titles and two Triple Crowns.

PHOTOGRAPHS BY HY PESKIN (LEFT) AND JOHN G. ZIMMERMAN

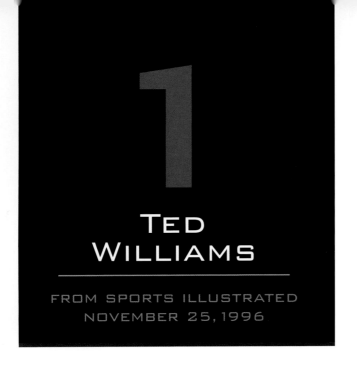

THE PURSUIT OF PERFECTION

The exactitude that made Ted Williams a .400 hitter
carried through all aspects of his life, up to his final years

BY S.L. PRICE

ARLY ONE TUESDAY MORNING in October, in a hilltop house nestled among live oaks dripping Spanish moss—a house set on the highest point in Citrus County, Fla., dominating all it surveys like a medieval castle—an old man struggles. He is close to blind. His long feet are wrapped in leather slippers with elastic across the instep so they won't fall off. A Boston Red Sox cap is on his head. A TV producer smiles and holds up a cue card that isn't helping.

Ted Williams says, "I know a young—"

"No, not 'I *know* a young man,'" the producer says. "'*This* young man.'"

"All *right*," Williams says. "This young man . . . said he'd go to prison himself before releasing prisoners early. And he's got . . . inmates working for the people of Middlesex County."

"That was good—the first part," the producer says. "But the second—"

"All right," Williams cuts in. "If you don't like the second, let's go again."

And with that the temperature in the cozy den ticks upward ever so slightly. Not good. Williams's temper has long been famous for its sudden, lung-tearing explosions, and everybody in the room—the producer; the cameraman; Frank Brothers, Williams's live-in aide; and Buzz Hamon, director of the Ted Williams Museum & Hitters Hall of Fame in Hernando, Fla.—has been grinning, cajoling, trying to take the edge off the morning's project. Williams is making a TV ad for Brad Bailey, a candidate for sheriff of Middlesex County, Mass. Problem is, three strokes in

five years have chipped away 75% of Williams's field of vision, so that he sees as if looking through a pipe, and it doesn't help that the glare of the TV light makes the phrases on the cue card nearly unreadable. Long ago Williams bent his life into a furious pursuit of perfection. Now here he is, in a roomful of people, tripping over words.

In 1941 Williams hit .406 for the Red Sox. In the 55 years since then, few players have come close to hitting .400, and the legend of The Kid's eyesight has only grown: He could follow the seams on a baseball as it rotated toward him at 95 mph. He could read the label on a record as it spun on a turntable. He stood at home plate one day and noticed that the angle to first base was slightly off; measuring proved him right, naturally, by two whole inches.

But that was long ago. Williams is 78 now. Since falling in his driveway and breaking his left shoulder two years ago, he has been unable to drive. This year, for the first time in five decades, he didn't go fishing. His buddies Jack Brothers, Joe Lindia, Sam Tamposi—and, worst of all, his longtime live-in girlfriend, Louise Kaufman—have died in the past five years.

And the parade of trouble didn't stop there. Looking to cash in on the late-1980s sports-memorabilia craze, he entangled himself in a partnership with a scam artist that, when it all crashed, cost Williams close to $2 million in losses and legal bills. Williams then signed up with the well-established trading card and collectibles company Upper Deck Authenticated, but that deal, too, unraveled in a messy whirl through the courts. Meanwhile, his clean, highly readable signature brought such a bonanza to forgers that the Ted Williams autograph—once a symbol of sporting quality—has become one of the most suspect in the business.

It has been, to say the least, a far more public and contentious walk through the sunset than Williams ever dreamed. And while nothing can threaten his legacy as one of the American Century's cultural icons, the result of all his travails is a bewildering new image of Ted Williams as dupe, Ted Williams controlled, that hardly jibes with nearly 60 years of tales depicting him as alternately cold and warm, bitter and sentimental, obnoxious and funny, tough and generous—but always savagely independent. This is, after all, a man who turned down a reported $100,000 and a chance to pal around with Robert Redford as an adviser on *The Natural* because Atlantic salmon were running. This is a two-war Marine pilot who flew half his 39 missions in Korea as John Glenn's wing man, but when they jetted deep into enemy territory, just as often it was Williams leading one of America's greatest pilots.

One summer in the early 1960s, Williams was at his baseball camp in Lakeville, Mass., when a call came in from nearby Hyannis Port: President Kennedy wanted to speak to him. "Tell him I'm a Nixon fan!" Williams roared.

And on this Tuesday morning? He will not be pushed. He does it his way: "No one has impressed me more in such a short time . . . as a man . . . . Ahhh . . . well, *hold* it there . . . turn it towa— . . . the right. . . . No one has impressed me more in such a short period of time as an up-and-coming young man: Brad Bailey . . . . I can't see that big print, for chrissakes!"

Then, abruptly, Williams nails it, the rhythm and tenor of a sweet endorsement: "Just wait till you meet Brad Bailey, and you'll be soooold yourself." The TV guys murmur how perfect it is. Williams beams and leans back in his chair as the men start packing. "That'll be *nice*," he says. "Why didn't you *bring* Cecil B. DeMille? All right!"

HE WAS NEVER CUDDLY. IN HIS playing days he was called Terrible Ted as much as he was called the Splendid Splinter. Disgusted by a home crowd that jeered and cheered him in the same inning of a game between the Red Sox and the Yankees in 1956, Williams trotted in toward the dugout spitting toward both the left- and rightfield stands. Then, to make sure everyone got the message, he stepped back out of the dugout and spit again. As he retells the story, he begins to boil again.

"I have compassion for Roberto Alomar," he says, his voice starting to rise as he refers to Alomar's spitting at umpire John Hirschbeck in September. "I know how upset you can get at a certain thing, and I was so upset!" His face twists, his mouth gapes to reveal a pair of incisors worn to nubs. "I had dropped a fly ball. Just as I started looking up to get the fly ball, bases loaded, a goddam raindrop came down, you know? And I lost just a little bit of the ball, and it hit my glove and bounced out. Well, I really got booed. Boy, I can understand how a guy can get so pissed. He hears that boo, boy, he wants to crack the goddam bark off!"

It's that odd, outsized passion, as much as his .344 lifetime average and his 4½ years of service in World War II and Korea, that always made Williams larger than life. So big that Boston just named a tunnel after him. Unlike DiMaggio, who carried himself with Olympian reserve, Williams was all too human, radiating flaws and ambition. Bats flew into the stands, fishing rods splintered and sank.

His wars with the Boston fans and media so scarred Williams that he refused to tip his hat after homering in his final at bat, in Boston in 1960. But in time this denial took on power, became a strange symbol of integrity. How else to explain why a thirtysomething candidate for sheriff in Massachusetts goes all the way to Florida to seek Williams's blessing? How else to explain why, in 1988, George Bush asked Williams to campaign for him during the New Hampshire primary? The two hit a fishing show in Manchester, and, Bush says, "I might as well not have existed."

SOMETIMES TED CLOSES HIS EYES, AND HIS MIND CONJURES UP the pitchers he beat and the ones who beat him long ago. But more and more he is haunted by visions of his happiest moments, alone with a line and a stream. "I dream of bonefish, I dream of salmon," he says. "I dream of casting for them, I dream of the beautiful spots I've been. And then I dream of some of the fish I've lost."

He speaks about his refuge on the Miramichi River in New Brunswick, Canada, and about spending hours tying thousands of flies and about the throat-catching moment after you've cast the fly and played the fish and you feel the hook dig in. Talking about fishing is not like talking about baseball or politics or history. No, Williams calls what he did in the water "a privilege" and lowers his voice as if describing something holy. And he keeps coming back to the same fish, that 35-pound salmon he hooked 3½ years ago on Quebec's Cascapedia River. It was the middle of the day. "Jeez, what a place!" he says. "Only kings and presidents and big shots and billionaires get to fish in there."

It was as big a salmon as he ever fought. "I made a helluva good cast because I was in kind of a narrow spot, and I was picking at it," he says. His hand slices back and forth across the kitchen table as if it were the surface of the river. His face is alight. "Picking at it this way, and I'm *shootin'* it that way! I was casting 60, 70 feet—a dry fly—and he took it."

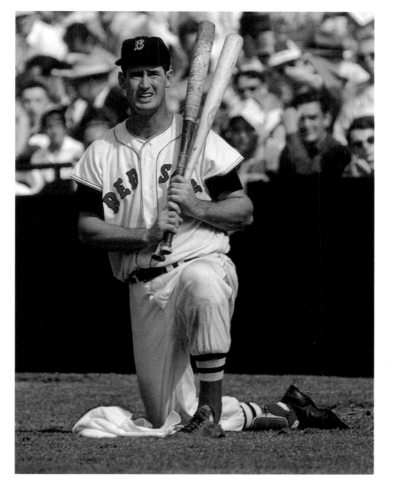

Williams's relationship with Red Sox fans had some notable ups and downs.

Williams leans forward, sets his feet and bears down. His face reddens. "And I fought him," he growls. "And I fought him a little *harder*. And I fought him really hard. I'm thinking, Jeez, I can't bring this fish home, and I'm really flossing it to him, see! And it's a deep little run there. He was down maybe 10 feet, and I couldn't see him . . . and I'm *really* lifting him up! Ummmmph!" He has an invisible fly rod in his hands, and he's trying like hell to pull the fish up through the kitchen floor.

"And then I let go," he says. The invisible rod drops. He crooks a finger in his mouth and tugs. "I had hooked him on this big, dry single hook, and I was just pulling him too hard! I tried the hard pull and he didn't break, so with a good bend I dragged him right up, and the hook pulled out just as he came out of the water." The salmon dropped with a splash. Gone.

It's over. Ted Williams comes back to himself, to a chair in a kitchen, with a fish show on TV. "I didn't get him," he says. "I'll always remember that moment when I close my eyes." He is asked to name the river again, and he repeats it: Cascapedia.

"The closest place to heaven I'll be," he says. "I know that." ∎

CARDINALS 1941–1944,
1946–1963

The three-time MVP and had 17 .300 seasons.

PHOTOGRAPH BY BETTMANN/CORBIS

2

STAN
MUSIAL

" As a consummate blend of power hitter
and contact hitter, he stands side by side
with Ted Williams, and Musial—my
number 1 choice here—was probably the
better defensive outfielder. The main
difference was that everybody liked
Musial. " —DAVID BAUER

▸ .331 CAREER AVERAGE
▸ 475 CAREER HOME RUNS

IT IS hard to consider his life without
feeling that he must have been invented
by Horatio Alger Jr. His is the story of
the poor boy who goes to the great city,
marries a lovely girl, becomes rich and
famous. But Horatio Alger wrote of
shoe clerks and newsboys; when Musial
stands at the plate, he is a warrior.

—Paul O'Neil, SI, December 23, 1957

3

RICKEY HENDERSON

A'S 1979–1984, 1989–1993,
1994–1995, 1998
EIGHT TEAMS THROUGH 2003

" "Rickey is the greatest leadoff hitter of all time," Rickey Henderson has said, and Rickey is right. He stole 100 bases in a season at age 21 and 66 at age 39 and augmented his speed with dangerous power. " —KOSTYA KENNEDY

▸ MLB RECORD 1,406 CAREER STOLEN BASES
▸ MLB RECORD 2,295 CAREER RUNS SCORED

DOC MEDICH was determined not to go down without a struggle. He threw to first base. Henderson scrambled back safely. The crowd—Medich's crowd!—booed him for crabbing the runner's act. Three more times Medich threw to first. Content that he had gotten a message across, Medich now addressed himself to the batter, Wayne Gross. Henderson was off with the first pitch. Ted Simmons had called a pitchout, and he bounded out to his left, and threw hard to second. Robin Yount caught the ball and swept down with his glove. Umpire Mike Reilly gave the "safe" sign. Henderson wrenched the bag loose from its moorings and held it aloft in triumph. The stolen base was transported by County Stadium functionaries to Lou Brock, the dethroned record holder, who waited at home plate for his successor.

—Ron Fimrite, SI, September 6, 1982

Henderson drew a record 2,129 unintentional walks.

PHOTOGRAPH BY V.J. LOVERO

4

BARRY BONDS

PIRATES 1986–1992
GIANTS 1993–2007

"A better batter through chemistry? Perhaps. But before he bulked up and achieved his historic power surge Bonds was an authentic five-tool star, and is the only player with more than 500 homers and 500 steals." —DICK FRIEDMAN

▸ MLB RECORD 762 CAREER HOME RUNS
▸ SEVEN-TIME NL MVP

FOR SOME REASON Bonds is reminded of his own childhood, of a play in which he performed in elementary school. He had to go onto the stage and introduce each new act, each time wearing a different costume. He remembers that for one introduction, he was supposed to wear a wet suit, but he didn't have time to don it and, instead, went out bare-chested. It wasn't much of a gaffe. But what he most remembers is that nobody booed. "You never see a five-year-old get booed," he said. "Always applauded, because they're trying. Always getting encouragement or praise. Because that little boy is trying." It's an odd thought for a rich superstar, years and MVPs removed from grade school. But then Bonds says something even odder. More that little boy than anyone might believe, he says, "That's the way it should always be."

—*Richard Hoffer, SI, May 24, 1993*

The home run leader also won eight Gold Gloves.

PHOTOGRAPH BY V.J. LOVERO

5

AL SIMMONS

A'S 1924–1932,
1940–1941, 1944
SIX OTHER TEAMS

" Righthanded-hitting Al Simmons violated the precept taught to every Little Leaguer: When he swung, he stepped toward third base. For "Bucketfoot Al," it sure worked. Simmons batted better than .300 and drove in more than 100 runs in each of his first 11 big league seasons. " —DICK FRIEDMAN

▸ .334 CAREER AVERAGE
▸ 307 CAREER HOME RUNS

FOR YEARS Simmons's line drives beat like distant drums off the right-centerfield fence at Shibe. For kids who haunted the perimeters of Shibe, Simmons was the grist of legend. This was a time when players often lived in private homes near the ballparks where they played. Simmons lived across the street from Shibe's rightfield fence, in a second-floor bedroom in the home of Mr. and Mrs. A.C. Conwell. Simmons was a notoriously late sleeper, and the discreet Mrs. Conwell would ask neighborhood boys to awaken the star so he would not miss batting practice. One of the lads was Jerry Rooney, whose family lived three doors away, and at age four, he recalls, he entered Simmons's room and whispered to him, "It's time to wake up, Al. You're in a slump, and it's time to go to batting practice."

—William Nack, SI, August 19, 1996

Simmons hit .381 in 1930 and .390 in '31.

CARL YASTRZEMSKI

RED SOX 1961–1983

" He'll always be remembered for his magical Triple Crown season in 1967, the year he led Boston to its first pennant in two decades. But Yaz also personified longevity: he ranks second on the alltime list for games played by any player and third in at bats. " —ALBERT CHEN

▸ 3,419 CAREER HITS
▸ 452 CAREER HOME RUNS

IT WAS NOT merely that Yastrzemski won baseball's rare Triple Crown. People will remember him for providing the spark to a team that had entered the season as a 100-to-1 shot—and for leading the American League through the wildest pennant race major league baseball has ever had. In the final two games of the season Boston needed victories in both to win the pennant. Yastrzemski got seven hits in eight at bats in the two games, and the Red Sox won both of them and the American League championship. In the World Series against St. Louis, Carl batted .400 and made several excellent defensive plays in a losing cause. In the last game of the Series, with the Sox hopelessly behind, Yastrzemski came up in the ninth and singled sharply. The crowd in Boston stood and roared its acclaim, probably because, more than anyone else, Carl Yastrzemski still believed in the dream.

—*Sports Illustrated, December 25, 1967*

The seven-time Gold Glover tamed the Green Monster.

PHOTOGRAPHS BY ART SHAY (LEFT) AND NEIL LEIFER

7

JOE JACKSON

A'S 1908–1909
INDIANS 1910–1915
WHITE SOX 1915–1920

" Separating fact from fiction is difficult in the story of Shoeless Joe. But this much is indisputable: He ranks third on the alltime career batting average list (.356) and was a giant of the Deadball Era. " —STEPHEN CANNELLA

▸ HIT .408 IN 1911
▸ FOUR 200-HIT SEASONS

Jackson hit .375 in the 1919 World Series.

PHOTOGRAPH BY CHARLES M. CONLON/TSN/ICON SMI

JACKSON WAS tried for throwing the Series, and a jury acquitted him. However, Kenesaw Mountain Landis banned Jackson. Baseball was then riddled with gambling, and Landis used this broad stroke to give the sport some credibility. Jackson was no villain; he was probably more an innocent victim or a scapegoat.

—*Nicholas Dawidoff, SI, June 12, 1989*

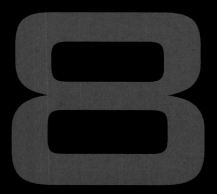

8

WILLIE STARGELL

PIRATES 1962–1982

" Few batters cut a more intimidating figure at the plate than Stargell, a 6'3", 225-pound lefthanded hitter who would windmill his bat before a pitch as if winding a crank. He blasted seven of the 16 balls ever hit completely out of Forbes Field. Stargell is remembered as much for his leadership qualities as he is for his big bat, particularly at the forefront of the 1979 "We Are Family" championship Pirates. " —TOM VERDUCCI

- 475 CAREER HOME RUNS
- 1979 NL MVP AT AGE 39

WHETHER HE is making a stretch run or mugging it up with the Pittsburgh fans, Stargell's pleasure comes from enjoying life and helping others to do the same. When Stargell is asked to sign an autograph, he makes the occasion even more memorable for the fans by engaging them in conversation. Stargell's view of baseball is refreshingly down home. "We're only playing out there," he says. "If we have to concentrate so damn hard that we can't have fun, we may as well put on a suit, sit in an office and give dictation to some secretary—that's how a business should be run. When I lose the desire to go out there every day, then I'll let some other excited youngster enjoy it. Until then someone will have to take it away."

—Anthony Cotton, SI, August 20, 1979

"Pops" was beloved both in and out of the clubhouse.

PHOTOGRAPH BY OZZIE SWEET

9

LOU BROCK

CUBS 1961–1964
CARDINALS 1964–1979

" Perhaps the finest base stealer produced on planet Earth (Rickey Henderson arrived from somewhere else), Brock took extraordinary pride in his craft. Yet Brock thought of himself as a hitter and not a runner. On the way to 3,023 hits he cracked .300 eight times. " —KOSTYA KENNEDY

▸ 938 CAREER STOLEN BASES
▸ .391 POSTSEASON AVERAGE

"I HAVE a decided advantage over the pitcher," Brock says, "because I can change my stealing technique, but a pitcher's motion is mechanical. He cannot alter it without risking injury to his arm. By using varying lengths and styles of leads and takeoffs, I minimize detection of my plans." At times Brock stands four or five steps off the base and rests his hands against his knees. At times he takes the same lead but puts his hands on his hips. Sometimes he stands motionless. "All this time," he says, "I'm getting ready to make my move." Pitchers have moves of their own, of course, and Brock has classified them. "All pitchers fall into four broad categories," he says. "I rate moves as fast, quick, moderate and slow. Believe it or not, you can be slow *and* quick. Add their tendencies to that, and, well, that's pretty much all there is to know."

—*Mark Mulvoy, SI, July 22, 1974*

Brock starred on two World Series winners in St. Louis.

PHOTOGRAPH BY WALTER IOOSS JR.

Ramirez played in four Fall Classics.

PHOTOGRAPH BY JOHN W. MCDONOUGH

10

MANNY RAMIREZ

INDIANS 1993–2000
RED SOX 2001–2008
THREE TEAMS 2008–2011

" The phrase "It's just Manny being Manny" held many connotations, but the one that applied the most to the often-flighty Ramirez was his ability to crush pitches. " —DAVID SABINO

▸ .312 CAREER AVERAGE
▸ 555 CAREER HOME RUNS

RAMIREZ'S FIRST coach wanted to make him a pitcher because he couldn't hit the ball. He refused, because it was hitting that lit him up from inside. It was hitting that spread the grin across his great Toltec face. He worked on the swing until the swing was the statement of who he was.

—*Charles P. Pierce, SI, July 5, 2004*

10 THE

BEST CENTERFIELDERS

A 1955 SI COVER STORY PONDERED THE QUESTION OF WHICH CENTERFIELDER WAS BETTER: DUKE SNIDER OF THE DODGERS OR HIS RIVAL ON THE GIANTS, WILLIE MAYS. "IT'S JUST PLAIN SILLY, COMPARING US," SNIDER SAID. "I THINK THE REAL FANS KNOW WHO'S THE BETTER BALLPLAYER. I MAKE MORE MONEY, DON'T I?"

SNIDER DID OUTEARN MAYS IN 1955, BY ROUGHLY $35,000 TO $25,000, BUT MORE NOTEWORTHY THAN CONTRACT DETAILS ARE THE RICHES THAT NEW YORK FANS ENJOYED AT THE TIME. FOR IN ADDITION TO SNIDER AND MAYS IN THE NL, NEW YORK'S AL TEAM HAD A YOUNG MAN NAMED MICKEY MANTLE. THREE OF SI'S TOP CENTERFIELDERS WERE IN THE SAME CITY AT THE SAME TIME, UNTIL MAYS AND SNIDER MOVED WITH THEIR TEAMS TO CALIFORNIA.

TWO OF OUR TOP 10, THOUGH, PLAYED FURTHER FROM THE SPOTLIGHT: NEGRO LEAGUE LEGENDS COOL PAPA BELL AND OSCAR CHARLESTON. WHEN HISTORIAN BILL JAMES CREATED HIS LIST OF THE TOP 100 PLAYERS EVER, HE EVALUATED NEGRO LEAGUE PLAYERS AND FOUND HIMSELF COMPARING STORIES TO STATS. "YOU WIND UP MAKING A LOT OF ASSUMPTIONS," JAMES TOLD SI IN 2005. JAMES RATED CHARLESTON FOURTH—NOT AS A CENTERFIELDER, BUT AS A PLAYER AT ANY POSITION. CHARLESTON DIDN'T SCALE QUITE THOSE HEIGHTS HERE, BUT THESE PLAYERS, DENIED THE BIGGEST STAGE, STILL MADE THEIR MARK ON HISTORY.

1

WILLIE MAYS

GIANTS 1951–1972
METS 1972–1973

❝ Mays defined *superstar* from the minute he set foot in Philadelphia's Shibe Park in 1951 at age 20 for his major league debut. Phillies pitcher Robin Roberts said after seeing Mays just in batting practice, 'I remember thinking, This has to be as good-looking a player as I ever saw. And it turned out he was the best player I ever saw.' ❞ —TOM VERDUCCI

‣ 3,283 CAREER HITS,
660 CAREER HOME RUNS
‣ 12 GOLD GLOVE AWARDS

A YOUNG and nameless pitcher, up for a tryout, sauntered out to face Willie in batting practice. "You got a curve?" Willie called. "Yeah," the youngster said. He heaved the ball. Willie smacked it over the fence. "You got something else?" Willie called. "Yeah," the youngster grunted. He heaved another ball. Willie smashed it solidly and it smacked the pitcher in the right leg a little above the knee. The young pitcher did not wince or grimace. Apparently he was manfully determined to show that getting his leg almost knocked off didn't faze him in the slightest. Willie looked with seeming bewilderment at the young pitcher, nonchalantly toeing up for another pitch. A grin began to tug at the corners of Willie's mouth, but, diplomatically, he kept it from spreading.

—*Joe David Brown, SI, April 13, 1959*

Mays robbed Cleveland's Vic Wertz (right) in the '54 Series.

2

TY COBB

TIGERS 1905–1926
A'S 1927–1928

" Ty Cobb's ornery reputation has endured through the years, but when the inaugural class of the Baseball Hall of Fame was selected, he received the greatest support from the voters, named on 98.2% (222 of 226) of the ballots cast. " —DAVID SABINO

▸ 4,189 CAREER HITS
▸ 897 CAREER STOLEN BASES

Cobb won nine consecutive batting titles.

HE DID more than just hit for average and steal bases. Almost contemptuously, Cobb bunted his way on base, forced errors, drew walks, slashed line drives . . . and then audaciously raced into the no-man's-land between bases, challenging his opponents to stop him if they dared.

—*Robert W. Creamer, SI, August 19, 1985*

3

JOE
DiMAGGIO

YANKEES 1936–1942, 1946–1951

"An extraordinary hitter who entered his final season with 349 career home runs and 333 strikeouts, DiMaggio unfurled the sport's enduring record, that 56-game hitting streak in the summer of 1941, when the nation turned its lonely eyes to him." —KOSTYA KENNEDY

‣ THREE-TIME AL MVP
‣ TWO BATTING TITLES

HE HAD fame that transcended mere celebrity. For nearly half a century after his playing days had ended, Joe DiMaggio remained a regal presence in the public eye, a species of American aristocrat. I've known people who couldn't tell an infield fly from a household pest who nevertheless held the Yankee Clipper in awe.

—Ron Fimrite, SI, March 15, 1999

In 1969 writers voted DiMaggio the greatest living player.

PHOTOGRAPH BY AP

4

MICKEY MANTLE

YANKEES 1951–1968

" He was the ultimate "five-tool player" long before anyone called it that. Without the injuries—the first serious knee injury, at age 19, initiated a decline in speed; a shoulder injury in '57 diminished his ability to switch-hit—he would have become the greatest all-around player ever. " —DAVID BAUER

▸ THREE-TIME AL MVP
▸ 1956 AL TRIPLE CROWN WINNER

HE WASN'T the greatest player who ever lived, not even of his time perhaps. He was a centerfielder of surprising swiftness, and he was given to spectacle: huge home runs (the Yankees invented the tape-measure home run for him), huge seasons, and one World Series after another. Yet he never became Babe Ruth or Joe DiMaggio—or, arguably, even Willie Mays, his exact contemporary. But for generations of men, he's the guy, has been the guy, will be the guy. And what does that mean exactly? A woman beseeches Mantle, who survived beyond his baseball career as a kind of corporate greeter, to make an appearance, to surprise her husband. Mantle materializes at some cocktail party, introductions are made, and the husband weeps in the presence of such fantasy made flesh. It means that, exactly.

—Richard Hoffer, SI, August 21, 1995

Mantle hit 18 World Series home runs.

PHOTOGRAPH BY HY PESKIN

THE MANTLE OF THE BABE

The sheer power of Mickey Mantle's home runs, even more than their quantity, led fans to compare number 7 to the greatest slugger of them all

BY ROBERT W. CREAMER

A THICK-BODIED, PLEASANT-faced young man, carrying a bat, stood at home plate in Yankee Stadium, turned the blond bullet head on his bull's neck toward Pedro Ramos, a pitcher in the employ of the Washington Senators, watched intently the flight of the baseball thrown toward him, bent his knees, dropped his right shoulder slightly toward the ball, clenched his bat and raised it to a near-perfect perpendicular. Twisting his massive torso under the guidance of a magnificently tuned set of reflexes, Mickey Mantle so controlled the exorbitant strength generated by his legs, back, shoulders and arms that he brought his bat through the plane of the flight of the pitch with a precision which propelled the ball immensely high and far toward the rightfield roof, so high and far that old-timers in the crowd—thinking perhaps of Babe Ruth—watched in awe and held their breath.

For no one had ever hit a fair ball over the majestic height of the gray-green façade that looms above the three tiers of grandstand seats in this, the greatest of ball parks.

Indeed, in the 33 years since the Stadium was opened not one of the great company of home run hitters who have batted there—the list includes Babe Ruth, Lou Gehrig, Joe DiMaggio, Jimmie Foxx, Hank Greenberg and about everyone else you can think of—had even come close to hitting a fair ball over the giant-sized filigree hanging from the lip of the stands which in both right and leftfield hook far into fair territory toward the bleachers.

Mantle hit the filigree. He came so close to making history that he made it.

The ball struck high on the façade, barely a foot or two below the edge of the roof. Ever since, as people come into the stadium and find their seats, almost invariably their eyes wander to The Spot. Arms point and people stare in admiration. Then they turn to the field and seek out Mantle.

On that same day that he hit the facade Mantle hit a second homer. This one was his 20th of the season and it put him at that date (May 30) 12 games ahead of the pace Babe Ruth followed when he established his quasi-sacred record of 60 in 1927. Other players in other years had excitingly chased Ruth's record. But Mantle, somehow, seemed different from earlier pretenders to Ruth's crown and different, too, from slugging contemporaries like Yogi Berra, whose great skill seems almost methodical, and Dale Long, who is still, despite all, an unknown quantity.

The excitement surrounding Mantle goes beyond numbers, beyond homers hit and homers and games to go. Like Ruth, his violent strength is held in a sheath of powerful, controlled grace. Like Ruth, he makes home run hitting simple and exciting at the same time. The distance he hits his home runs (the approved cliché is "Ruthian blast") takes away the onus of cheapness, a word often applied to the common variety of home run hit today, and leaves the spectator aghast, whether he roots for Mantle or against him.

All this holds true despite the hard fact that heretofore in his five years in the major leagues the most home runs Mantle has hit in one season is 37, whereas Ruth hit 40 or more 11 different times, and two dozen others have hit 40 or more at least once.

Yet where others impress, Mantle awes. Harvey Kuenn, the shortstop of the Detroit Tigers and a topflight hitter in his own right, listened as sportscaster Howard Cosell, an eyewitness, described the Memorial Day home run to him.

"Did he really hit it up there?" Kuenn asked, knowing but not believing. "Really?" He shook his head. "His strength isn't human," he said. "How can a man hit a ball that hard?"

Marty Marion, the unexcitable manager of the Chicago White Sox, described a homer Mantle had hit against the Sox with two out in the ninth to tie a game the Yankees eventually won. "It went way up there," Marty said, with a wry little grin, pointing to the far reaches of the upper stands in deep right-center field. "He swung just as easy and whup! It was gone. Way up there. I never saw anything like it."

As for the nonprofessional, there is no question that Mantle is the new excitement, the new Ruth. Like Ruth, he is known to those who don't know baseball, magically, the way Ruth was. A 7-year-old boy, just on the edge of interest in baseball and in bed getting over the measles, watched part of a Yankees game on television. Later he was not quite sure what teams had been playing and he wasn't positive of the score, but when he was asked if he had seen Mickey Mantle bat, his red-speckled face lit up and he said, excitedly, "He hit a big one!"

Some time, maybe, Mantle will have the curiosity to go back some 29 years, to a day of grandeur such as he may live to enjoy himself. If so, this is what he will read in *The New York Times* of October 1, 1927.

"Babe Ruth scaled the hitherto unattained heights yesterday. Home Run 60, a terrific smash off the southpaw pitching of Zachary, nestled in the Babe's favorite spot in the rightfield bleachers. . . . The boys in the bleachers indicated the route of the record homer. It dropped about halfway to the top. Boys, No. 60 was some homer, a fitting wallop to top the Babe's record of 59 in 1921."

Whether Mickey himself will ever know a similar moment depends as much on his ability to emulate Ruth's poise and presence and competitive spark as it does on his bat, but his broad, broad back seems ready to receive the mantle of the Babe. ∎

5

TRIS SPEAKER

RED SOX 1907–1915
INDIANS 1916–1926
TWO TEAMS 1927–1928

" Speaker was the best player of the 1910s not named Ty Cobb. A wizard with the glove—they called him the Grey Eagle for his range—he still holds the record for most doubles (792). " —ALBERT CHEN

▸ .345 CAREER AVERAGE
▸ MLB RECORD HOLDER FOR CAREER ASSISTS IN OUTFIELD

SPORTSWRITERS CALLED Speaker "the fifth infielder." Batters and base runners could have explained why. Speaker concocted a pair of dazzling set plays involving second base. In one, he would hesitate on a short line drive in his direction, appearing to lose the ball—or to be planning to take it on a bounce. The runner would take off toward third. Then the Gray Eagle would soar in at full speed, catch the ball on the run and continue to second base. Unassisted double play. Speaker's other favorite involved no fewer than five fielders. With a runner on second, the pitcher and catcher would stall, as if confused over signs. The shortstop and second baseman would distract the runner, yet remain far from the bag. Speaker would charge in from short center, whereupon the pitcher would turn and throw. The astonished runner would find Tris waiting there to tag him out.

—*Noel Hynd, SI, June 30, 1986*

Speaker won World Series in Boston and Cleveland.

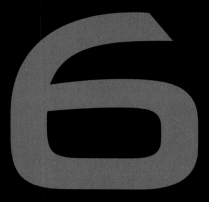

KEN GRIFFEY JR.

MARINERS 1989–1999, 2009–2010
REDS 2000–2008
WHITE SOX 2008

" Forget for a moment the home runs and the Gold Gloves: In his prime Junior stood out for his smiling abandon on the field. Watching Griffey was a joyful reminder that it's a kid's game at heart. " —STEPHEN CANNELLA

‣ 630 CAREER HOME RUNS
‣ 1997 AL MVP

JUNIOR'S ACHIEVEMENTS might get more notice if the man himself worked up more enthusiasm for them. He has been consistently uninterested in his statistics throughout his career. Such a lack of self-indulgence is no surprise, coming from someone who still plays with the insouciance of a child in a pickup game. He doesn't bother stretching with the team before games, saying with his typical coyness, "Why should I stretch? Does a cheetah stretch before it chases its prey?" He doesn't exactly push his body with training. He denied that he had hired a personal trainer this year ("C'mon. Do I look like I have a trainer?" he said) and ended his one experimentation with the muscle-building supplement creatine after only two days. "I got cramps," explains Griffey. "Besides, I don't need it. I play centerfield. I've got to run all the time."

—Tom Verducci, SI, May 17, 1999

The 13-time All-Star won 10 Gold Gloves.

7

The Silver Fox soared for a catch at Ebbets Field.

" Playing third fiddle in '50s New York to Willie Mays and Mickey Mantle, the Duke still made himself heard. Batting lefty, he took full advantage of the cozy dimensions at Ebbets Field, whacking 40 or more homers five seasons in a row. " —DICK FRIEDMAN

▸ 11 WORLD SERIES HOMERS
▸ EIGHT-TIME ALL-STAR

DUKE SNIDER

IN EVERY SENSE, the contemporary hero of Flatbush, prematurely gray at the temples in his 29th year, is a picture player with a classic stance that seldom develops a hitch. Next to Ted Williams, Snider probably has the best hitting form in the game. And, like Williams, he has amazing eyes— large, clear, calm and probing.

—*Sports Illustrated, June 27, 1955*

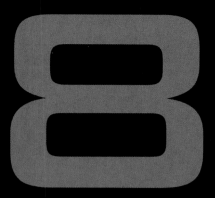

8

OSCAR CHARLESTON

NEGRO LEAGUES
11 TEAMS FROM 1915 TO 1941

" Many who saw Charleston swear that he was the greatest centerfielder ever and maybe the greatest player, period. The stats are sketchy but awe-inspiring, such as an otherworldly .451 batting average for the Harrisburg (Pa.) Giants in 1925. " —DICK FRIEDMAN

▸ ELECTED TO BASEBALL HALL OF FAME IN 1976
▸ .339 CAREER AVERAGE

TEAMMATES AND opponents stampeded to proclaim his greatness. One of the few still standing, Buck O'Neil testifies that "a better player never drew breath." Dizzy Dean, who faced him while barnstorming in the 1930s, described pitching to Charleston as a throw-it-and-duck proposition. Ted Page, a splendid outfielder, told historian John B. Holway that Charleston introduced himself to the great Walter Johnson before an exhibition game by saying, "Mr. Johnson, I've done heard about your fastball, and I'm gonna hit it out of here." In Page's account, which may qualify as legend become fact, a home run was indeed what Charleston hit. But all that is mere preamble to the proclamation that John McGraw issued: "If Oscar Charleston isn't the greatest baseball player in the world, then I'm no judge of baseball talent."

—*John Schulian, SI, September 5, 2005*

Charleston's range in the outfield was prodigious.

PHOTOGRAPH BY NATIONAL BASEBALL HALL OF FAME

9

KIRBY PUCKETT

TWINS 1984–1995

" The heart and soul of two Twins championship teams, Puckett was one of the game's most popular players because he was an Everyman superstar—just 5' 8", 220 pounds during his prime, he hit for average, and for power, and gunned players down at home from deep in the outfield. " —ALBERT CHEN

▸ .318 CAREER AVERAGE
▸ SIX GOLD GLOVES

BOBBY COX brought in lefthander Charlie Leibrandt to face the righthanded-hitting Puckett, who was leading off in the bottom of the 11th. Why Leibrandt? He had won 15 games in the regular season, Cox pointed out later. But Cox may as well have said what was on everybody's mind—that it didn't matter whom he put on the mound. The man was going to hit a home run no matter what. Puckett did just that, and the tortured Leibrandt walked off the field, his face buried in the crook of his right arm. Afterward, teammates filed almost sheepishly past Puckett's locker, some shaking his hand, others embracing him, most of them without any words to say. He acknowledged he was having difficulty grasping the enormousness of the evening: "Ten, 30, 50 years from now, when I look at it, it might be different," he said. "Right now? Unbelievable, man. Unbelievable."

—*Steve Rushin, SI, November 4, 1991*

Puckett had five seasons with 200-plus hits.

PHOTOGRAPH BY JOHN BIEVER

10

COOL PAPA BELL

NEGRO LEAGUES
SEVEN TEAMS FROM 1922 TO 1946

"His speed is the stuff of legend. Confined to the Negro leagues, he never played a game in the majors, but there are those who say there's never been a better leadoff hitter than the swift, switch-hitting Bell." —DAVID BAUER

▸ ELECTED TO BASEBALL
  HALL OF FAME IN 1974
▸ .341 CAREER AVERAGE

THEY CAN'T chart the speed of Papa Bell. "Why he could turn out the light," says Satchel Paige, "and jump in bed before the room got dark!" Others also embellish: he could hit a hard groundball through the box and get hit with the ball as he slid into second; he was so fast that he once stole two bases on the same pitch. "People kin sure talk it, can't they?" says Papa. Papa says he did steal two bases on one pitch, which was a pitchout. "The catcher, why he was so surprised the way I was runnin' that he just held the ball," says Papa. "I ask him later what he doin' holdin' that ball, and he say he didn't know, 'cept he *never* seen a man run like that before in his life." . . . He would never make more than $450 a month, although his ability was such that later he would be ranked on Jackie Robinson's alltime team in the same outfield with Henry Aaron and Willie Mays.

—Mark Kram, SI, August 20, 1973

Bell played until he was 47 years old.

10

THE

BEST RIGHTFIELDERS

THE TOP 10 AT THIS POSITION INCLUDES THE MOST FAMOUS COUPLE IN BASEBALL HISTORY, EVEN THOUGH THE TWO PLAYERS NEVER MET. WHEN BABE RUTH DIED IN 1948, HANK AARON WAS A MERE 14 YEARS OLD. IT WAS THE MERE PROSPECT OF AARON'S ECLIPSING THE HOME RUN RECORD OF BASEBALL'S MOST CELEBRATED FIGURE THAT HELPED LAND THE ATLANTA BRAVES RIGHTFIELDER ON HIS FIRST SI COVER IN 1969, AT THE LATE AGE OF 35.

THE STORY ENDEAVORED TO EXPLAIN WHY, "DESPITE HIS ABILITY . . . THE FAME THAT WAS ACCORDED MANTLE, MAYS AND MUSIAL HAS NEVER BEEN GRANTED TO AARON. PERHAPS THIS HAPPENED BECAUSE HE DID NOT PLAY IN NEW YORK . . . OR THAT HE DID NOT COME INTO THE BIG CITY AND TEAR APART THE FENCE IN EBBETS FIELD THE WAY STAN DID IN THOSE DAYS WHEN HE SEEMED TO EXIST JUST TO KILL THE DODGERS. BEING IN MILWAUKEE DID NOT HELP AARON'S PUBLICITY VALUE AT ALL. . . . " AND SO ON.

THE STORY'S SUBJECT SHRUGGED OFF THE MATTER—WHILE GETTING IN A SUBTLE DIG. "AARON HIMSELF CONCLUDES IT IS YOUNGSTERS WHO HAVE APPRECIATED HIM MOST OVER THE YEARS, BECAUSE 'ADULTS TEND TO JUST READ THE HEADLINES SOMETIMES. KIDS READ EVERYTHING, ALL THE WAY DOWN THROUGH THE BOX SCORES AND THE STATISTICS.' " PEOPLE OF ALL AGES WILL NOT HAVE TO READ TOO FAR DOWN OUR LIST TO FIND MR. 756.

1

BABE
RUTH

RED SOX 1914-1919
YANKEES 1920-1934
BRAVES 1935

" With his home runs and his outsized personality, Babe Ruth was a game-changer and is still the sport's most titanic figure. How far above his contemporaries was the Bambino? In 1920, the Babe slammed 54 homers—more than all but one team in the majors. " —DICK FRIEDMAN

▸ 714 CAREER HOME RUNS
▸ .342 CAREER AVERAGE

BAN JOHNSON had said that Ruth had the mind of a 15-year-old boy. But can today's teenagers tell you who Ban Johnson was? They know who Ruth was just as they know who Daniel Boone was. Ruth— because he came along when he did—saved the national game. Without Ruth and the home runs that were like no home runs any slugger has hit before or since, it is just possible that the game would have died. Baseball, in one shameful instance, had been faked. People had been betrayed. Kids were learning to say, "Aw, it's all fixed." But when Ruth —his big head cocked, his matchstick legs together, his pigeon toes turned in— drove a ball out of the park, nobody could say that was fixed or rigged or faked. People who saw Babe Ruth hit a home run never forgot it.

—*Gerald Holland, SI, December 21, 1959*

Ruth holds the career record for slugging percentage.

Aaron passed the Babe with this swing.

BRAVES 1954–1974
BREWERS 1975–1976

" He's now second on the alltime list, but he's still the Home Run King. The feat that made him a celebrity also made it too easy to forget his long career as one of the most consistent sluggers the game has ever seen. " —STEPHEN CANNELLA

▸ 755 CAREER HOME RUNS
▸ MLB RECORD 2,297 RBI

THEY CALLED him Hammerin' Hank, an encomium to his bluntly effective hitting but one that works just as well as a tribute to his overall ethos. Hammering is the life's work of commoners, not kings. In hammering as in Aaron, there is an understated nobility that only the passage of time adequately reveals.

—Tom Verducci, SI, July 23, 2007

HANK
AARON

THE DRIVE TO GLORY

In front of a home stadium filled with celebrities and frenzied fans, Hank Aaron stroked a fastball down the middle and broke the most cherished record in baseball

BY RON FIMRITE

ENRY AARON'S ORDEAL ended at 9:07 p.m. Monday, April 8. It ended in a carnival atmosphere that would have been more congenial to the man he surpassed as baseball's alltime home-run champion. But it ended. And for that, as Aaron advised the 53,775 Atlanta fans who came to enshrine him in the game's pantheon, "Thank God."

Aaron's 715th home run came in the fourth inning of the Braves' home opener with Los Angeles, off the Dodgers' Al Downing, a lefthander who had insisted doggedly before the game that for him this night would be "no different from any other."

Downing's momentous mistake was a high fastball into Aaron's considerable strike zone. Aaron's whip of a bat lashed out at it and snapped it in a high arc toward the 385-foot sign in left-centerfield. Dodgers centerfielder Jimmy Wynn and leftfielder Bill Buckner gave futile chase, Buckner going all the way to the six-foot fence for it. But the ball dropped over the fence in the midst of a clutch of Braves' relief pitchers who scrambled out of the bullpen in pursuit. Buckner started to go over the fence after the ball himself, but gave up after he realized he was outnumbered. It was finally retrieved by reliever Tom House, who even as Aaron triumphantly rounded the bases ran hysterically toward home plate holding the ball aloft. It was, after all, one more ball than Babe Ruth ever hit over a fence, and House is a man with a sense of history.

House arrived in time to join a riotous spectacle at the plate. Aaron, his normally placid features exploding in a smile, was hoisted by his teammates as Downing and the Dodgers infielders moved politely to one side. Aaron shook hands with his father Herbert, and embraced his mother Estella. He graciously accepted encomiums from his boss, Braves board chairman Bill Bartholomay, and Monte Irvin, representing commissioner Bowie Kuhn, who was unaccountably in Cleveland this eventful night. Kuhn is no favorite of Atlanta fans and when his name was mentioned by Irvin, the largest crowd ever to see a baseball game in Atlanta booed lustily.

"I just thank God it's all over," said Aaron, giving credit where it is not entirely due.

No, this was Henry Aaron's evening, and if the Braves' management overdid it a bit with the balloons, the fireworks, the speeches and allround hoopla, who is to quibble? There have not been many big baseball nights in this football-oriented community and those few have been supplied by Aaron.

Before the game the great man did look a trifle uncomfortable while being escorted through lines of majorettes as balloons rose in the air above him. There were signs everywhere—MOVE OVER BABE—and the electronic scoreboard blinked HANK. Sammy Davis Jr. was there, and Pearl Bailey, singing the national anthem in Broadway soul, and Atlanta's black mayor, Maynard Jackson, and Governor Jimmy Carter, and the Jonesboro High School band, and the Morris Brown College choir, and Chief Noc-A-Homa, the Braves' mascot, who danced with a fiery hoop.

This is not the sort of party one gives for Henry Aaron, who through the long weeks of on-field pressure and mass media harassment had expressed no more agitation than a man brushing aside a housefly. Aaron had labored for most of his 21-year career in shadows cast by more flamboyant superstars, and if he was enjoying his newfound celebrity, he gave no hint of it. He seemed to be nothing more than a man trying to do his job and live a normal life in the presence of incessant chaos.

Before this most important game of his career he joked at the batting cage with teammate Dusty Baker, a frequent foil, while hordes of newsmen scrambled around him, hanging on every banality. When a young red-haired boy impudently shouted, "Hey, Hank Aaron, come here, I want you to sign this," Aaron looked incredulous, then laughed easily. The poor youngster was very nearly mobbed by sycophants for approaching the dignitary so cavalierly.

Downing, too, seemed unaware that he was soon to be a party to history. "I will pitch to Aaron no differently tonight," said he, as the band massed in rightfield. "If I make a mistake, it's no disgrace."

Downing's "mistake" was made with nobody out in the fourth inning and with Darrell Evans, the man preceding Aaron in the Braves' batting order, on first base following an error by Dodgers shortstop Bill Russell. Downing had walked Aaron leading off the second inning to the accompaniment of continuous booing by the multitudes. Aaron then scored on a Dodger error, the run breaking Willie Mays' alltime National League record for runs scored.

This time, with a man on base, Downing elected to confront him mano a mano. His first pitch, however, hit the dirt in front of the plate. The next hit the turf beyond the fence in leftfield.

"It was a fastball down the middle of the upper part of the plate," Downing lamented afterward. "I was trying to get it down to him, but I didn't. He's a great hitter. When he picks his pitch, he's pretty certain that's the pitch he's looking for. Chances are he's gonna hit it pretty good. When he did hit it, I didn't think it was going out because I was watching Wynn and Buckner. But the ball just kept carrying and carrying."

It was Aaron's first swing of the game—and perhaps the most significant in the history of baseball. ∎

Robinson had 586 career home runs and 2,943 hits.

PHOTOGRAPH BY TONY TRIOLO

3

REDS 1956–1965
ORIOLES 1966–1971
THREE TEAMS THROUGH 1976

———————————————

" Frank Robinson was all about winning, and the numbers back him up. He placed among the top 10 position players in Wins Above Replacement nine times during his career. " —DAVID SABINO

———————————————

▸ MVP IN AL AND NL
▸ 1966 AL TRIPLE CROWN WINNER

FRANK ROBINSON

"I'D PLAY in the park until it got dark, and then I'd go over to the community center and we'd play indoors," Robinson said. "I can't remember having a hot meal from the time I was 12 until I signed with the Reds. I'd get home when everybody was in bed and there'd be my supper in a cold pot on the stove."
—*Morton Sharnik, SI, June 17, 1963*

4

ROBERTO CLEMENTE

Clemente was great with his bat and in the outfield.
PHOTOGRAPH BY NEIL LEIFER

" He inspired with his grit and generosity. After Clemente died in a plane crash at 38, three months after stroking his 3,000th hit, he became the first and still the only player for whom the Hall of Fame's five-year waiting period was waived. " —KOSTYA KENNEDY

▸ FOUR NL BATTING TITLES
▸ 1966 NL MVP

THE DODGERS put Clemente on their Triple A roster, which meant he could be drafted by another team at the end of the '54 season. The Pirates did just that. Pirates G.M. Branch Rickey delighted in stealing Clemente away from Rickey's former club and denying them an outfield of Clemente, Duke Snider and Carl Furillo.

—*Steve Wulf, SI, December 28, 1992*

5

REGGIE JACKSON

A'S 1967–1975, 1987
YANKEES 1977–1981
TWO OTHER TEAMS

" Has there ever been a player more fit for the bright lights of New York than the original Mr. October? One of the game's greatest clutch players, Jackson was a World Series MVP for the A's in 1973 and also the Yankees in '77, when he gave his iconic three-home run performance in Game 6. " —ALBERT CHEN

▸ 563 CAREER HOME RUNS
▸ 1973 AL MVP

IN SPRING TRAINING Jackson told a *Sport* magazine writer that the Yankees' star catcher, Thurman Munson, was jealous of him and coined a phrase that would haunt him for months. "I'm the straw that stirs the drink," Jackson said to the writer over beers at the Banana Boat in Fort Lauderdale. "It all comes back to me. Maybe I should say me and Munson, but really he doesn't enter into it." After the article was published, Fran Healy, the Yankees' backup catcher at the time, remembers Munson walking around the clubhouse holding the magazine in his hand, saying, "Can you believe this? Can you believe this?" Healy said something about parts of the article being out of context. Healy recalls Munson's incredulous response: "For four pages?"

—*William Nack, SI, August 4, 1980*

Jackson was known for big swings in big moments.

PHOTOGRAPH BY WALTER IOOSS JR.

6

MEL OTT

GIANTS 1926–1947

"The undersized (5' 9") Ott, who became a New York Giant at age 17, is an often overlooked prewar treasure: He was the first National Leaguer to hit 500 home runs and complemented his fierce power with his uncanny ability to get on base and his mastery of the tricky Polo Grounds rightfield." —STEPHEN CANNELLA

▸ 511 CAREER HOME RUNS
▸ LED NL IN HOME RUNS SIX TIMES

HE WAS BOYISH, mannerly, square. The most famous baseball use of the phrase "nice guy" applies to Ott. "Nice guys finish last," is what Leo Durocher is supposed to have said when Ott was managing the Giants and Leo the Brooklyn Dodgers. Frank Graham, the sportswriter who first wrote the story, said that Red Barber had chided Leo about not being a "nice guy." Durocher scoffed. "Nice guys. Look at Ott. There's not a nicer guy in the world than Mel Ott. But he's in last place." Durocher was, of course, wrong in his implication that Ott was a loser. A poor manager, yes, but in his playing days he was a winner, all the way. The point is, even rowdy Leo Durocher recognized the fact that Mel Ott was a man to admire. He was an awfully nice guy.

—*Sports Illustrated, December 1, 1958*

Ott was both a slugger and a gentleman.

PHOTOGRAPH BY BETTMANN/CORBIS

7

PETE ROSE

REDS 1963–1978, 1984–1986
PHILLIES 1979–1983
EXPOS 1984

" Before his name became forever linked with Hall of Fame controversy, The Hit King thrilled fans with his headfirst slides, line drives into the gap, World Series heroics and his outsized personality. " —ALBERT CHEN

▸ MLB RECORD 4,256 HITS
▸ 1973 NL MVP

WHEN HE first became a professional baseball player in 1960, fresh from Cincinnati's Western Hills High School, Rose was often ridiculed. Neither his teammates nor his opponents could fathom his rapturous manner, his unbridled rah-rahism. "They couldn't believe he was for real," says Reds pitcher Jack Billingham, who played against Rose in the Florida State League in '61. "They'd talk about him on buses. I'd hear all about this kid who runs out walks and never stops talking." When he advanced to the majors, he was shunned at first by his own teammates. The Reds were notably cliquish then, and the brash young hustler did not fit the accepted mold of professional nonchalance. Rose found his friends among the team's blacks, Frank Robinson and Vada Pinson, who recognized in him, if not soul, at least miles and miles of heart.

—Ron Fimrite, SI, December 22, 1975

Rose holds the MLB record for games played (3,562).

407 FT.

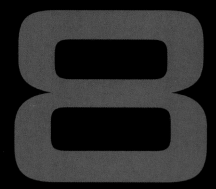

8

AL KALINE

TIGERS 1953–1974

" Noted for a phenomenal arm but perhaps obscured by his quiet consistency, Kaline is one of the game's most underappreciated players. In a 13-season stretch from age 20 to 32, he never had fewer than 15 home runs or 68 RBIs a year, won 10 Gold Gloves and made every All-Star team. " —DAVID BAUER

▸ 3,007 CAREER HITS
▸ 399 CAREER HOME RUNS

KALINE IS one of the last of an almost prehistoric type of ballplayer, the kid who makes it not because of physique but in spite of it. Walk into a baseball clubhouse nowadays and you see The Body Beautiful all around you. But not many years ago you would see bandy-legged little guys who make it on gristle and shank, on skills honed in thousands of games on sandlots that no longer exist. Al Kaline is not bandy-legged, but neither is he a strong athlete, and he has had to overcome physical limitations that would have driven a lesser man to pack it in long ago. He has always had osteomyelitis, a persistent bone disease, and when he was eight years old doctors took two inches of bone out of his left foot, leaving jagged scars and permanent deformity. This slowed Kaline down only slightly, and only temporarily.

—*Jack Olsen, SI, May 11, 1964*

The steady Kaline was an 18-time All-Star.

PHOTOGRAPHS BY HERB SCHARFMAN (LEFT) AND WALTER IOOSS JR.

TONY GWYNN

PADRES 1982–2001

❝ The most adept contact hitter of his generation, placement artist Tony Gwynn won eight NL batting titles and has the highest lifetime average (.338) of any player whose career began after World War II. ❞ —DICK FRIEDMAN

▸ 3,141 CAREER HITS
▸ 19 CONSECUTIVE .300 SEASONS

FIFTEEN YEARS to the day on which he played his first major league game, San Diego Padres outfielder Tony Gwynn hunches over a small monitor propped up on a battered blue steamer trunk in the visitor's clubhouse of Miami's Pro Player Stadium, studying a video of his batting stroke—the sweetest swing since Glenn Miller's. *Land softly on the front foot . . . cock the top hand slightly toward the pitcher . . . stay back . . . pow!* The checkpoints are as constant as the engraved notches on a dipstick. Gwynn, having had one hit in five at bats the previous night against the Florida Marlins, is half a quart low. "I'll fix it," the master mechanic says. The checkup is unremarkable except for this: 2,037 games after his debut he was at work last Saturday more than six hours before game time, well ahead of coaches, rookies and vendors. Padre Time marches on.

—*Tom Verducci, SI, July 28, 1997*

Gwynn's best batting average was .394, in 1994.

Waner had extra-base hits in a record 14 straight games.

PHOTOGRAPH BY NATIONAL BASEBALL HALL OF FAME/MLB PHOTOS/GETTY IMAGES

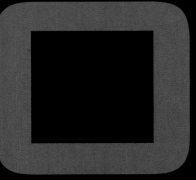

10

PAUL WANER

PIRATES 1926–1940
THREE TEAMS THROUGH 1945

"He whacked pitches the way he did corncobs thrown to him as a kid growing up on a farm in Oklahoma. From a closed stance and choking up on his thick-handled bat, Waner slashed line drives while rarely striking out—just 376 times in 20 seasons." —TOM VERDUCCI

▸ .333 CAREER AVERAGE
▸ 3,152 CAREER HITS

AT HIS best playing weight, 140 pounds, he could have passed for an ex-jockey sidling up to tout a favorite horse. Yet Fred Fitzsimmons, a pitching coach with the Cubs, said Waner hit the ball through the box harder than any other hitter that Fitz faced in the major leagues.

—*Jim Brosnan, SI, March 7, 1960*

10 THE

Best Righthanded Pitchers

HE THREW SEVEN NO-HITTERS, 12 ONE-HITTERS, WON 324 GAMES AND TOSSED AN ALLTIME RECORD 5,714 STRIKEOUTS. WHICH MAKES IT ALL THE MORE AMAZING THAT NOLAN RYAN DIDN'T CRACK OUR LIST OF THE TOP RIGHTHANDED PITCHERS OF ALL TIME. HE FINISHED JUST OUTSIDE THE TOP 10, AS DID THE LEGENDARY SATCHEL PAIGE, WHO ADVISED NEVER TO LOOK BACK, BECAUSE SOMETHING MIGHT BE GAINING ON YOU.

WHAT RYAN AND PAIGE WOULD SEE IF THEY LOOKED AT WHO WAS BEHIND THEM IN THE VOTE COUNT MIGHT PROVIDE SOME CONSOLATION, BECAUSE MANY HALL OF FAME RIGHTIES DIDN'T EVEN GET A SINGLE VOTE ON ANY BALLOT. MORDECAI BROWN, DIZZY DEAN, ROBIN ROBERTS AND JIM PALMER ARE JUST THE BEGINNING OF A LONG LIST OF THOSE ON THE WRONG SIDE OF A SHUTOUT.

IN SHORT, IF YOU'RE LOOKING FOR THE TOUGHEST LIST TO CRACK IN THIS BOOK, YOU'VE FOUND IT. WHICH MAKES SENSE. ON A TYPICAL 25-MAN BASEBALL ROSTER, NEARLY HALF THE SPOTS ARE DEVOTED TO PITCHERS, AND WITH RIGHTIES BEING MORE COMMON THAN THEIR SOUTHPAW COUNTERPARTS, THERE ARE SIMPLY MORE PLAYERS TO CHOOSE FROM HERE THAN AT ANY OTHER POSITION. SO WHEN IT COMES TO SELECTING GREATS, THIS POSITION IS LIKE A SUPERMARKET BEFORE A STORM: IF YOU'RE GOING TO GET STUCK IN A LONG LINE ANYWHERE, IT'S HERE.

1

WALTER JOHNSON

SENATORS 1907–1927

" The Big Train created the archetype of the intimidating power pitcher. Ty Cobb said that the first time he faced the fireballing Johnson was "the most threatening sight I ever saw in the ball field." " —STEPHEN CANNELLA

▸ 417 CAREER WINS
▸ MLB RECORD 110 SHUTOUTS

HE THREW only fastballs, blazing fastballs. His unique, fluid motion—a kind of casual sidearm, almost submarine delivery, in which his right arm whipped around and across his chest—became simultaneously the most recognizable but least imitated in all of baseball, although why legions of major leaguers don't throw the way he did is one of the game's enduring mysteries. Johnson complained only once of a sore arm, even though he pitched 5,914 innings, third on the alltime list. His pendulum delivery was a natural motion, unlike an overhander's. His motion looks peculiar today because he never seemed to snap his wrist or elbow. He gained his exceptional speed from the sweep of his broad back and shoulders and his right arm. Johnson would turn away from the batter as he began his motion and then pivot in a burst of energy, the ball shooting out from his body toward the plate.

—*William Taaffe, SI, October 26, 1987*

The hard-throwing Johnson struck out 3,509 batters.

PHOTOGRAPH BY AP

GIANTS 1900–1916
REDS 1916

Mathewson led the majors in ERA five times.

2

" Christy Mathewson was never better than in a span of six days in October 1905 when he threw three complete game shutouts to take Games 1, 3 and the deciding Game 5 of the World Series against the Athletics. " —DAVID SABINO

‣ 373 CAREER WINS
‣ 2.13 CAREER ERA

WAS THERE ever a pitcher whose mere presence was so mesmerizing? Here he comes, marching to the mound, wearing a long white linen duster, removing it to stand there tall, broad-shouldered and square-jawed, and then starting to toss effortlessly, with consummate grace.

—Frank Deford, SI, August 25, 2003

CHRISTY MATHEWSON

3

CY YOUNG

PHOTOGRAPH BY CHICAGO HISTORY MUSEUM/GETTY IMAGES

CLEVELAND SPIDERS 1890–1898
RED SOX 1901–1908
THREE OTHER TEAMS

Young won two games in the first World Series.

"What is the most remarkable statistic of Cy Young's career? His unapproachable 511 wins? We'll take this one: 749 lifetime complete games—103 more than his closest competitor, Pud Galvin." —DICK FRIEDMAN

▸ 2.63 CAREER ERA
▸ 15 20-WIN SEASONS

TRYING OUT, Young was pitching to the team's slugger, who was backed up against the grandstand because no catcher was around. Afterward, the manager told how Young had splintered the boards on the wall and made the place "look like a cyclone had just passed." "After that," Young said, "they always called me Cy."

—*Sports Illustrated, November 14, 1955*

GREG MADDUX

CUBS 1986–1992, 2004–2006
BRAVES 1993–2003
TWO TEAMS THROUGH 2008

" No one ever executed the art of pitching better than Maddux. At the height of his mastery, a four-year stretch from 1992 through '95, Maddux went 75–29 with a 1.98 ERA and won the Cy Young Award every season. " —TOM VERDUCCI

▸ 355 CAREER WINS
▸ 18 GOLD GLOVES, AN MLB RECORD FOR ALL POSITIONS

WHAT SETS Maddux apart is a mind that constantly processes information no one else sees. At home in Las Vegas he is a formidable poker player, detecting when an opponent has a good hand by the way he strokes his chin or suddenly stops fiddling with his chips. But he is even better at analyzing hitters—so good that four times this year, while seated next to John Smoltz in the dugout, he has warned, "This guy's going to hit a foul ball in here." Three of those times a foul came screeching into the dugout. This seeming omniscience is complemented by Maddux's mastery of the movement and location of his pitches. That's how he can dominate without a signature pitch, without anything close to the menace of Bob Gibson's fastball or the treachery of Sandy Koufax's curve.

—Tom Verducci, SI, August 14, 1995

Maddux went from Chicago to Atlanta as a free agent.

PHOTOGRAPH BY HEINZ KLUETMEIER

5

TOM
SEAVER

METS 1967–1977, 1983
REDS 1977–1982
WHITE SOX 1984–1986
RED SOX 1986

" Flawless mechanics made for a picture
perfect delivery, with that right knee
scraping the dirt, and made him one of
the most consistently dominant pitchers
of any era. It's hard for anyone to
remember Seaver, in his prime, having a
bad outing. " —DAVID BAUER

‣ 311 CAREER WINS
‣ THREE CY YOUNG AWARDS

DURING 1969 Seaver ran off winning
streaks of eight and 10 games,
which helped spare the Mets any
long losing sieges, but win or lose he
brought some special characteristics
to a young baseball team. He
expected his team to win. Yet he had
a way of handling defeat that helped
everyone. An icy realist, he had no
use for alibis. When he pitched a bad
game, he would say he was lousy.
If others were lousy, he attempted
to break the mood. Once when he
thought the bench was too quiet he
walked along the dugout plucking
spiders from the walls and throwing
them in the laps of the silent. Seaver
could get away with this, of course,
only because he had earned the
respect of the Mets with his talent
and attitude—but, having won the
respect, he made maximum use of it.

—*William Leggett, SI, December 22, 1969*

Tom Terrific struck out 3,640 batters.

6

GROVER CLEVELAND ALEXANDER

PHILLIES 1911–1917, 1930
CUBS 1918–1926
CARDINALS 1926–1929

" The farmboy from Nebraska, the game's original control artist, won the first of three pitching Triple Crowns in 1915, when he led the Phillies to their first-ever pennant. " —ALBERT CHEN

▸ 373 CAREER WINS
▸ FIVE FULL SEASONS WITH SUB-2.00 ERA

HE TOOK four warmup pitches on the mound—that's all—and he was ready. Alec was a little bit of the country boy psychologist out there. I guess a lot of the great pitchers are. He knew it was Tony Lazzeri's rookie year, and that here it was, seventh game of the [1926] World Series, two out and the bases loaded and the score 3–2. The pressure was something. Lazzeri *had* to be anxious up there. This is not to take anything from Lazzeri—he was a great hitter—but he was up against the master. And don't think when Alec walked in he didn't walk slower than ever. He wanted Lazzeri to wait as long as possible, standing at the plate thinking about the situation. And he just knew Tony's eyes would pop when he saw his fastball.

—Donald Honig, as told by Les Bell, SI, October 9, 1978

Alexander led the majors in strikeouts six times.

7

ROGER CLEMENS

RED SOX 1984–1996
BLUE JAYS 1997–1998
YANKEES 2000–2003, 2007
ASTROS 2004–2006

❝ There's no doubting the dominance of Roger Clemens during his tenure with the Red Sox, when he struck out 20 batters in a game—twice, and 10 years apart. His totals and late-career accomplishments have been tainted by performance enhancing drug allegations, but that doesn't subtract from his early-career successes. ❞ —DAVID SABINO

▸ MLB RECORD SEVEN CY YOUNG AWARDS
▸ 354 CAREER WINS, 4,672 CAREER STRIKEOUTS

"I WATCHED perfect games by Catfish Hunter and Mike Witt, but this was the most awesome pitching performance I've ever seen," said Boston manager John McNamara. Even Seattle pitching coach Phil Regan, who was Sandy Koufax's teammate, called it "the best game I've ever seen." "It's not just the strikeouts that make it great," said Gorman Thomas, whose seventh-inning homer had spoiled Clemens's shutout. "It's the zero next to the 20." Years from now, when someone studies the box score and sees CLEMENS (W, 4–0) 9 3 1 1 0 20, he may think it impossible that a pitcher could strike out 20 batters without giving up a walk.

—Peter Gammons, SI, May 12, 1986

Clemens twice finished seasons with a sub-2.00 ERA.

PHOTOGRAPH BY HEINZ KLUETMEIER

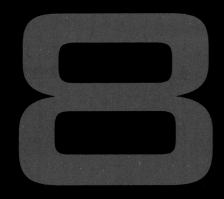

PEDRO MARTINEZ

EXPOS 1994–1997
RED SOX 1998–2004
METS 2005–2008
TWO TEAMS 1992–2009

" No starter in the live-ball era has allowed fewer base runners per nine innings—and he did it in a time dominated by cartoonish, chemically enhanced sluggers. One game to win, against any lineup in baseball history? Give me Pedro in his prime. " —STEPHEN CANNELLA

▸ THREE CY YOUNG AWARDS
▸ LED MAJORS IN ERA FIVE TIMES

BY CONVENTIONAL STANDARDS, Pedro Martinez is a freak. He's listed at 5' 11" and 170 pounds, but appears even smaller in person. He has scant muscle definition, and his long, soft face makes him look about as intimidating as a mall cop. While his stuff says Randy Johnson or Roger Clemens, his body says Rafael Belliard. When his unimposing appearance is mentioned, Martinez smiles and says, "Why don't you grab a bat? Then we'll see. I can look as mean as a man 6' 10" when I'm on the mound." Indeed, Martinez may have soft, friendly features, but that description doesn't apply to his eyes. The eyes belong to a killer, a man with a mean streak as deep and wide as the Charles River.

—Gerry Callahan, SI, April 20, 1998

Martinez dominated with a deep repertoire of pitches.

PHOTOGRAPH BY CHUCK SOLOMON

ON TOP OF HIS GAME

Pedro Martinez's final start for the Red Sox came in Game 3 of the 2004 World Series, and his masterly performance helped put an end to the fabled curse

BY TOM VERDUCCI

HERE LIES THE CURSE OF the Bambino, born Dec. 26, 1919, the day Red Sox owner Harry Frazee sold Babe Ruth to the Yankees, and died Oct. 27, 2004, the day a group of wild-haired, self-styled Idiots completed one of the most one-sided sweeps in World Series history, not to mention the greatest reversal of fortune the sports world may ever have witnessed.

"It is," general manager Theo Epstein said after his team's domination of the St. Louis Cardinals, "the ultimate cleansing."

Though he was to be the starting pitcher in Game 3, Pedro Martinez did not bother sitting in on the pregame meeting with his catcher and coaches to review the St. Louis hitters. Of course, he never sits in. "I'm telling you," catcher Jason Varitek said, shaking his head, "we have some different people around here."

Maybe Pedro figured, Why bother? Why break down the tendencies of a World Series opponent when you can command the baseball like a yo-yo on a string? Why clutter the mind with scouting reports when it is the men with the bats in their hands who should be on the defensive?

In the first World Series start of his brilliant career, Martinez rose to the occasion. He did not have vintage 1999 velocity, but he did exhibit mastery of a different sort. With impeccable location on all his pitches, Martinez shackled the potent Cardinals lineup with seven shutout innings in the manner of a true virtuoso: He made it look easy.

Behind Martinez, Boston made a 4–1 win seem like a blowout; St. Louis did not get on the board until Larry Walker homered against reliever Keith Foulke in the bottom of the ninth. Martinez allowed three hits—two infield hits and an opposite-field double—struck out six and retired the last 14 batters he faced. The Cardinals had been 6–0 at home in the postseason before they ran into Martinez.

"It's emotional for me," Varitek said, "because I've been with him a long time, and for him to put up with the stuff he's had to put up with and have a performance like that, I tip my hat to him."

Asked just what "stuff" Martinez had endured, Varitek said, "Every time he pitches it's, 'What's wrong with Pedro?' because he's not striking out 19. I'm just really happy for him. This is his moment."

With free agency pending, Martinez knew the start might have been his last in a Boston uniform.

"Performing like I did tonight and in previous games in the playoffs is not bad," Martinez said. "If I have to leave, I will leave, and I'll be proud."

Martinez seemed wobbly at the start. He walked two batters around an infield single by Albert Pujols while throwing mostly fastballs, cutters and sliders. Then Jim Edmonds hit a shallow pop fly to Manny Ramirez in leftfield. Pujols wandered so far off second base in anticipation that the ball might drop that Walker decided he must tag from third and make an attempt to score. It was a desperate decision. Ramirez easily threw out Walker at the plate.

The Cardinals would have one more chance to bloody Martinez, and they would blow that, too, with shoddy baserunning. Starting pitcher Jeff Suppan was at third and Edgar Renteria at second with no outs in the third when Walker rolled a grounder to Mark Bellhorn. The Red Sox conceded the run in that situation, keeping Bellhorn back near the outfield grass. Bellhorn flipped to first baseman David Ortiz for the out.

Suppan, however, panicked. He started for home, stopped, broke back for third, broke again for home and then, upon seeing Ortiz spot him, tried to scamper back to third. It was too late. Ortiz threw to Bill Mueller, who tagged Suppan out for a dagger of a double play.

St. Louis would never get another runner against Martinez. He threw mostly changeups over his final four innings, exploiting the Cardinals' urgency to get back into the game and the Series.

"A phenomenal performance," pitcher Curt Schilling called it. "They had one shot at him, and they missed. And then he ran with that."

Said Martinez, "Once they didn't score in that inning, I said, 'It's up to me now.' "

Boston then gave Martinez breathing room. Consecutive two-out hits in the fourth put the Sox up 2–0. Ramirez and Mueller added RBI singles in the fifth for a 4–0 lead.

Buoyed by the lead, Martinez attacked the strike zone. He went to a three-ball count against only three of his final 18 batters.

Martinez had waited his entire career for this start; he turned 33 the day before Game 3. The start pushed him to 244 innings for the season, a new career high. He was in uncharted land. He was a World Series winner.

Taking the baton from Martinez, who had taken it from Schilling, Game 4 starter Derek Lowe handcuffed once again what had been the National League's most potent offense. Schilling, Martinez and Lowe threw 20 innings without allowing an earned run.

Lowe was one of the first players to sprint out of the dugout as Foulke flipped the baseball to Doug Mientkiewicz for the final out. What followed was a celebration unlike any other in recent years, at least in the depth of its meaning. This one was 86 years in the making.

As the players hugged and jumped and skipped—yes, there was Martinez, skipping across the infield grass like a little boy—there was at last a perfect order to the Red Sox' universe. Above them, even the moon, the sunlight refracted from the earth's atmosphere, glowed red. ∎

9

BOB FELLER

INDIANS 1936–1941, 1945–1956

" You could hear his fastball pop in the catcher's glove from the upper deck, and his curveball, the Yankees' Charlie Keller once said, 'behaved like an epileptic snake.' Baseball's most dominant pitcher of the 1940s (despite three missing prime years in the Navy) Rapid Robert led the league in strikeouts seven times. " —KOSTYA KENNEDY

> 266 CAREER WINS
> SIX 20-WIN SEASONS

IT IS DIFFICULT to imagine now what a marvel Feller was when he burst upon the scene, a callow youth of 17. Many athletes are great. Bob Feller was seminal. In that long-ago time, it was unheard of for teenagers to succeed in the big top of athletics. Perhaps in all the world only Sonja Henie had previously excelled at so young an age in any sport that mattered, and, after all, she was but a little girl wearing tights and fur trim, performing dainty figure-eights. Feller dressed in the uniform of the major league Cleveland Indians, striking out American demigods. In his first start Bobby Feller struck out 15, one short of the league record. Then, later in the season, he broke the mark, fanning 17, one for each year of his life, in the only professional team sport that mattered then in the United States.

—Frank Deford, SI, August 8, 2005

Feller tossed three no-hitters and 12 one-hitters.

CARDINALS 1959–1975

The hard-throwing Gibson pitched five 20-win seasons.

PHOTOGRAPH BY MARVIN E. NEWMAN

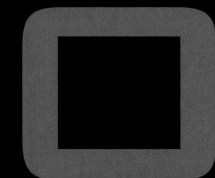

" No pitcher was more intimidating than the Cardinals great who stared hitters down with his famous scowl. Gibson was the ultimate big-game pitcher, and his 1968 season—he put up a 1.12 ERA, the lowest since 1914—is one of the greatest ever. " —ALBERT CHEN

BOB GIBSON

▸ 1968 NL MVP
▸ TWO-TIME WORLD SERIES MVP

"AS I RECALL he didn't make one bad pitch over the plate that year," says Lou Brock of 1968. "That whole season," continues Tim McCarver, "he could hit an area six inches by six inches right above the hitters' knees. We'd call it the cock box. He could put it in that box whenever he wanted to. At will."

—*Steve Rushin, SI, July 19, 1993*

10 THE

BEST LEFTHANDED PITCHERS

"ARE LEFTIES HUMAN?" WAS THE QUESTION ASKED, WITH PERHAPS A HALF-GRAIN OF SERIOUSNESS, IN AN SI STORY BY ROBERT W. CREAMER IN 1956. THOUGH THE COVER BOY FOR THE STORY WAS THE LEVEL-HEADED WARREN SPAHN, THE POINT OF CREAMER'S INVESTIGATION WAS TO TRACE THE ODD BEHAVIOR ATTRIBUTED TO LEFTHANDED PITCHERS. LEFTY GOMEZ, OUR NO. 10 LEFTY, WAS RESPONSIBLE FOR SOME OF THE REPUTATION, BUT THE SOURCE OF THIS PARTICULAR NILE WAS A PITCHER NAMED RUBE WADDELL.

SOME OF WADDELL'S MORE NOTABLE ANTICS: "HE WAS MISSING AT GAME TIME ONE DAY IN 1900 WHEN HE WAS SUPPOSED TO PITCH FOR PITTSBURGH AGAINST BROOKLYN. HE WAS FOUND UNDER THE STANDS PLAYING MARBLES WITH SOME LITTLE BOYS. ONCE WHEN HE WAS MISSING FROM THE BALLPARK HE WAS FOUND ACTING AS AN AUTOMATON IN A STORE WINDOW." THAT'LL DO IT.

WADDELL FINISHED OUT OF OUR TOP 10, RECEIVING JUST ONE NINTH-PLACE VOTE. IN GENERAL IT WAS A CATEGORY OF HIGH UNANIMITY, AS EIGHT OF OUR TOP 10 PITCHERS APPEARED ON EVERY BALLOT. THE MOST INTERESTING CHOICE: ONE PANELIST CAST A FIFTH-PLACE VOTE FOR BABE RUTH, WHO IN 1916 WENT 23–12 AND LED THE MAJORS WITH AN ERA OF 1.75. LATER IT WAS REALIZED RUTH MIGHT BE DOING SOMETHING BETTER WITH HIS TIME THAN PITCHING—AND IT WASN'T PLAYING MARBLES.

1

SANDY KOUFAX

DODGERS 1955–1966

" After struggling with control and confidence for six seasons, Koufax put together six seasons that stand as baseball's equivalent of the Sistine Chapel ceiling: 129–47 with a 2.19 ERA, not including a 0.94 ERA in three World Series in that span. And then, at age 30, he was gone—retired with a painful arthritic elbow " —TOM VERDUCCI

‣ THREE 25-WIN SEASONS
‣ THREE NL CY YOUNG AWARDS

"HE'S THE greatest pitcher I ever saw," says Ernie Banks. "I can still see that big curveball. It had a great arc on it, and he never bounced it in the dirt. And he had the fastball of a pure strikeout pitcher. It jumped up at the end. The batter would swing half a foot under it." Koufax was so good, he once taped a postgame radio show with Vin Scully before the game. He was so good, the relief pitchers treated the night before his starts the way a sailor treats shore leave. On one rare occasion in which Koufax struggled to go his usual nine innings, manager Walter Alston visited his pitcher while a hungover Bob Miller warmed in the bullpen. "How do you feel, Sandy?" Alston asked. "I'll be honest with you, Skip," Koufax said. "I feel a hell of a lot better than the guy you've got warming up."

—*Tom Verducci, SI, July 12, 1999*

Koufax had two complete-game wins in the '63 Series.

PHOTOGRAPH BY NEIL LEIFER

A'S 1925–1933
RED SOX 1934–1941

Grove, a strikeout master, won the 1931 AL MVP.

" Connie Mack controversially paid a record sum to acquire Grove, and Grove rewarded him by being the cornerstone of the A's dynasty teams of 1929 through '31, winning the pitching Triple Crown twice during those years. " —ALBERT CHEN

TALES OF Grove's exploits abound. One afternoon while leading the Yankees 1–0 in the ninth inning, Grove gave up a triple to the leadoff hitter, shortstop Mark Koenig. Throwing nothing but darts, Grove then struck out Babe Ruth, Lou Gehrig and Bob Meusel. On nine pitches.

—*William Nack, SI, August 19, 1996*

▸ NINE ERA TITLES
▸ 300 CAREER WINS

LEFTY GROVE

3

WARREN SPAHN

BRAVES 1942, 1946–1964
TWO TEAMS 1965

"The winningest southpaw ever, he also helped inspire one of the most winning baseball battle cries: "Spahn and Sain, and pray for rain."" —DICK FRIEDMAN

▸ 363 CAREER WINS
▸ 13 20-WIN SEASONS

SPAHN RECALLED the trauma of his major league debut as an obscure 20-year-old lefthander with the wartime Boston Braves. It was 1942, and Casey Stengel summoned him from the bullpen to face the Dodgers' Pee Wee Reese. "Kid," Stengel said, "this hitter has been beaned and got his skull broke. I want you to throw your first two pitches at his head." Spahn was a magnificent competitor, but he was also a sportsman. He threw two fastballs shoulder-high inside, neither near Reese's head, then walked the Brooklyn shortstop. Stengel made his way back to the mound. "Yer outta the game," he said, "and when you get to the dugout, keep walking till you reach the clubhouse. There's gonna be a bus ticket there back to Hartford. You'll never win in the major leagues. You got no guts." Proceeding with this narrative, Spahn uttered a put-down for the ages. "A few years later," he said, "after I won the Bronze Star during the Battle of the Bulge. . . "

—Roger Kahn, SI, December 8, 2003

Spahn's curveball befuddled hitters for years.

PHOTOGRAPH BY MARVIN E. NEWMAN

Johnson is second on the career strikeouts list.

PHOTOGRAPH BY JOHN IACONO

4

MARINERS 1989–1998
DIAMONDBACKS 1999–2004, 2007–2008
FOUR TEAMS 1988–2009

" The media guides said that Randy Johnson stood 6' 10", but those who tried to hit his 99-mph missiles are forgiven for believing the Big Unit was 12 feet tall. " —STEPHEN CANNELLA

▸ 303 CAREER WINS
▸ 4,875 CAREER STRIKEOUTS

RANDY JOHNSON

BEFORE A game in 1993, the home plate umpire told catcher Dave Valle, "He's so good they don't need you. Let me call the pitches tonight." "I let him call every pitch," recalls Valle, to whom the umpire whispered pitches under his breath. Johnson went the distance in a victory.

—*Tom Verducci, SI, May 25, 2009*

5

WHITEY FORD

YANKEES 1950, 1953–1967

" Casey Stengel once said that if his life depended on one game, he wanted Ford pitching it. With a modern-baseball best .690 career regular-season win-loss percentage, Stengel knew what he was talking about. " —DAVID SABINO

▸ 236 CAREER WINS
▸ MLB RECORD 33²/₃ CONSECUTIVE SCORELESS WORLD SERIES INNINGS

"I'LL TELL YOU one secret about Ford," said Yankees pitching coach Jim Turner. "He looks like a little boy out there on the mound. But he isn't. He's a man. People think he's one of these cuties, has to fool the batters. But he's got plenty of stuff on the ball." "I weigh 180," Ford demurred gently. "I know because I just weighed myself. I don't want to get fat." He smiled, a cheerful, amused little smile, as if this were a personal joke. "When I tried out for the Yankees in 1946 I was five seven and weighed 140. I was a first baseman. Krichell [Paul Krichell, the Yankees' chief scout] told me I was too little to be a first baseman. He told me to try pitching." Ford grinned again, as if he had just thought of something funny. "Maybe Krichell was just kidding," he said, "because I was so little. I wonder if he was. Though I could always throw pretty good."

—Robert W. Creamer, SI, September 10, 1956

Ford's nickname was Chairman of the Board.

6

STEVE CARLTON

CARDINALS 1965–1971
PHILLIES 1972–1986
FOUR TEAMS THROUGH 1988

" Carlton's fastball hummed from the start; he refined a dastardly slider; and he threw both of them over the top, primary weapons in a prolific career decorated with a shelf of Cy Young Awards—four of them in all. " —KOSTYA KENNEDY

▸ 329 CAREER WINS
▸ 4,136 CAREER STRIKEOUTS

UNLIKE MANY pitchers, Carlton's not afraid of losing, because he considers failure to be a steppingstone to success. When he sits in the trainer's room going over the hitters, he just thinks of the guys he gets out. He's taken note of the guys who hit him and made mental adjustments, but he doesn't dwell on them. Lefty reads widely in psychology and Eastern philosophy, things like Taoism and Buddhism. I understand many Eastern thinkers don't think of experiences as positive or negative, just useful. Lefty's like that. He acts the same after every game, win or lose. He's as conscientious about his preparation between starts as he is his pitching. Nothing in life overwhelms him, probably because he believes in reincarnation. He sees life as a journey, and when this one ends, another one begins.

—Tim McCarver, with Jim Kaplan, SI, July 21, 1980

The 6' 4" Carlton was an intimidating mound presence.

PHOTOGRAPH BY CLIFF WELCH/ICON SMI

WHEN LEFTY SPOKE

*Steve Carlton stopped granting interviews in later years,
but not before the master of control invited a reporter
along for a night in Miami that nearly went a little wild*

BY RON FIMRITE

THE TALL YOUNG ATHLETE IN the checkered sport coat walked quickly past the swimming pool as old men in flowered bathing trunks scuttled in his wake, their wrinkled limbs pumping below protruding bellies. "Hey, Steve," one of them trumpeted, "gonna win 30 this year?" Steve Carlton, baseball's best pitcher, smiled gamely, but his small darting dark eyes betrayed the uneasiness he experiences when trapped in a crowd. "Sure," he said without looking back. The old man guffawed, shaking his head as if that were the most preposterous boast he had heard in a lifetime of suffering braggadocios. Wasn't that Steve a caution. . . .

Carlton had come to the improbably named Waikiki Resort Motel in Miami Beach to revive old times, not old-timers. Ten years ago he had been a pool boy there, a youth so tall and gaunt he seemed an Ichabod Crane to the septuagenarian clientele. But he had been good at his job, just as he had been good at almost everything then that did not involve books or classrooms.

Young Steve Carlton was a Dade County Paul Bunyan. Why, he could knock a line of birds off the telephone wires with nothing more than a handful of rocks. Once, while walking in the woods, he came upon a quail and scared it into the branches of an oak. He took an ax in his big left hand and flung it hard. The blade cut that little bird's head off as neatly as a surgeon's knife. The ax, stained red, just hummed in the trunk of the tree until Steve fetched it.

At the Waikiki, he could stack mats higher than any pool boy and he was the champion comic diver. One day he dived off the roof of the pool shack to rescue a little girl from drowning. He was something.

He was something else now, suddenly, after adult years of mostly humdrum competence. In an erratic career with the Cardinals—he lost 19 games one season, won 20 the next—he had had a background of salary disputes, the last of which led to the trade that sent him to Philadelphia just before spring training last year, a consignment, it was believed at the time, to purgatory. Instead, grimly determined, he compiled in 1972 perhaps the most extraordinary record of any pitcher in history.

He set major league marks by winning 27 games for a last-place team and by accounting for 45.8% of all his team's victories. He led the National League in wins, complete games (30), innings pitched (346), strikeouts (310) and earned run average (1.97). Only Sandy Koufax among NL lefthanders had won as many games in a single season, and Koufax in 1966 was pitching for a pennant winner, not a last-place team.

Carlton's mental preparation for a pitching assignment is considered monastic by the congenial standards of the diamond. He shuts himself off the day of a game, entering, as former teammate Dal Maxvill describes it, "a little dark room of the mind." But win or lose he emerges from this self-inflicted catatonia with renewed verve.

Carlton protests that neither his uppers nor his downers are as high or as low as they are made out to be. His pregame meditation, he says, is merely a device to banish the "variables" that would otherwise shatter his concentration. "People are always throwing variables at you," he says, as if variables were hard objects to be ducked.

It was a warm, breezy Miami evening. The Carlton entourage—Steve, Joe, Mom and intrepid adviser Dave—had opted for mackerel and stone crab at the Mike Gordon Seafood Restaurant on 79th Street.

There was trouble almost from the start. The lines of waiting diners were long and quarrelsome. When the group was finally seated it was determined that it was not large enough for the appointed table. Would the Carltons accept lesser accommodations? Certainly not.

"Let's go someplace else," said Dave.

"The food here is good," said Steve.

Drinks were ordered—a Beefeater on the rocks with a twist for Steve, a vodka martini for Dave, bourbon and water for the elder Carltons.

Joe was quiet. Mom—Mrs. Anne Carlton—wondered what everyone was going to order. Steve was worried about his shape. All those damn banquets. Variables, all of them. Beverley and the kids were still in St. Louis. He had not seen much of them this winter.

The drinks arrived. Dave sipped his, then brought his fist down heavily on the table. "This is gin! I ordered vodka. Let's go someplace else!"

Steve watched with rising irritation as the waitress poured a single shot of Beefeater into a large glass filled with ice and lemon. The liquid barely occupied the bottom of the glass.

"That does it," he bellowed, more angry now even than Dave. "A single shot! What kind of a cheapskate is this Mike Gordon?"

"We wanna see Mike Gordon," said Dave.

"He's doing the dishes," said the waitress.

Stories of how Steve had been known to stage scenes in bars and restaurants sprang to mind.

"We're just gonna have to do something to this place," he said ominously. He was eying two expensive nautical lanterns on the shelf behind him. Visions flashed of the lanterns in smithereens, of angry voices, a great commotion. . . .

"Yes," said Steve, "we definitely gotta do something." He looked furious. He grabbed the menu, a slim paper volume. He held it before him. Then, theatrically, ripped it in two. He smiled a satisfied, good inner smile. He had caught himself. Almost, anyway.

"Vindictiveness," he said very slowly, "is a variable."

"Why don't we go someplace else," said Dave. ∎

167

7

GIANTS 1928–1943

Hubbell won an MLB record 24 consecutive games.

" Hubbell's brilliant run from 1933 to '37 may be the best five-season stretch a pitcher has ever had. The master of the screwball's gradual decline that followed suggest the high-stress pitch took its toll on his arm, or his career numbers would be even gaudier. " —DAVID BAUER

HUBBELL'S SCREWBALL bordered on the unhittable. He had used it in striking out Babe Ruth, Lou Gehrig, Jimmie Foxx, Al Simmons and Joe Cronin consecutively in the 1934 All-Star Game. Batters didn't hit it very often, and when they did, they didn't connect solidly.

—*Noel Hynd, SI, April 20, 1987*

CARL HUBBELL

▸ TWO-TIME NL MVP
▸ 253 CAREER WINS

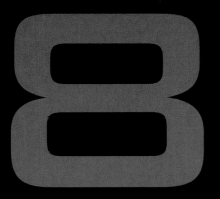

8

EDDIE PLANK

A'S 1901–1914
TWO TEAMS THROUGH 1917

" Plank took his sweet time on the mound and slung the ball sidearm and preferred to throw a curveball rather than the heat. The m.o. led to eight 20-win seasons, slender ERAs and a southpaw record that might stand forever: 69 shutouts." —KOSTYA KENNEDY

▸ 326 CAREER WINS
▸ 2.35 CAREER ERA

WHY WAS Plank one of the only pitchers from his era to excel after age 35? Because Plank didn't pitch professionally until he was 25. Plank was such an economical pitcher that he hated to throw to first base to keep runners close to the bag. He had his best year (26–6, 2.22 ERA) when he was 36. And in his final season five years later, his ERA was 1.79.

—*Albert Kim, SI, May 22, 1989*

Plank pitched for six pennant winners in Philadelphia.

PHOTOGRAPH BY THE BAIN COLLECTION/LIBRARY OF CONGRESS

BRAVES 1987–2002, 2008
METS 2003–2007

Glavine was the 1995 World Series MVP.

PHOTOGRAPH BY AL TIELEMANS

9

TOM GLAVINE

" The cornerstone on which Atlanta's 1990s dynasty was built. Only two NL lefties—Warren Spahn and Steve Carlton—won more career games than Glavine, and only Carlton had more strikeouts. " —DAVID SABINO

▸ 305 CAREER WINS
▸ TWO NL CY YOUNG AWARDS

GLAVINE PERSONIFIED fortitude. His signature game was the 1995 World Series clincher over the Cleveland Indians. Locked in a scoreless duel in the fifth inning, Glavine shouted to his teammates, "Will somebody hurry up and score here? Because they sure as hell won't." The Braves won 1–0.

—Tom Verducci, SI, February 22, 2010

10
LEFTY GOMEZ

YANKEES 1930–1942
SENATORS 1943

"Ace of the 1930s Yankees juggernaut, Lefty Gomez was renowned for his wisecracking wit, but when he took the ball the southpaw was deadly serious, going 189–102 in 14 seasons. In seven World Series starts, he went 6–0 with a 2.86 ERA." —DICK FRIEDMAN

▸ TWO PITCHING TRIPLE CROWNS
▸ FOUR 20-WIN SEASONS

WHEN YOU watched Gomez you were always aware that this, after all, was a game. For Lefty had fun. One day rightfielder George Selkirk said, "Lefty, you are the slowest man I ever saw. I'll bet you five dollars that I can beat you to the dugout at the end of an inning." Gomez said, "You got a bet." The next inning, with two men on base and two out, the batter laid heavily on one of Gomez's fastballs and drove it to left centerfield. Gomez watched it go, saw Joe DiMaggio loping after it and then glanced toward rightfield. Here came Selkirk, racing like a sprinter. Gomez took off for the bench. They pounded down the dugout steps and landed one-two on the bench just as DiMaggio took the third out into his glove. "[Manager] Joe [McCarthy] wasn't at all pleased," Lefty recalled. "But I won the bet."

—Robert W. Creamer, SI, June 25, 1956

Gomez pitched in seven consecutive All-Star games.

10

THE

BEST RELIEF PITCHERS

MAYBE THE ODDEST THING YOU'LL SEE IN THIS BOOK IS THE JUXTAPOSITION OF THE PHOTOS OF OUR NO. 2- AND NO. 3-RANKED RELIEVERS. IF YOU'RE LEAFING THROUGH QUICKLY, THEY CAN LOOK LIKE THE SAME GUY IN THE SAME UNIFORM, WITH SOMETHING CLOSE TO THE SAME MUSTACHE—THOUGH OF COURSE ROLLIE FINGERS'S IS DIFFERENTIATED FROM DENNIS ECKERSLEY'S BY THE SIGNATURE TWIRL AT THE END. THEY ARE BUT TWO OF THE MANY HIRSUTE HURLERS IN THIS SECTION.

ANOTHER TREND AMONG OUR TOP RELIEVERS IS THAT SEVERAL OF THEM WERE ONE-TRICK PONIES, ACHIEVING LONG-STANDING SUCCESS LARGELY BY MEANS OF A SINGLE PITCH. WE'VE GOT MARIANO RIVERA WITH HIS CUTTER, HOYT WILHELM WITH HIS KNUCKLEBALL, BRUCE SUTTER WITH HIS SPLIT-FINGER PITCH AND DAN QUISENBERRY BRINGING THE THUNDER FROM DOWN UNDER.

THE TOP-10 RELIEVERS ARE ALL OF RELATIVELY RECENT VINTAGE, WHICH IS TO BE EXPECTED, GIVEN THAT THE RELIEF SPECIALIST IS A MODERN PHENOMENON. BUT ONE OLD-TIMER DID GARNER A SINGLE 10TH-PLACE VOTE—FIRPO MARBERRY, WHO LED THE AL IN SAVES FIVE TIMES FOR THE SENATORS BETWEEN 1924 AND 1932. A SIGN THAT HE CAME FROM A DIFFERENT ERA: IN ONE OF THOSE SEASONS, 1929, HIS LEAGUE-LEADING TOTAL WAS A MERE 11 SAVES. ALSO, HE HAD NO FACIAL HAIR WHATSOEVER.

1

MARIANO RIVERA

YANKEES 1995–2013

"Throwing the cutter almost exclusively—his catcher, Jorge Posada, at times didn't waste a superfluous sign for it—Rivera saved more games than any pitcher and became one of the greatest postseason weapons, putting up a 0.70 ERA and a record 42 saves in 96 postseason games" —TOM VERDUCCI

▸ 608 SAVES THROUGH 2012
▸ 11 SEASONS WITH ERA BELOW 2.00

JUST THREE months into his new role as the closer for a budding Yankees dynasty, Rivera was suddenly unable to throw his signature four-seam fastball straight. He was gripping the ball the same way he always had, releasing it the same way he always had. The wicked movement just . . . happened. And continued to happen while Rivera warmed up one late-June night in the bullpen at Tiger Stadium. Rivera didn't have an explanation, and though he says he "didn't have any idea where the ball was going," his results did not suffer. He got the save in that game, then in the next three. Still, for a month, he worked to eliminate the cutting action. Then he said, 'I'm tired of working at this. Let's let it happen.' And since that day we didn't try to straighten it out anymore." He smiles. "And the rest is history."

—Tom Verducci, SI, October 5, 2009

Rivera helped the Yankees to five World Series titles.

PHOTOGRAPHS BY CHUCK SOLOMON (LEFT) AND PORTER BINKS

RELIEF PITCHERS

Eckersley had six seasons with single-digit walks.

PHOTOGRAPH BY V.J. LOVERO

RED SOX 1978–1984, 1998
A'S 1987–1995
THREE TEAMS 1975–1997

❝ He spent 12 seasons as a very good starter before he revolutionized the closer's role when Tony La Russa began using him exclusively as a ninth-inning specialist. ❞ —ALBERT CHEN

▸ 1992 AL MVP
▸ 0.61 ERA IN 1990

"I GET fired by fear," says the Eck. "I'm scared of failure every time I go out there. I can remember Carl Yastrzemski telling me that it never gets easier, that the game just got tougher and more nerve-racking every year. Boy, was he ever right. The 45th save was tougher than the first one."

—Peter Gammons, SI, December 12, 1988

DENNIS ECKERSLEY

3

ROLLIE FINGERS

A'S 1968–1976
PADRES 1977–1980
BREWERS 1981–1982, 1984–1985

" Reliable, rollicking Rollie Fingers popularized the handlebar moustache and the role of closer. The unflappable Fingers led his league in saves three times and won the AL Cy Young and MVP for the Brewers in '81, when he had a 1.04 ERA. " —DICK FRIEDMAN

▸ 341 CAREER SAVES
▸ 1.35 ERA IN 16 WORLD SERIES APPEARANCES

THE RELIEF PITCHER is the least predictable of players. As often as not, the rally-dousing Fireman of the Year one season becomes the arm-weary Flop of the Year the next. So when Ray Kroc, the McDonald's magnate who also owns the Padres, signed a free-agent reliever to a six-year, $1.6 million contract, he figured to be called a meatball by the experts. He wasn't, simply because the man he hired was Rollie Fingers, who in eight full years at Oakland had suffered none of the vicissitudes of his trade. The tireless Fingers has never been named the year's best reliever, having been edged out several times by men who are no longer stars. If he performs well for San Diego, a new title may have to be created just for him: Fireman of the Decade.

—Ron Fimrite, SI, April 11, 1977

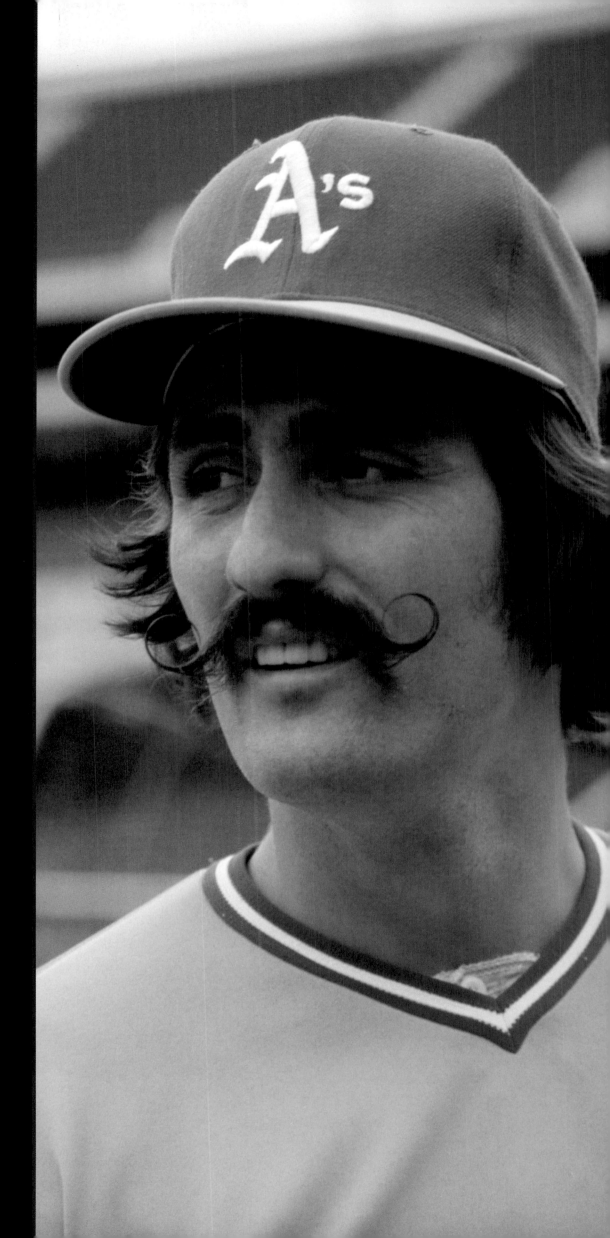

Fingers won the 1974 World Series MVP.

PHOTOGRAPH BY FRED KAPLAN

4

Gossage was named to nine All-Star teams.

WHITE SOX 1972–1976
YANKEES 1978–1983, 1989
SEVEN TEAMS THROUGH 1994

" What set the Goose apart from the specialists of today was his effectiveness over multiple innings. Nearly two thirds of his career saves (62.2%) came in games in which he managed at least four outs. " —DAVID SABINO

‣ 310 CAREER SAVES
‣ 0.77 ERA IN 1981

RICH GOSSAGE

CRANKED UP by the noise of the crowd, Gossage goes right to work, winning through intimidation. At 6' 3", 217 pounds, he takes a slump-shouldered Incredible Hulk stance and scowls at the hitter. Then he uncorks a 95–100-mph fastball that baffles the batters, even though they're fully expecting it.

—Jim Kaplan, SI, September 29, 1980

5

TREVOR HOFFMAN

MARLINS 1993
PADRES 1993–2008
BREWERS 2009–2010

" Drafted by the Reds as a shortstop in 1989, he converted to pitcher in '91, was left unprotected in the '92 expansion draft and selected by the Marlins, traded in '93 to the Padres, where he was booed and robbed of velocity by rotator cuff surgery in '95. Hoffman's shoulder trouble, though, prompted him to develop the pitch that would be his calling card: the changeup. " —TOM VERDUCCI

▸ 601 CAREER SAVES
▸ 2.87 CAREER ERA

ON JULY 25, 1998, inspired by the use of the song "Wild Thing" in the movie *Major League*, Hoffman added musical accompaniment to his trot to the mound. As Hoffman jogged in from the bullpen, the ominous, slow cadence of heavy bells played on the stadium loudspeakers, followed by more of "Hell's Bells" by AC/DC. Hoffman snuffed out the Houston Astros that night for what was then a record-tying 41st consecutive save. The streak, but not the music, ended the next night. His signature moment is one of the most electrically charged in sports: Padres fans rising and roaring, in Pavlovian fashion, upon hearing the first bell toll, the foreboding bonging like something out of Hitchcock as Hoffman enters slowly, stage right.

—*Tom Verducci, SI, May 13, 2002*

Hoffman averaged 9.4 strikeouts per nine innings.

HOYT WILHELM

GIANTS 1952–1956
ORIOLES 1958–1962
WHITE SOX 1963–1968
SIX TEAMS THROUGH 1972

" The first true reliever, and the first elected to the Hall of Fame, his success changed the game. He didn't throw his first major league pitch until he was 29, he threw his last at age 49; and he did it all with the knuckleball. What's not to love? " —DAVID BAUER

▸ MLB RECORD 124 WINS
AS RELIEVER
▸ 2.52 CAREER ERA

WILHELM GRIPS the ball with his thumb and the very tip of his index and middle fingers and lets fly with a relatively easy sidearm motion. From that point on neither he, nor the batter, nor his own catcher knows what course it is going to take. For most of its journey to the plate the ball does nothing much but float easily and almost enticingly toward the expectant batter. This, as it turns out, is only a sly come-on, for suddenly it begins to bob and weave like Floyd Patterson moving in to throw a left hook. It wobbles, it flutters. It dances and dips. And then, finally, it darts dizzily off in one direction or another—sometimes down, sometimes sideways, occasionally even up—while the batter bludgeons the air and the catcher makes his frantic lunge.

—Roy Terrell, SI, June 29, 1959

Wilhelm said his grip was all about the fingertips.

7

BRUCE SUTTER

CUBS 1976–1980
CARDINALS 1981–1984
BRAVES 1985–1986, 1988

" With his devastating split-fingered pitch—hitters couldn't hit it and they couldn't lay off—the long-fingered Sutter led the National League in saves a record five times. In 1979 he saved 37 for a sub-.500 Cubs team; in '84 he saved 54% of the Cardinals wins, and though he struggled some in the '82 World Series, St. Louis would never have won the title without him. " —KOSTYA KENNEDY

▸ 1979 NL CY YOUNG WINNER
▸ 300 CAREER SAVES

BRUCE SUTTER is baseball's counterpart of that singular character in the Rodgers and Hart song "Johnny One Note." Sutter has only one pitch, but like Johnny's note, it is unique and overpowering. Sutter calls his magic pitch a "split-fingered fastball," which is an accurate-enough description in that his fingers are spread apart when he releases the ball. But the fastball part is debatable for the simple and—for hitters— maddening reason that the ball's speed changes at least once, maybe twice, in the course of its flight. "It's unhittable," says Montreal manager Dick Williams, "unless he hangs it, and he never does. It's worse than trying to hit a knuckleball."

—Ron Fimrite, SI, September 17, 1979

Sutter was a six-time All-Star.

PHOTOGRAPH BY JERRY WACHTER

8

DAN QUISENBERRY

ROYALS 1979–1988
TWO TEAMS 1988–1990

"He wasn't an intimidator, but Quiz was dominant nonetheless, a one of a kind with an unmistakable submarining pitching style. The righthander was key in Kansas City's two pennants and its 1985 World Series win." —ALBERT CHEN

▸ LED AL IN SAVES FIVE TIMES
▸ 2.76 CAREER ERA

QUISENBERRY WAS introduced to his role model, Pittsburgh's Kent Tekulve, during spring training, and the two sidearmers discussed their exotic pitch. As a result, he began bending even closer to the ground. "The lower one gets," he explains, "the more pronation occurs and the more the ball sinks." Whatever, it works.

—*Ron Fimrite, SI, June 9, 1980*

THE COMIC RELIEVER

*The down-under throwing motion that befuddled
so many hitters was just one of many funny things
about the bullpen artist known as "The Australian"*

BY STEVE WULF

A TYPICAL INTERVIEW WITH Dan Quisenberry occurred after he earned his sixth save by getting himself into and out of a scary situation against the Yankees.

Reporter: "Did you know your records this year are actually better than they were at this time last year?"

Quisenberry: "How did you know? I'm into classical this year instead of pop."

Reporter: "Did the weather affect your performance?"

Quisenberry: "Actually, I think my problem is that I haven't been clipping my toenails properly. The club is after me to change that."

Says reliever Mike Armstrong, Quisenberry's locker neighbor, "The day I came up he treated me very seriously, telling me how to settle in and everything. But that night, after I heard how he talked to reporters, well, I couldn't believe it. I'd never heard anybody do that before."

Offstage, Quisenberry is genuinely funny, with a fine feel for the absurd. When he's leading someone to his house by car, for instance, he likes to pull up to a huge mansion in the K.C. suburb of Mission Hills, get out and walk to the gate as if it were his. The mansion happens to belong to Ewing Kauffman, who also owns the Royals.

"I enjoy his sense of humor," says Royals manager Dick Howser. "I enjoy his pitching even more."

Quisenberry's, of course, is what sets him apart. If you're a batter, you see him wind up like a normal pitcher, but then he pivots, does a fleeting imitation of a flamingo, steps toward third base, pulls his right hand out from what seems like his left back pocket, whips his arm around and throws from what seems like the tops of third baseman George Brett's shoes. Then he follows through with a little jump that leaves him squarely facing the plate. "He comes," says Milwaukee's Rick Manning, "from a different zone."

Submariners—a silly way to describe them, actually—are not to be confused with sidearmers. In the minor leagues they call what sidearmers do "throwing Laredo," Laredo being in the bottom of Texas. Quisenberry says his style is more "throwing Sydney."

Much of Quisenberry's effectiveness is derived from batters' unfamiliarity with his motion. But that doesn't explain all his success. His control is phenomenal. Last year he walked one batter every 11 innings. The three little words which mean the most to any manager in baseball are he throws strikes. Quisenberry throws strikes.

He also throws sinkers. His pitch isn't very fast, 80 to 85 mph, but the ball feels like lead when it hits a bat. He has no secret. He just holds the ball with the seams and lets his arm and wrist do their thing. "He's not tough to put the ball in play against," says Detroit's Alan Trammell. "It's just tough to put it where you want it."

And because Quisenberry doesn't strike out many hitters, Howser has to use him differently. "I have to bring Dan in one batter earlier than I would a Gossage," says Howser. "I know he's not going to get out of a jam with a strikeout, and the ground ball I want him to get might go through for a hit."

If Quisenberry were a fluke the batters would have caught on by now. But not only does he throw sinkers, he also throws sliders, occasional changeups and, ta-da, knuckleballs. Says Oakland's Rickey Henderson, "I didn't know he had a knuckleball until he threw me one with two strikes. I had no chance. I just froze and let it go by. I stared at him, but he just turned his back. And I'm thinking, 'That's not fair.'"

And now we thought we'd give the ball to Quisenberry. Herewith relief writing by The Australian:

In Kansas City I go out to the bullpen at 7:27. I do that because I used to go out with Renie Martin at that time, and the reason he did that was because his number was 27. I just never changed.

One thing I like to watch for in the bullpen is The Look. Whenever the alarm goes off during a game, somebody gets this look in his eye, depending on where we are in the game. The Look is a stare that goes for 30 yards and focuses on nothing. I know I get it. Your mind starts playing visions of embarrassment and greatness against each other, and you become a blend of fear and hope and confidence. When the danger's passed, The Look goes away. You breathe a sigh of relief but also a sigh of disappointment because you wanted to be in the game.

Early in the season, we killed a night off in Cleveland by writing a song. Ron Johnson was then our Black & Decker—our tool, our bullpen catcher—and he's pretty good with a guitar, so we came up with something called "Secret Bullpen Man," which is sung to the tune of "Secret Agent Man," the old song by Johnny Rivers. In the song we make fun of each other's inadequacies. Everybody is lit up in this thing, and some of it would be pretty embarrassing. But the chorus is, "Secret Bullpen Man, Secret Bullpen Man,/ You can always call his number,/ But don't put him in the game." The song ends with us singing, "No, no, not me,/ No, no, not you,/ No, no, not him." Here's my verse:

"The ace down here is Dan Quisenberry. He likes to make the games kind of scary. He's got a bag of tricks. But mostly takes his licks. He makes the skipper head straight for the sherry."

It has a good beat and you can dance to it. I give it an 85.

It's funny. The bullpen is a closed environment, but I get a sense of freedom there that I don't get in the dugout or the clubhouse. I guess I just like being locked in a closet, taking verbal abuse from a lot of hostile people. ∎

9

**LEE
SMITH**

CUBS 1980–1987
SEVEN TEAMS THROUGH 1997

Smith's fastball reached 101 mph.

PHOTOGRAPH BY WALTER IOOSS JR.

" Number 3 on the alltime saves list and, at 6' 5", 220 pounds, with a nasty beard, a ferocious face and a scary fastball, he's No. 1 on the alltime most physically intimidating closer list. (Goose Gossage? A distant No. 2.) " —DAVID BAUER

▸ 478 CAREER SAVES
▸ SEVEN-TIME ALL-STAR

WHEN MIKE ROARKE was the pitching coach for the Cubs, he talked to Smith about moving to the bullpen. He got a cool reaction. "I thought the big man always started," recalls Smith. "I told him I might quit and play hoops." Roarke said, "Your fastball's a lot better than your jump shot. So get your butt out to the bullpen."

—Peter Gammons, SI, April 4, 1988

10

BILLY WAGNER

ASTROS 1995–2003
METS 2006–2009
THREE TEAMS THROUGH 2010

"A scary thought: Wagner, the most intimidating lefthanded reliever ever, wasn't even a natural lefty—he taught himself to throw that way after breaking his right arm as a kid. Only four closers saved more games than Wagner, and no one who has pitched at least 900 innings has struck out more men per nine innings." —STEPHEN CANNELLA

▸ 422 CAREER SAVES
▸ 11.9 STRIKEOUTS PER NINE INNINGS FOR CAREER

BILLY WAGNER, the Astros' smaller-than-life closer, comes into games after 20 warmup pitches and trots to the mound calmly. There's nothing menacing or imposing about him. He doesn't have a crazed stare. He doesn't hide behind a sinister-looking goatee. He is 28 and has the body of a high school kid; he stands a couple of inches under six feet and would tip the scales at his listed weight of 180 pounds only after a third helping of grits. He tucks his glove under his left arm, his throwing arm, and says a prayer. Then he brings it. First pitch, fastball, 95 mph. Strike one. Second pitch, fastball, 97 mph. Strike two. Third pitch, fastball, 98 mph. Next victim.

—*Michael Eamberger, SI, September 20, 1999*

Wagner had a career ERA of 2.31.

10

THE

Best Managers

"THE THREE THINGS YOU NEED TO BE A GOOD MANAGER," WHITEY HERZOG CONFIDED IN THE PAGES OF SPORTS ILLUSTRATED, IN 1981, "ARE PLAYERS, A SENSE OF HUMOR AND, MOST IMPORTANT, A GOOD BULLPEN. IF I'VE GOT THOSE THREE THINGS, I GUARANTEE YOU I'LL MAKE THE HALL OF FAME. A MANAGER DOESN'T NECESSARILY WIN GAMES, BUT HE CAN LOSE A LOT OF GAMES."

WHILE HERZOG, WHO WON A WORLD SERIES WITH THE CARDINALS IN 1982 AND MADE THE HALL OF FAME IN 2010, DOWNPLAYED THE VALUE OF HIS EFFORTS, SOME CONTEMPORARIES ARGUED MANAGERS DESERVED MORE CREDIT. FRANK ROBINSON, SKIPPERING THE GIANTS IN '81, SAID, "A MANAGER HAS SOME INFLUENCE ON EVERY GAME PLAYED. FIRST OF ALL, HE'S RESPONSIBLE FOR PREPARING HIS TEAM TO PLAY . . . HE MAKES IMPORTANT DECISIONS THROUGHOUT THE GAME, NOT JUST IN THE EIGHTH OR NINTH INNINGS."

WHICHEVER SIDE YOU TAKE, THERE'S NO DOUBT THAT THE MEN ON OUR TOP 10 LIST BENEFITED FROM WORKING WITH GREAT TALENT. EACH MANAGED AT LEAST THREE, IF NOT MORE, OF THE TOP-10 PLAYERS IN THIS BOOK. MAYBE YOU THINK IF WOULD BE HARD TO LOSE IF YOU HAD, SAY, MICKEY MANTLE, YOGI BERRA AND WHITEY FORD AT YOUR DISPOSAL, AS CASEY STENGEL DID. BUT IT'S LIKE HERZOG SAYS: MAYBE THESE MANAGERS DIDN'T WIN THE GAMES, BUT THEY DIDN'T EXACTLY LOSE THEM EITHER.

McGraw's innovations included the hit-and-run.

1

ORIOLES 1899, 1901–1902
GIANTS 1902–1932

" McGraw was the game's dominant figure at the beginning of the 20th century, with his outsized, fiery personality and unstoppable Giants teams. " —ALBERT CHEN

‣ 2,763 CAREER WINS
‣ TWO WORLD SERIES TITLES, 10 NL PENNANTS

JOHN MCGRAW

MUGGSY [MCGRAW] was the earthy scuffler, an odd duck, unrepentant, but who—surprise!—is inspiring and brilliant. His heirs are many: George Halas, Casey Stengel, Red Auerbach, Leo Durocher, Vince Lombardi, Bear Bryant, Earl Weaver, Billy Martin, Scotty Bowman, Bill Parcells, Bob Knight.

—*Frank Deford, SI, August 25, 2003*

2

JOE McCARTHY

CUBS 1926–1930
YANKEES 1931–1946
RED SOX 1948–1950

❝ He won a record 61.5% of his regular season games. Marse Joe won the World Series so often that his off-season directive from New York owner Jacob Ruppert was usually a simple, "Do it again next year." ❞ —DAVID SABINO

▸ SEVEN WORLD SERIES TITLES
▸ NL PENNANT WITH CUBS

MCCARTHY, THROUGHOUT his tenure, had an essentially established club. Consequently, he should not be criticized for being basically a percentage manager. With men of the caliber of Gehrig, Dickey, DiMaggio, Rolfe, Crosetti and Gordon around, that's what he had to be. But he believed in making changes when necessary, and he tried to make at least one important shift a year because he thought it perked up the team. Joe seldom complained about anything. Only once I remember, after he had won three pennants in a row in 1943, he harked back to his close third-place finish in 1940, which had been preceded by four successive flags, and remarked that if we had brought up Phil Rizzuto to play shortstop that year instead of a year later he might have won eight in a row.

*—Yankees G.M. George M. Weiss,
as told to Robert Shapien, SI, March 13, 1961*

McCarthy's teams had winning records every season.

PHOTOGRAPH BY AP

3

CASEY STENGEL

DODGERS 1934–1936
BRAVES 1938–1943
YANKEES 1949–1960
METS 1962–1965

" Behind all the lovable, quotable Stengelese was a savvy tactician. "Most ball games are lost, not won," he said, meaning that Stengel probably didn't give himself much credit for winning seven World Series. " —DAVID BAUER

▸ 10 AL PENNANTS WITH YANKEES
▸ 1,905 CAREER WINS

DESPITE THE patronizing nicknames of Ol' Case and the Perfessor, he was not lovable and he was not cute. He was a tough man, as sure of himself as anyone you are ever likely to know. He was a gifted public clown but not a private one. Oh, he could entertain friends— and anyone else within hearing distance—and leave them helpless with laughter, but he never played the fool for them, not even when he was lying on the floor of a hotel lobby at two in the morning, demonstrating the proper execution of the hook slide. He was noted for saying, "You could look it up," but a more significant pet expression was, "Now let me ask you this." Like Socrates, he would pursue a theme with his listeners—his students— and the insights he would develop were sometimes astonishing.

—*Robert W. Creamer, SI, October 13, 1975*

The Mets, like the Yankees, retired Stengel's number.

PHOTOGRAPHS BY NEIL LEIFER

4

TONY LA RUSSA

WHITE SOX 1979–1986
A'S 1986–1995
CARDINALS 1996–2011

❝ Master and commander of any situation, crusty Tony La Russa shrewdly mixed and matched intuition and numbers to win more victories than any manager except Connie Mack and John McGraw. ❞ —DICK FRIEDMAN

▸ THREE WORLD SERIES TITLES
▸ 2,728 CAREER WINS

IN THE 2006 NL Division Series against the Padres, La Russa courted disaster when he pulled ace Chris Carpenter with a 5-1 lead in the seventh inning of Game 1 and when he yanked Jeff Weaver, pitching a two-hitter, after only five innings in Game 2. Both times La Russa threw in his lot with his relief corps—three rookies (Tyler Johnson, Josh Kinney, Adam Wainwright) and a second-year man (Randy Flores). "Take out your ace and go to four rookies? Take out a guy pitching a two-hitter and go to four rookies?" says La Russa, grouping Flores with the others. "Either one of those [games] gets away, and it would be: Tony, you screwed up another Series." But this time it worked. It all worked. "He's relentless, and he has no fear," says Detroit manager Jim Leyland. "He's the most creative manager I've ever managed against."

—*S.L. Price, SI, June 4, 2007*

While a player, La Russa studied law in the off-season.

PHOTOGRAPH BY HEINZ KLUETMEIER

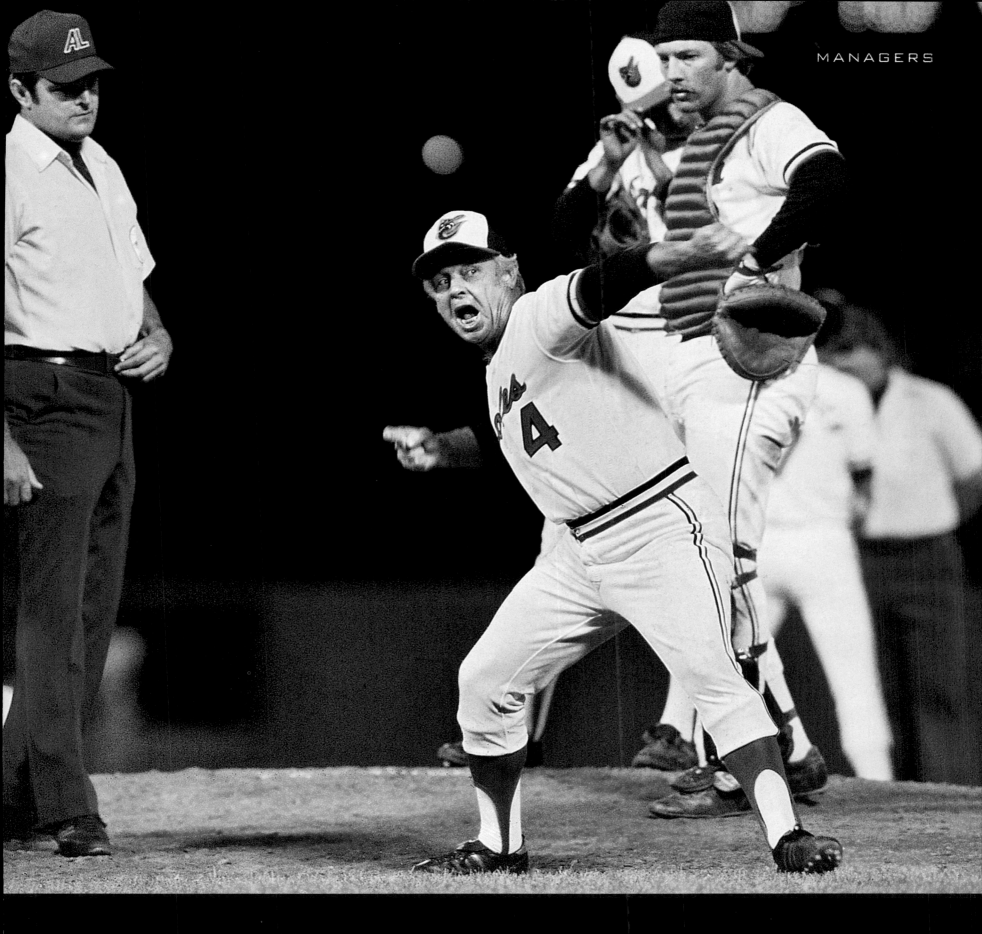

ORIOLES 1968–1986

Weaver was a stat man with a temper.

PHOTOGRAPH BY MANNY MILLAN

5

" The cigar-smoking, umpire-antagonizing Earl of Baltimore wasn't just a wonderfully colorful personality; he was the smartest man in the ballpark. He was a "Moneyball" manager decades before *Moneyball* existed. " —ALBERT CHEN

WEAVER, HALF-NAKED in his dressing room, looked up from his postgame can of beer and shook his head like a damp spaniel. "Nobody's been able to explain [my] charts yet," he said. "I can't even explain them to you. Just say this is something that has helped us win three championships in a row. O.K.?"

—*Ron Fimrite, SI, July 10, 1972*

▸ FOUR AL PENNANTS, ONE WORLD SERIES TITLE
▸ 1,480 CAREER WINS

EARL
WEAVER

6

SPARKY
ANDERSON

REDS 1970–1978
TIGERS 1979–1995

" An inveterate worrier whose hair turned home-plate white before he was 40, Anderson was beloved by his players in Cincinnati and again in Detroit as he presided over 18 consecutive winning seasons from 1972 through '88. " —KOSTYA KENNEDY

▸ THREE WORLD SERIES TITLES
▸ 2,194 CAREER WINS

"IT'S SO important to remember where you came from. I used to joke with Johnny Bench," Anderson said. "He was born in Binger, Oklahoma, and I was born in Bridgewater, South Dakota. 'Don't forget where you came from,' I'd yell at him, and he'd yell it right back at me. Baseball guys are mostly people from poor families, and they should never forget it."

—*Ron Fimrite, SI, June 11, 1984*

Anderson won a title in Detroit after taking two in Cincy.

PHOTOGRAPH BY JOHN WEISS

7

CONNIE MACK

PIRATES 1894–1896
A'S 1901–1950

" Mack cut a regal, if unusual, figure in a major league dugout. There never was or will be anyone like him. He was a gentleman who didn't curse or drink, who called his players by their given name (not their nickname), and who sought educated ballplayers to play a cerebral brand of baseball. " —TOM VERDUCCI

▸ FIVE WORLD SERIES TITLES
▸ 3,731 CAREER WINS

IN THREE DIFFERENT eras he built clubs that are ranked among the greatest that ever played baseball. Connie Mack also had some dreadful ball clubs and never pretended otherwise. You might wonder how he even endured it, for this courtly, kindly, priestly old man was as fierce a competitor as John McGraw or Joe McCarthy or Leo Durocher. He'd always been able to dish it out, and in 1921 he taught himself to take it. That year the Athletics were trying to avoid running last for the seventh consecutive season. They went to Chicago, where the White Sox were in a slump. Connie was confident, but the A's lost every game in Chicago. When they went to Cleveland, Connie couldn't go along. He had a nervous breakdown. "I told myself after that," he says, "that I'd never let it happen again. I'd always be ready to take the bad with the good."

—Red Smith, SI, October 25, 1954

Mack preferred to manage in a business suit.

PHOTOGRAPH BY JACOB HARRIS/AP

8
BOBBY COX

BRAVES 1978-1981, 1990-2010
BLUE JAYS 1982-1985

" He's been sometimes unfairly discounted because he had so much talent in his dugout, but Cox knew how to make it work—and how to not mess it up—year after year after year. Eleven consecutive division titles speaks for itself. " —DAVID BAUER

▸ 1995 WORLD SERIES TITLE
▸ 2,054 CAREER WINS

COX WAS named the Braves G.M. in October 1985. "There was a decision to rebuild by drafting and developing pitchers," says John Schuerholz, who took over as G.M. in 1990, the year Cox became field manager. "It is a great credit to Bobby that he didn't make trades while everybody was lusting after [his] guys."

—Steve Rushin, SI, April 5, 1993

IN THROUGH THE OUT DOOR

On his way to being ejected from more games than any other manager, Bobby Cox may have ticked off the umps, but he also earned the respect of the guys in the dugout

BY THOMAS LAKE

BEFORE WE TALK ABOUT sacrifice, or phantom blackbirds, or the Chipper Jones Momentum-Turn Hypothesis, let me tell you about the time Bobby Cox demolished a toilet with one bare hand.

It happened at Shea Stadium. Braves shortstop Darrel Chaney slid into home, and the plate umpire called him out, and Chaney raised enough Cain to get himself ejected. Cox was so furious on his player's behalf that he went to the bathroom by the dugout and visited justice upon the toilet. Chaney saw the shattered tank, the gushing water, and he loved the skipper for what he had done.

Chaney decided he would do anything for Bobby Cox, even ride the bench without complaint, which he did for most of the 1979 season. He played so seldom in the dusk of his career that he basically forgot how, and by mid-September his average had fallen to .111. Cox called him into the office.

They're not renewing your contract, he said. They're gonna release you. But I'll play you as much as I can these last two weeks, so other clubs can see you.

Chaney was a career .217 hitter. He went out those last two weeks and hit .333 for Bobby Cox. And then he retired.

According to the Chipper Jones Momentum-Turn Hypothesis, the ejection of Bobby Cox from any baseball game imparts a certain heat and energy to his players, who respond by playing better. Thus the momentum turn and, perhaps, victory.

Cox, who will retire after this season, has managed 4,438 games, fourth-most in baseball history. But Tony La Russa has managed more games than Cox and has barely half the ejections. Joe Torre has managed almost as many games and has fewer than half the ejections. Connie Mack managed for 53 years, and he's not even among the top 10 ejectees. Bobby Cox hasn't just been around a long time. He's been *getting thrown out a lot for a long time.* The previous record holder—McGraw, the New York Giants' manager from 1902 to '32—was known for kicking umpires with his cleats and getting ejected on purpose so he could go bet on horses. Bobby Cox has gotten booted at a rate about 50% higher than McGraw's rate as a manager.

The mystery, then, is why. Why would a man who hates attention draw it to himself so frequently? More to the point: Why would the same man become one of the most successful managers of all time? Is there a connection?

The Chipper Jones Momentum-Turn Hypothesis implies one. But it has not been accepted as scientific fact. "People think you can spark teams by [getting ejected]," Nationals manager Manny Acta told *The Washington Post* in 2007. "It's just not true. [The Braves] never won any of those games because he got thrown out of the game."

But there is no way to know how many times Cox has saved a player from ejection. The number must be large. David Vincent found that since Cox took over in 1990, the Braves' player-ejection rate has been about half the major league average.

We found evidence of at least six times that Cox took an ejection to keep a player from getting tossed. Then we looked at how those players used their second chances.

The salvation backfired once, on June 8, 1996, when Tom Glavine allowed 12 hits and seven runs after Cox rescued him.

Four other times it succeeded. Steve Avery pitched 2⅓ innings more without allowing a hit. Tim Hudson cruised through the next six innings to get the win. Chipper Jones had a walk-off double against the Giants. It even happened once in the World Series, Game 6 in 1996, when Marquis Grissom exploded over a blown call at second base and Cox was ejected after helping other coaches restrain the Atlanta outfielder. In the ninth inning Grissom hit a two-out single to bring in a run and put the tying run on second. The Braves could have sent it to extra innings if Mark Lemke hadn't popped up to end the Series.

The sixth time is notable in its own way. On May 4, 1998, Ryan Klesko was in the dugout, airing various grievances to umpire Joe Nauert, when Nauert walked toward the bench to shut him up. It was the eighth inning. Klesko had already made his final plate appearance and was scheduled for defensive replacement in the ninth. Cox stepped up and took the ejection anyway.

By now, maybe you see what his players see.

That getting tossed can be an act not of hubris but of humility, because it means Bobby Cox values himself less than the man he's saving, and because he will inhabit the place he hates most—the spotlight—in order to save him.

That it can be an act not of aggression but of sacrifice.

That the ocean of numbers matters less than the knowledge that Bobby Cox will fight for his players, right or wrong, whether or not it makes tactical sense, in the first inning or the 13th, in a rain delay in Toronto or in the washroom at Shea Stadium, with water gushing from a shattered toilet.

The 150th ejection came to pass on July 29, 2009, after a Braves player in the dugout yelled something at Bill Hohn, and Hohn took off his mask and came over brandishing his lineup card. He didn't know who'd done the yelling, but someone would have to pay.

"I have to throw somebody out," he said, or something like that, and the players were not surprised to see what Bobby Cox did next. ∎

9

JOE TORRE

YANKEES 1996–2007
FOUR TEAMS 1977–2010

" Yes, he's fifth on the alltime wins list and won four World Series. But more impressive was his ability to turn any dugout into a zen garden: No manager was better at creating an aura of calm amid chaos. " —STEPHEN CANNELLA

▸ 2,326 CAREER WINS
▸ 13 CONSECUTIVE
POSTSEASON APPEARANCES

NO MAN in baseball history had waited this long to participate in the World Series—4,272 games as a player and manager, spanning 37 years. . . . If you were looking for a real World Series logo—not the garish patches on the side of the Braves' and the Yankees' caps—you could do worse than this: a middle-aged man with a shadowy mug straight out of an Edward G. Robinson flick, weeping in the dugout. Joe Torre cried right there after the Yankees closed out the Orioles in five games in the ALCS. That moment made his wife Alice think about 1984, shortly after Torre had suffered the second of his three firings as a manager. The two of them were watching television. A TV commentator asked a celebrity, "How would you like to be remembered?" Alice said, "Joe, how would you answer that?" Torre shook his head and said, "I never realized my dream."

—Tom Verducci, SI, October 28, 1996

Torre's Yankees had four 100-win seasons.

PHOTOGRAPH BY JOHN W. MCDONOUGH

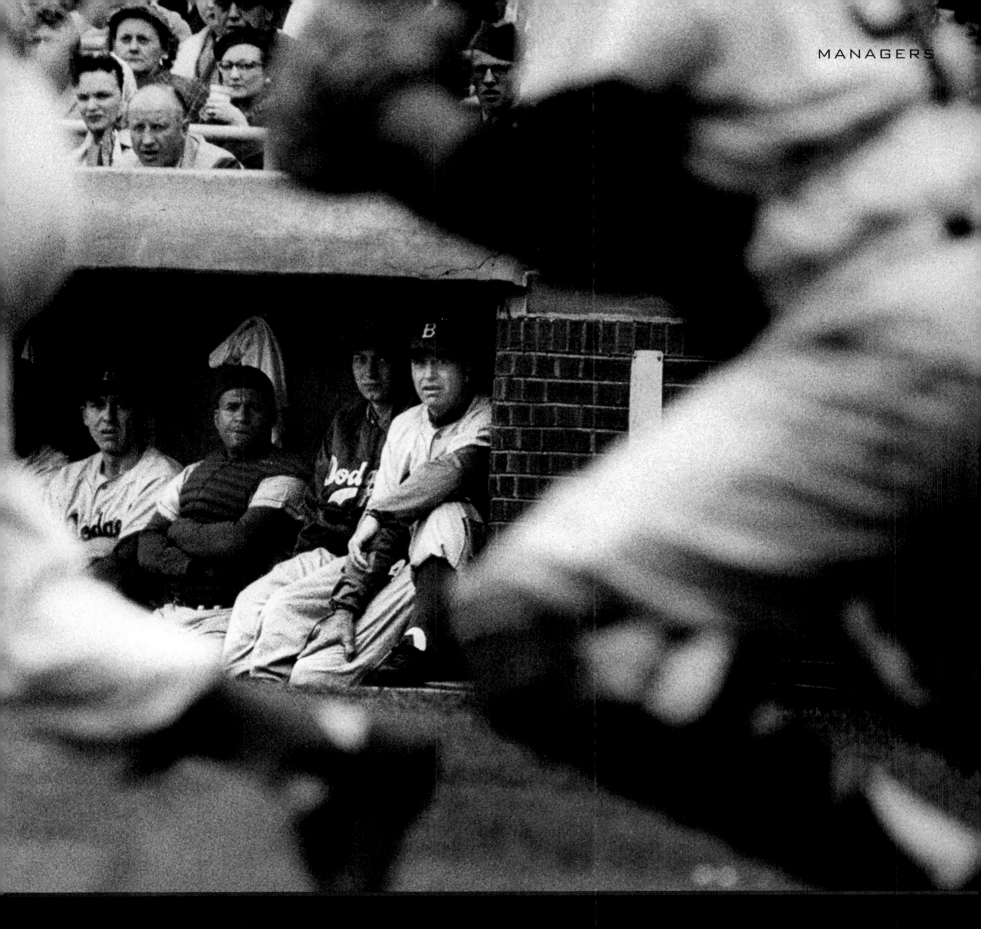

Alston's manner was quiet but blunt.

10

DODGERS 1954-1976

" Only Connie Mack and John McGraw had longer runs with one team. Alston won four World Series in Brooklyn and Los Angeles, including 1955, when "Dem Bums" won the Dodgers' first title in franchise history. " —DAVID SABINO

▸ 2,040 CAREER WINS
▸ SEVEN NL PENNANTS

HE IS a small-town boy in a glittering city, and he shows it. He seldom offers an opinion, keeps his own counsel and goes home to Ohio in the winter. He is tough to interview because his answers are obvious ("Why did you put Roebuck in for Miller?" "I thought he'd do better.")

—Robert W. Creamer, SI, May 13, 1963

WALTER ALSTON

10

THE

BEST GAMES

A HORRIBLE MISTAKE IN THE TOP OF THE NINTH COST THE PIRATES A CHANCE TO CLINCH THE 1960 WORLD SERIES AGAINST THE YANKEES. WITH ONE OUT IN GAME 7, PITTSBURGH FIRST BASEMAN ROCKY NELSON FIELDED A GROUNDER AND STEPPED ON THE BAG. HE COULD HAVE THROWN TO SECOND AND ENDED THE GAME, BUT HE CHOSE TO ATTEMPT TO TAG THE BASE RUNNER, MICKEY MANTLE. THE MICK ELUDED NELSON AND MADE IT SAFELY BACK TO FIRST. WITH THAT EXTRA OUT, THE YANKEES SCORED TO TIE THE GAME.

NELSON'S MISPLAY IS LITTLE REMEMBERED BECAUSE IT WAS WASHED AWAY BY BILL MAZEROSKI'S HOME RUN IN THE BOTTOM OF THE NINTH—IN FACT, MAZEROSKI'S HEROICS WERE ONLY MADE POSSIBLE BY NELSON'S MISPLAY. SEVERAL OF OUR BEST GAMES WERE MADE GREAT BECAUSE OF SOMEONE'S NOT-SO-GREAT MOMENT.

THE INFAMOUS GAFFES OF BILL BUCKNER AND STEVE BARTMAN DEFINE TWO GAMES ON OUR TOP 10 LIST—AND THE PUBLIC PROFILES OF ONE EXCELLENT BALLPLAYER AND ONE OTHERWISE PRIVATE PERSON. AS UNDENIABLY AMAZING AS BOTH GAMES WERE, IT'S ALSO HUMAN TO FEEL SYMPATHY FOR BUCKNER AND BARTMAN AND THE CONTINUAL RELIVING OF THEIR WORST MOMENTS. TAKE SOLACE IN KNOWING THAT THE LEGENDARY "MERKLE'S BONER" GAME—FRED MERKLE WAS, IN SHORT, THE BUCKNER OF 1908—APPEARED ON ONLY ONE BALLOT, IN EIGHTH PLACE. PEOPLE FORGET, EVENTUALLY.

home run." —TOM VERDUCCI

▸ DWIGHT EVANS SNARED
SSIBLE JOE MORGAN HOME
RUN IN 11TH INNING
▸ REDS WON GAME 7 4-3

"FISK WAS leading off for the Red Sox. On the second pitch, a low inside sinker thrown by the eighth and last of the Reds' pitchers, Pat Darcy, Fisk took a mighty cut. The ball described a high arc toward the wall in left, curving as if to spin foul. Fisk stood several feet down the line, frantically urging the ball fair with his hands. It hit the yellow foul pole above the wall, a home run. A game-winning home run. The Red Sox had won this epic struggle. It was V-J Day at home plate when Fisk arrived, a hero of heroes in one of the finest games ever played. Said Fisk, "I don't think anybody in the world could ask for a better game than this one."

—*Ron Fimrite, SI, November 3, 1975*

2

1986 WORLD SERIES GAME 6

METS 6, RED SOX 5

"The Red Sox were about to win the Series for the first time in 68 years. But Mookie Wilson battled reliever Bob Stanley until the seventh pitch, which sailed wild inside and past the catcher. Kevin Mitchell scored to tie it. And then Wilson hit a ground ball down the first base line, and Bill Buckner bent to get it. . . ." —KOSTYA KENNEDY

▸ RED SOX HAD SCORED TWO IN TOP OF THE 10TH
▸ METS WON GAME 7 8–5

WILSON COULD see that Buckner was playing him deep, perhaps 30 feet behind the bag. He knew he had a chance to beat out a ball hit down the line. Buckner knew that too, and when Wilson hit the next pitch directly at him, the first baseman decided against going to his knees, knowing that a throw from that position might not have enough on it. The ball was not hit all that solidly. "It bounced and bounced and then it didn't bounce," said Buckner. "It just skipped." It skipped under his glove and between his aching legs as Ray Knight hopped crazily home with the winning run. "I can't remember the last time I missed a ground ball," said Buckner. "I'll remember that one." So, he must know, will a lot of people.

—*Ron Fimrite, SI, November 3, 1986*

Buckner's agony was the Mets' elation.

ATL LINEUP
Winston
BRAVES
TWINS
WCCO TIME
BALLS STRIKES OUTS
AB AVERAGE
11:01
Bud
AMERICAN LEAGUE
Enjoy
Coca-Cola
Budweiser
MN LINEUP
TCF
Bud Dry
TOYOTA
1101
WCCO AM Radio 830
BUD LIGHT
43 ft.
3
29
6

3

1991
WORLD SERIES
GAME 7

TWINS 1, BRAVES 0

" This may have been the best World Series ever, and it ended with the first Game 7 to go into extra innings in 67 years. Jack Morris pitched all 10 innings for Minnesota in an epic, cuticle-ruining performance. " —STEPHEN CANNELLA

▸ GENE LARKIN'S SINGLE WON GAME IN 10TH INNING
▸ SERIES HAD THREE EXTRA-INNING GAMES, FIVE ONE-RUN GAMES

MORRIS OUTLASTED the 24-year-old John Smoltz. On this night it appeared he would have outlasted Methuselah. When the seventh game and the Series had finally been bled from the bodies on both sides, when the two teams had stopped their cartoon brawl, raising ridiculous lumps by alternately slugging each other over the head with a sledgehammer, when all of 60 minutes had passed after the last game, [Twins third baseman Mike] Pagliarulo stood wearily at his locker. "This was the greatest game," he said. "How could the TV guys describe it? They had a chance to win—but they didn't. We had a chance to win—but we didn't. Then we did. I kept thinking of the '75 Series tonight. This is why baseball is the greatest game there is."

—Steve Rushin, SI, November 4, 1991

Larkin's pinch hit scored Dan Gladden from third.
PHOTOGRAPH BY RICHARD MACKSON

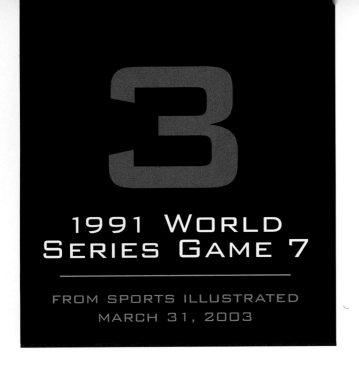

3

1991 WORLD SERIES GAME 7

FROM SPORTS ILLUSTRATED
MARCH 31, 2003

FOR AS LONG AS IT TAKES

*Jack Morris and John Smoltz dueled pitch for pitch in a
game that would turn on a startling baserunning error*

BY TOM VERDUCCI

ACK MORRIS AWOKE ON THE morning of Oct. 27, 1991, without a doubt in his mind. There was only one thing in his life that mattered that day, and he knew how it would turn out. As he prepared breakfast for himself, his parents and his two boys, Morris knew exactly how the game would end. What bothered him was that his father, Arvid, and mother, Dona, who flew in from Michigan to stay with him during the Series, were not so certain. His father was too quiet. His eyes betrayed his anxiety. "Don't worry, Dad," he said. "We're going to win the World Series."

"I was amazed," Arvid says. "He had never done anything like that before. It had always been a 'Let the chips fall . . .' type thing with him."

"When Kirby [Puckett] hit that [Game 6] home run [forcing Game 7], a calm came over me that I never had felt in the game," Morris says. "Growing up, I always envisioned being on the mound in Game 7, bottom of the ninth. I had this calm come over me knowing that I had mentally prepared for this game my whole life."

There was, however, something Morris never counted on: an opposing pitcher with the same kind of resolve.

John Smoltz grew up in Lansing, Mich., 90 minutes from Tiger Stadium. John was a huge Tigers fan. "Never missed a game," he says. He liked all those Tigers—Kirk Gibson, Alan Trammell, Sweet Lou Whitaker and the rest—but one player stood out above all others: Jack Morris.

In the summer of 1985 Detroit drafted him. Smoltz signed too late to play in rookie ball, so the Tigers let him spend two weeks with the major league club. Morris was there, but Smoltz didn't have the nerve

to say hello. Then one day somebody said something funny in the clubhouse, and Smoltz laughed. Morris gave Smoltz one of his icy glares.

"Go ahead and laugh, kid," Morris said. "You're trying to take our jobs." Smoltz stopped laughing.

Morris has no memory of Smoltz's being with the team, had no knowledge of him two years later when the Tigers traded Smoltz to Atlanta to get Doyle Alexander, had no idea that his Game 7 opponent grew up idolizing him.

In that game Smoltz, then 24, matched Morris zero for zero, clutch pitch for clutch pitch. After seven innings neither team had scored.

Smoltz got three ground ball outs to end the seventh then, exhausted, trudged up the four flights of stairs from the dugout to the clubhouse for some rest. He flopped into a chair in front of a television and cried out, "Please, *please* can we score?" They would not. Morris, with some help from Lonnie Smith, would not allow it.

Smith checked his swing on the second pitch of the eighth inning, sending the ball softly into rightfield for a single. Morris missed with his first pitch to Terry Pendleton, and the bullpen phone vibrated. Pitching coach Dick Such wanted Steve Bedrosian and Mark Guthrie to warm up.

With the count 1 and 2 on what was Morris's 100th pitch, Pendleton crushed a fastball toward the gap in left centerfield. The speedy Smith seemed certain to score. Except there was a problem—Smith had broken toward second on a delayed steal but committed a fundamental mistake by not peeking toward home to pick up the ball when it was hit. Now he was looking to his left, then to his right. Where was it? Smith knew Pendleton's hit was in play. He just had no clue where.

As Smith searched, Chuck Knoblauch, the second baseman, crouched as if fielding a ground ball, then threw an invisible baseball to shortstop Greg Gagne, who raced to cover second base, finishing the pantomime double play. A legend was born: Knoblauch deked Smith. It may have looked that way on television, but it wasn't true.

"In no way was I faked out by Knoblauch." Smith says. "If I did think Knoblauch had the ball, why didn't I slide?"

Leftfielder Dan Gladden chased the ball. Smith pulled into second standing up and rounded it, stopping four steps past the bag. He then froze, staring into left centerfield. Puckett, the centerfielder, was nowhere near the ball, but his reputation for the impossible catch made Smith indecisive.

Up in the clubhouse Smoltz yelled at the television *"Go! Go! Go!"*

Smith took two more hop-steps. Jimy Williams, the third base coach, never gave Smith any direction. Finally, only after the ball had bounced in front of the wall, off the wall, into the air like a little pop-up and eventually into Gladden's glove, Smith took off for third base. Williams finally threw his left hand up, the signal for Smith to stop there. Pendleton easily pulled into second with a double.

Ron Gant, the number 3 hitter, grounded meekly to first base. David Justice was intentionally walked. Now the bases were loaded. Four pitches later Morris hung a forkball to Sid Bream. It was a lousy pitch, the kind that sometimes causes a hitter to jump at it. Bream topped the ball to first baseman Kent Hrbek, who fired a strike to catcher Brian Harper to force Smith at home. Harper made a perfect return throw to Hrbek. Double play. Inning over.

The bottom of the inning was just as wild. Smoltz, pitching with one out and a runner at first, yielded a hit-and-run single to Knoblauch. Braves manager Bobby Cox walked to the mound to remove a disgusted Smoltz.

"I felt like Jack did," Smoltz says. "I was going to go as long as it took— 10, 11 innings."

"Cactus Jack" seemed to grow stronger as the game reached extra innings.

Reliever Mike Stanton intentionally walked Puckett to load the bases. Then Knoblauch made an even worse baserunning gaffe than Smith's. He took off from second on Hrbek's soft liner to second baseman Mark Lemke and was doubled off. Inning over.

Morris had reached the big leagues in 1977, a time when no one paid much attention to pitch counts or rotator cuffs or knew what a closer was. He was 22 years old when he made his first major league start. He walked the first four batters he faced. Manager Ralph Houk left him in for nine innings. He struck out 12; heaven knows how many pitches he threw. Houk's successor, Sparky Anderson, reinforced the tenet that Morris should not look to the bullpen for help.

"Sparky left me out there to rot because he was teaching me something," Morris says. "He believed in me, believed I had the best stuff on the team. Once I got what he was doing, I wasn't going to let him take the ball from me ever again. I always looked at it this way: If the relievers came into the game, I screwed up."

One day Morris was losing 5–4 in the fifth inning when he noticed "our 20th pitcher warming up." He saw Anderson leave the dugout for the mound, his second visit of the inning, which required Morris's

removal once Anderson had crossed the third base line. Morris walked toward Anderson and grabbed him before he reached that line. "Get the hell out of here," he yelled, "because what you've got warming up is no better than what I've got right now."

Morris breezed through the ninth inning, getting three outs on eight pitches. He had thrown 118 pitches in the game. Tom Kelly thanked him in the dugout, told him "Great job, that's all we can expect from you," and walked away . . . even though no one was throwing in the bullpen.

"I'm fine," Morris said. "I'm fine."

The pitching coach grabbed Kelly by the arm and said, "TK, he said he's fine."

Kelly paused, then said, "Oh, hell. It's only a game."

So Morris pitched the 10th inning, the only starting pitcher to do so in the World Series since Tom Seaver, one of his heroes, did it in 1969. It made no sense. A 36-year-old pitcher, working a second straight time on short rest, throwing 10 shutout innings . . . and he was getting *stronger*.

Morris was prepared to go back out for the 11th, but Minnesota loaded the bases with one out against Alejandro Peña in the last of the 10th. Kelly sent Gene Larkin to pinch-hit. Larkin hit the first pitch over the leftfielder's head, and Gladden danced home with the game's only run. Morris was the first player to get to home plate, waving Gladden in.

Morris never pitched again for the Twins after that Game 7. He exercised his option for free agency and signed with Toronto. Then he again pitched his team into the World Series, in 1992, and pitched against the Braves again, though poorly in Game 5. He gave up a grand slam— to Lonnie Smith. Smoltz was the winning pitcher. Morris knew that a night like Oct. 27, 1991, would not happen again.

"It was the epitome of everything I'd ever tried to achieve in my life," Morris said. "And yet within 24 hours this sadness came over me, knowing I might not be back in Minnesota and I might not ever pitch a game like that for the rest of my life. . . . I wish everybody could experience what I experienced that day. The joy. Total joy. The world would be a better place if everybody could feel that at least once."

On that Sunday morning when Morris woke up and knew he would win Game 7, an old baseball wizard with gleaming white hair awoke with a similar premonition. Sparky Anderson met his friends for his daily game of golf that day in Sunset, Calif. The boys were talking about how the Braves would win the Series. The man with the white hair laughed.

"Tell you what to do," Anderson told them. "Go home and get your bankbook. Clear it out and send it to Vegas. Morris is pitching. He will beat Smoltz. I promise you that."

"How do you know?" they said.

"Boys, I know that guy," Anderson said. "He's an animal. If he doesn't have a real challenge, he's liable to give up six runs. But don't get him in a position where you challenge him."

Anderson laughs when he tells the story. "[Jack] was the last of them," he says. It was 12 years ago. Another era. "When you talk to Cactus Jack, tell him he's still the meanest man I ever met." ∎

4

2011
WORLD SERIES
GAME 6

CARDINALS 10, RANGERS 9

"As a Texan and a Rangers fan, it pains me even to recall this game, much less commemorate it. David Freese? Really? But when a team is twice down to its last strike and comes back to win the game and then the Series, well, that's an instant classic." —DAVID BAUER

▸ GAME WENT 11 INNINGS
▸ FREESE ENDED IT WITH
   LEADOFF HOME RUN

IN THE first 106 World Series, 105 teams stood one strike away from the championship and eventually won it. The only exception was the 1986 Red Sox. In the 107th World Series, Ron Washington's Rangers became the '86 Red Sox' fraternal twin. Texas somehow managed twice—in successive innings in Game 6—to slip on infamy's banana peel at the cruelest possible moment, blowing two-run leads in the ninth and 10th innings before losing 10–9 in the 11th. Opportunity, like a rolling die, is many-sided, however. The double-dog dare that was Game 6 became one of glory for the champion Cardinals, the signature moment for a team that stood on the abyss so often over its last 50 games that it could paint the view from memory like Van Gogh could Arles.

—*Tom Verducci, SI, November 7, 2011*

Freese, raised outside St. Louis, was welcomed home.

OFFICIAL WATCH

LONGINES
WITTNAUER

LONGINES

AMERICAN

P RP   1 2 3 4 5 6 7 8 9 10

SCORE CARD

NEXT GAME *HERE* PITTSBURGH

265FT.

BATTER
9

BALL STRIKE
1

OUT

UMPIRES
1ST 2ND 3RD
Home Plate

NATIONAL

P RP
1 9 2 3   N. YORK
3 2 3 1   PITTS.

SCORE CARD

5

1960
WORLD SERIES
GAME 7

PIRATES 10, YANKEES 9

___

" Bill Mazeroski had just 11 homers all season before hitting his immortal, ninth-inning, Series-ending shot, and he did it as the leadoff hitter on a 1–0 count. The shock value alone was historic. Mickey Mantle later said it was the only loss that ever made him cry. " —DAVID BAUER

___

▸ ONLY WALK-OFF HOME RUN IN GAME 7 OF WORLD SERIES
▸ YANKEES HAD TIED GAME IN TOP OF NINTH

___

BILL MAZEROSKI came to bat. He had produced the deciding margin in two earlier Pirates victories, with a two-run homer in the first game, which Pittsburgh won 6–4, and a two-run double in the fifth game, which Pittsburgh won 5–2. He let one of Ralph Terry's fastballs go by. Then he hit the next one over the leftfield fence. There was noise in Forbes Field then, and it went on for more than an hour. Mazeroski took off his cap and swung it around his head as he went leaping and frolicking around the bases. The fans spilled out of their seats and mobbed the Pirates, especially Mazeroski, who had to fight his way to home plate. A man ran out with a spade and dug up home plate, which may be hanging over some mantel in Pittsburgh right now.

—*Roy Terrell, SI, October 24, 1960*

Mazeroski's shot set off Pittsburgh pandemonium.

METS 7, ASTROS 6

"This 16-inning series-clinching thriller featured a three-run ninth-inning rally by the Mets and seven runs scored in extra innings, including a game-tying home run by Houston's Billy Hatcher in the 14th." —DAVID SABINO

1986 NLCS
GAME 6

▸ METS SCORED THREE RUNS
IN TOP OF 16TH INNING
▸ ASTROS SCORED TWO IN
16TH, LEFT TWO RUNNERS ON

THEY SURVIVED a two-hit, 12-strikeout masterwork [in Game 5] by Nolan Ryan for nine innings and then won on Gary Carter's run-scoring single in the 12th. That was a throbber, all right, but it was tame beside the pennant clincher. This was the longest of all postseason games—4 hours, 42 minutes— and possibly the most exciting.

—Ron Fimrite, SI, October 27, 1986

This win made possible the Mets '86 World Series title.

PHOTOGRAPH BY RICHARD MACKSON

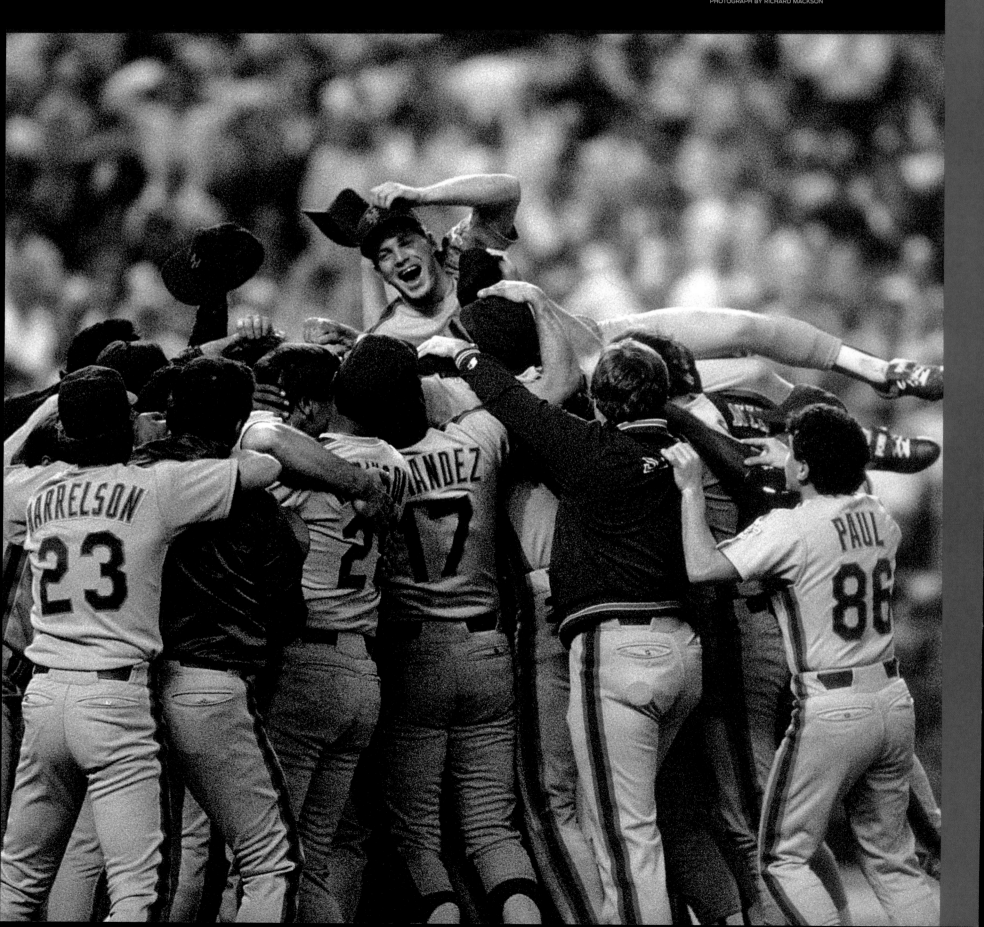

7

1951 NL Pennant Series Game 3

Thomson hit his three-run Shot Heard Round the World.
PHOTOGRAPH BY AP

" The radio call of Bobby Thomson's home run by play-by-play man Russ Hodges—"The Giants win the pennant! The Giants win the pennant!"—forever will resound. " —DICK FRIEDMAN

▸ GIANTS AND DODGERS DECIDED PENNANT WITH THREE GAME TIE-BREAKER
▸ DODGERS HAD 13-GAME DIVISION LEAD IN AUGUST

THE PITCH came in high and tight, just where Ralph Branca had wanted it. Thomson swung hard and the ball sailed out toward left. "I got a chance at it," thought Andy Pafko, bolting back toward the wall. Then the ball was gone. For seconds, which seemed like minutes, the crowd sat dumb. Then came the roar.

—Roger Kahn, SI, October 10, 1960

Gonzalez's bloop hit brought down the Yankees.

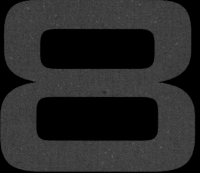

DIAMONDBACKS 3, YANKEES 2

" Roger Clemens and Curt Schilling started, Randy Johnson came on in relief, and one of the most dramatic Series finished with Luis Gonzalez hitting a game-winning single off the great Mariano Rivera. " —ALBERT CHEN

► RIVERA ENTERED IN 8TH WITH ONE-RUN LEAD
► YANKEES WERE THREE-TIME DEFENDING CHAMPIONS

THE WINNING RUN scored on a bases-loaded, 140-foot, broken-bat, chili-dipped single by Luis Gonzalez. In its fourth season Arizona became only the sixth team to win a winner-take-all World Series game on the last swing; the first to knock out a defending champion that way.

—Tom Verducci, SI, November 12, 2001

2001 WORLD SERIES GAME 7

9

1956 WORLD SERIES GAME 5

YANKEES 2, DODGERS 0

"Twenty-seven up, 27 down. Pivotal Game 5 at Yankee Stadium. Sheer perfection on the grandest stage, achieved by the Yankees' Don Larsen against the Brooklyn Dodgers in the 1956 World Series. The no-windup specialist's feat will never be topped—unless someone is perfect in a Game 6 or 7." —DICK FRIEDMAN

▸ LARSEN STRUCK OUT SEVEN
▸ YANKEES SCORED ON MICKEY MANTLE HOME RUN, HANK BAUER SINGLE

THOUGH HE pitched well for two more years for the Yankees, Larsen never again had a brush with greatness. By the summer of '59 there was talk of moving him, because of his strong bat, to the outfield (which never happened), and after that season he was traded to Kansas City, where he went 1–10. He finished with a lifetime record of 81–91. "People said I didn't do enough in my career," Larsen says, "and maybe they're right. But I had one great day." In 1993, after 24 years as a paper salesman in California, Larsen moved to Hayden Lake, Idaho. He and his wife Corrine built a home on the shore of a sheltered cove. "That was an amazing thing that happened," he says. "I'm just glad that it happened to me."
—Kostya Kennedy, SI, October 14, 1996

Catcher Yogi Berra leaped into Larsen's arms.

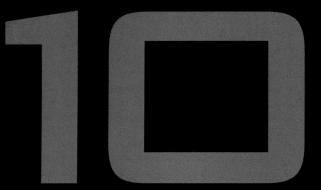

10

2003 NLCS GAME 6

MARLINS 8, CUBS 3

" Baseball's most cursed franchise was five outs from the World Series when Steve Bartman reached out on a foul ball. What's always overlooked is Alex Gonzalez's one-out error at shortstop that should have been a double play; instead, the Marlins scored eight runs in the game's fateful eighth inning. " —ALBERT CHEN

▸ CUBS WERE UP 3-0 IN 8TH
▸ MARLINS WON GAME 7 9-6

MOISES ALOU drifted across the leftfield line and jumped to make a backhand catch, his glove just above the green railing atop the wall. Three fans seated in the first row, their eyes fixed not on Alou but on the falling baseball, also reached for the pop-up. It was Bartman who touched it. The ball clanked off his left hand. By sunrise Bartman's life would become a nightmare. News helicopters hovered over his suburban home; his phone had to be disconnected; he could not go to the consulting firm at which he worked; people were planning their Bartman Halloween costumes; and actor Kevin James was preparing a pitch for a movie titled *Fan Interference*. A Chicago alderman, Tom Allen, told the *Chicago Sun-Times*, "He better get a new address. He ought to move to Alaska." Florida governor Jeb Bush offered Bartman asylum.

—Tom Verducci, SI, October 11, 2004

Bartman made his infamous reach.

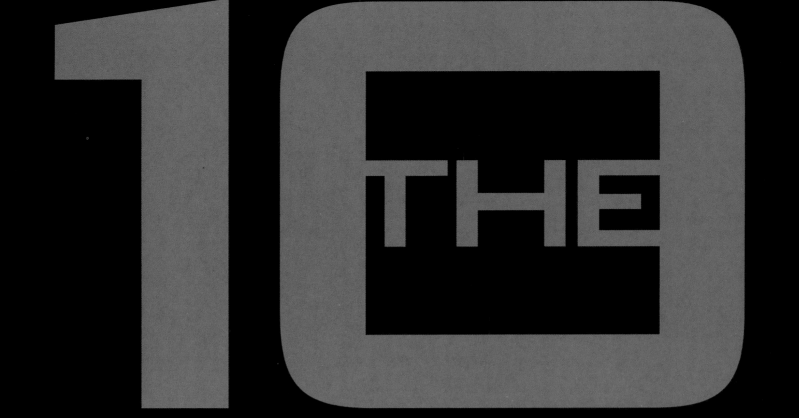

THE 10

BEST BALLPARKS

BY NOW THE VIRTUES OF OLD BALLPARKS ARE EVIDENT TO ALL CONCERNED. FENWAY PARK AND WRIGLEY FIELD WILL LIKELY FOLLOW THE PATH OF ROME'S COLOSSEUM, WHICH IS TO STAND FOR AS LONG AS THEY ARE ABLE. NOT TOO LONG AGO, THOUGH, THIS COURSE WAS NOT SO OBVIOUS.

IN A 1988 STORY SI'S RON FIMRITE FELT COMPELLED TO ARGUE FOR THE SURVIVAL OF THE GRAND OLD BUILDINGS—WRIGLEY, FENWAY, TIGER STADIUM AND COMISKEY PARK—AMID A SEA OF CHARMLESS MULTIUSE FACILITIES AND DOMES. "THESE ANCIENT HALLS ARE AS REPRESENTATIVE OF BASEBALL'S FORMATIVE YEARS AS THE STATELY HOUSES OF GOVERNMENT IN WASHINGTON ARE OF THE NATION'S," HE WROTE. "IT'S NO SMALL THING TO WATCH A GAME IN A PLACE WHERE TY COBB PLAYED. AND THE OLD PARKS HAVE THE CHARACTER OF AGE. I DEFY ANYONE TO TELL ME THE DIFFERENCE BETWEEN THREE RIVERS STADIUM AND RIVERFRONT STADIUM. BUT YOU AREN'T LIKELY TO FORGET WRIGLEY FIELD. THESE OLD BUILDINGS DESERVE PRESERVATION, IF FOR NO OTHER REASON THAN TO SHOW SUCCEEDING GENERATIONS WHAT A REAL BASEBALL PARK LOOKS LIKE."

TWO OF THE FOUR PARKS HE TALKED ABOUT STILL STAND TODAY. THE OTHER TWO HAVE BEEN DEMOLISHED. ALL OF THEM MAKE OUR TOP 10 LIST, THOUGH, WITH THE TWO STILL OPEN FOR BALLGAMES TAKING OUR TOP SPOTS. THEIR VALUE, NOW, IS CERTAINLY APPRECIATED.

1

FENWAY PARK

BOSTON

" The ballpark is filled with attractions that can make it feel like a tourist trap: Look kids, the Green Monster! And there's Pesky's Pole! But Fenway is a living museum, a monument to the seamless connection between baseball's past and present. And if you can get put up with seats made for 1912-sized backsides, a darn good place to watch a game. " —STEPHEN CANNELLA

▸ OPENED 1912
▸ CAPACITY 37,493

FENWAY PARK belongs not to one but to all, its physical shape nipped and tucked many times over but its soul— the game of baseball played in urban environs as a communal treasure— left untouched. One day before a game in 2011, Red Sox second baseman Dustin Pedroia sat in the shoebox of a home dugout, where players must still navigate around pillars, and said in wonderment, "A hundred years. This place is a hundred years old? Imagine that." It was easy to imagine Tris Speaker or Ted Williams or Carlton Fisk or Roger Clemens taking in the same view from the same dugout. The ballpark has made for a rare unbroken line that connects those who have worn the Red Sox uniform, as well as those who have rooted for them.

—Tom Verducci, SI, November 24, 2011

The seats atop the Green Monster were added in 2003.

755 BOTTLES
OF BEER ON
THE WALL
Miller Lite

EAMUS
CATULI!

AC036198

CHICAGO

Fans on neighboring rooftops enjoy the action too.

2

"Never mind the ivy and the scoreboard and the charm; Wrigley was the last park to succumb to lights, in 1988, and remains the sanctuary of day baseball. Because baseball is better by day and this park revels in it, Wrigley is forever No. 1 on my list." —DAVID BAUER

▸ OPENED 1914
▸ CAPACITY: 41,019

WRIGLEY FIELD is a ballpark. If there was one way to rile Philip K. Wrigley, the retiring gentleman who owned the Chicago Cubs between 1932 and his death in '77, it was to refer to Wrigley Field as a stadium. It is a park, with spiders and grasshoppers and vines an inch around on the field of play.

—E.M. Swift, SI, July 7, 1980

WRIGLEY FIELD

HAPPY TO BE HERE

With the Cubs leading their division in September, the author took in a Labor Day homestand at Wrigley and learned that there's nothing better than a lost cause

BY GARY SMITH

GRABBED A BEER AND BEELINED TO THE bleachers, packed nearly an hour before the game. I needed to locate the diehards, the leathery lifers … the scar tissue. I found an enclave in center and squeezed among them. Judy Caldow, the retired phys-ed teacher who keeps score at every game and has over 3,000 scorecards organized at home in plastic tubs. Howard Tucker, the blind man with the cowbell and black transistor in his hands. Fred Speck, the lawyer with the Hawaiian shirt, sunglasses and black cane who noticed me scribbling into a notepad beside him and announced, "You know, I was a journalism major at the University of Illinois, wrote for the *Daily Illini* and various minor publications. But then I found I just couldn't stick my nose up the asses of all the a-------."

"Oh, really? Obviously, I've had no trouble whatsoever!" I *almost* blurted. Instead I bought us each a beer, made Fred's acquaintance and jumped into the Batter Game, a gambling contest that a young blogger named Eammon Brennan and six other fans in front of me, including two young women, were initiating: buck an at bat to play, pass the cupful of bills to the next player for each successive batter, win a buck if your hitter singles, two if he doubles, three if he triples, four if he homers, and if you're lucky, like we were, one of the contestants will keep her stash in her bra. Here was a vestige of Cubs bleacher life from its grimmest days, when the regulars diminished the horror by betting on every pitch—ball, strike, hit, foul—and even on whether the ball, rolled toward the mound after the last putout each inning, would reach dirt or fall short and end up on the grass.

I came out smoking in the Batter Game, three of my first four hitters delivering. Fred sniffed. He'd been through every stage of Cubs fanhood: from the child in the early '60s who loved them unconditionally to the hoarse heckler in the '70s venting his ire from the near empty bleachers to the 53-year-old man today sitting Buddhalike amidst the frenzy, unattached to each transient turn of fate.

"September baseball in the bleachers used to be the Cubs 20 games out, me and eight other people rooting for a totally lost cause with complete passion," Fred said. "There's nothing better than a lost cause. It's like being at a party at 3:30 in the morning, when the 90 people who were there at midnight are gone, and it's down to eight of you in the kitchen. That's the most priceless part of the party. A big part of me wants this team to sweep everything—first round of the playoffs, second round, World Series—then go right back into the toilet so I get my stadium back."

Yes, the audience had changed. Yes, many of the roughly 150 bleacher season-ticket holders resented the frat party they now found themselves in. And yes, there was a Spiderman standing just behind Fred at this very moment, defrocked of his mask by security guards because God knew what havoc a superhero, emboldened by anonymity and a dozen Pabst Blue Ribbons, might wreak. A Spidey from Scotland, of all places, here for—of course—his bachelor party on the eve of his wedding to a woman from Japan whom he'd met in the Caymans; what hath God and Wrigley wrought?

"I've been all over the world," Fred continued, unperturbed. "I've scuba-dived the Great Barrier Reef and motorcycled the Icefields Parkway in the Canadian Rockies, and, yes, they're both *beautiful*. But I realized when I first came here 45 years ago that this ballpark on a sunny day was one of the most beautiful things I'd ever seen, and that it *still* is today. Winning or losing stopped making me happy or sad years ago. I just love to be here."

I sprang to the concession stand to snag us two more beers and returned just in time to begin singing "Take Me Out to the Ballgame" only to notice, out of the left corner of my eye … yes, another marriage busting out, a young man on one knee offering up the big question and the big rock to a young woman in a sleeveless Cubbie T-shirt.

The woman, 21-year-old Megan Bart, slipped on the ring and flushed. The man, 27-year-old former Padres minor leaguer Rusty Moore, rejoiced. "Why here?" I asked him.

"Because the atmosphere is unmatched," he replied. "This year, for once, I just don't think something bad is going to happen," he said.

Something bad happened. Ryan Howard, as Rusty spoke, poleaxed a pitch to dead center: 4–1 Phillies.

Freddie Scar Tissue just sat and sipped, transcending. "In the early '60s," he said, "I saw the Cubs give up a three-run homer on a *bunt*. How can life disappoint you after that?"

It was time, I decided, to put the Buddha's detachment to the ultimate test. Yes … *Bartman*.

Bartman, the young man wearing earphones and a Cubs hat in a seat near the leftfield line who, on the evening of Oct. 14, 2003—with Chicago leading 3–0 and five outs away from a World Series berth—rose and touched a foul pop-up just as Cubs leftfielder Moises Alou reached for it, possibly preventing him from catching it, initiating a catastrophic sequence of events.

"Yes, I was here on Bartman night," said Fred. "The woman I came with was crying. I walked out of this stadium after Game 7 like John Wayne, and I realized, They can't hurt me. That's the moment I knew. I'd hit the Zen spot—no one or nothing could touch me."

Fred, just before departing, told me which one of the three dozen Wrigleyville bars to meet him at, and he finally let down his scar tissue. "If they win it all," he confessed, "I'll cry like a baby and laugh like a hyena for a week." ∎

NEW YORK CITY

The stadium also hosted football, boxing and the Pope.

3

YANKEE STADIUM

" With its magisterial design, its majestically pinstriped lineups, a regular World Series role and orotund public address announcer Bob Sheppard, Yankee Stadium was the game's most iconic stadium from its first pitch to its last. " —DICK FRIEDMAN

▶ 1923–2008
▶ 56,936 CAPACITY AT CLOSE

"CLOSE YOUR EYES and you can see Lou Gehrig listening to the echoes of his farewell speech in 1939 . . . Reggie Jackson driving a knuckleball for his third home run in the final game of the '77 Series . . . Yogi Berra leaping into Don Larsen's arms . . . the dying Ruth, bracing himself on a bat, waving that last, long goodbye.

—William Nack, SI, June 7, 1999

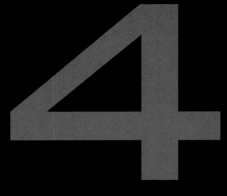

4

EBBETS
FIELD

NEW YORK CITY

" It felt like it was family and
friends had gathered to cheer on
members of the neighborhood at
this quirky building in Flatbush,
with its shallow rightfield fence and
structural beams throughout the
stands. " —DAVID SABINO

▸ 1913–1957
▸ CAPACITY: 31,902

YOU SCRAMBLED to get there, riding a
subway or a trolley car, and you walked
steep runways with a loping gait. Two
runways and a quick, sharp turn and
there the diamond lay, so close you
felt that you could reach it in 10 strides.
There were the Dodgers, gabbling
through infield drill, standing so near
that you could almost hear their chatter.
—*Roger Kahn, SI, August 5, 1974*

Ebbets's classic facade inspired the Mets' Citi Field.

PHOTOGRAPH BY RICHARD MEEK

5

CAMDEN YARDS

BALTIMORE

"The gem on the inner harbor of Baltimore changed baseball. Camden Yards had every modern convenience, including luxury boxes, but its red-brick feel bowed to Fenway Park, Wrigley Field and other cozy, early 20th century ballparks. It was such an artistic and financial hit that it kicked off a building boom of so-called retro ballparks, none of which topped it." —TOM VERDUCCI

▸ OPENED 1992
▸ CAPACITY: 45,971

ORIOLE PARK at Camden Yards is built on the site of a saloon once owned by the father of Babe Ruth. The short rightfield porch is guarded by a 25-foot-high wall that's decorated with advertising (the last park to have ads in the field of play was Philadelphia's Connie Mack Stadium, which closed in 1970) and holds the out-of-town scoreboard. This is a ballpark full of feelings, the strangest being the one you get while watching a game. As you squint in the sunlight, there is a sense that you've already seen a thousand games in this place. "You get the feeling this wasn't the first game played here," said Baltimore shortstop Cal Ripken after the exhibition opener. Indeed, it's as if this ballpark comes equipped with memories.

—Tim Kurkjian, SI, April 13, 1992

The B&O warehouse is just beyond rightfield.

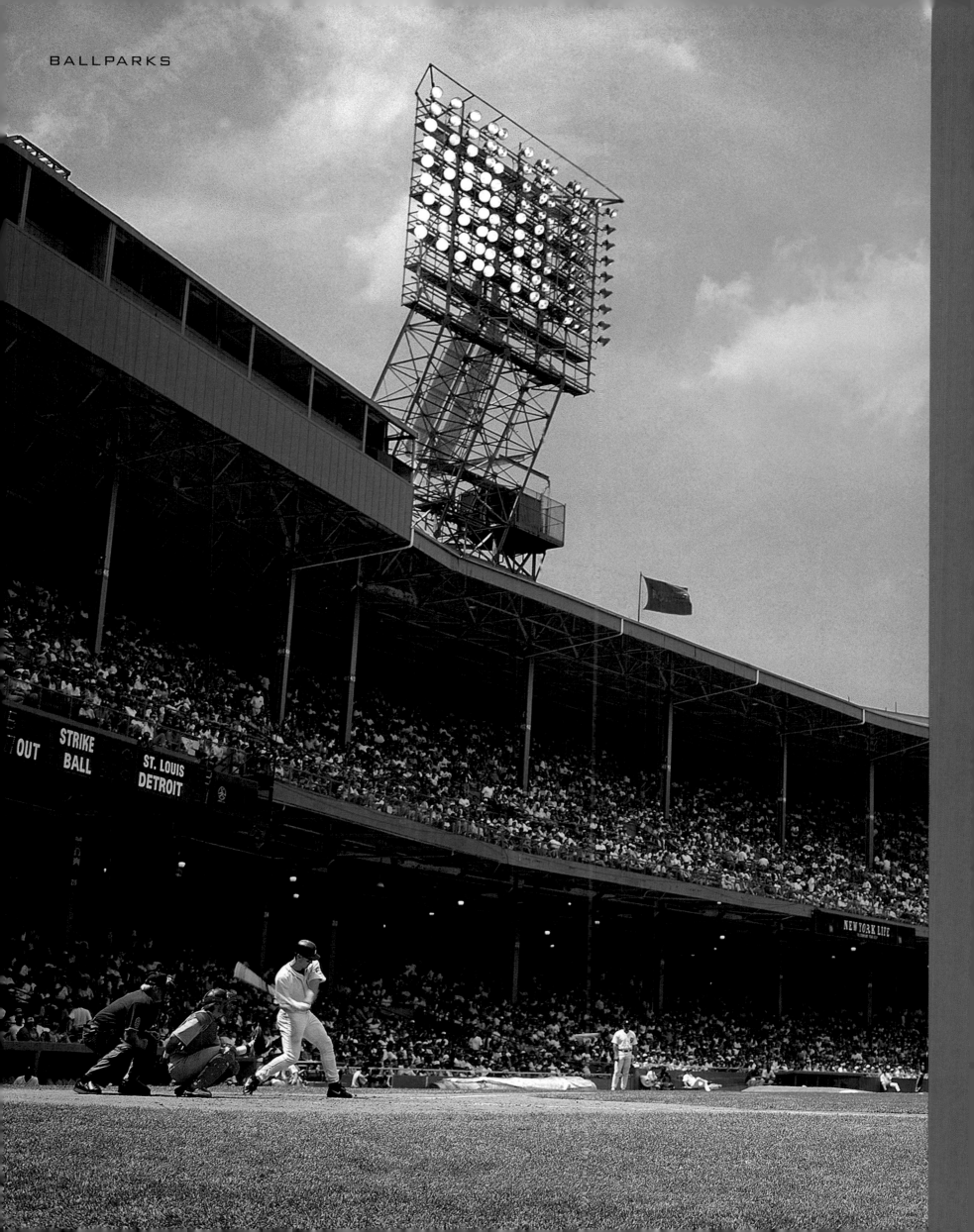

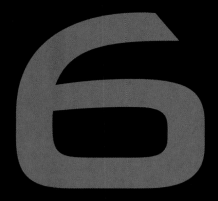

TIGER
STADIUM

DETROIT

"The Corner, the beautiful, blue-rinsed bandbox in the Corktown neighborhood, was the grande dame of ballparks. It was wonderfully quirky, and the site of Babe Ruth's 700th home run and Lou Gehrig's first missed game." —ALBERT CHEN

▸ 1912–1999
▸ CAPACITY: 52,416

THE PARK sits like a large, down-at-the-heels amusement ride, at its famous corner. The games continue, but there is the overwhelming feeling that the show soon will pack up and move along. The signs on the outfield walls, the logos changing from those of pizzas to those of health-care plans by the inning, seem an intrusion, a last stab at modernization that could never work. The famous sign on one door—VISITORS CLUBHOUSE. NO VISITORS—has disappeared. The best seats in baseball are still at Tiger Stadium, maybe 10,000 of them that put the spectator closer to the game than he would be at any other stadium. The worst seats in baseball, too many to count and all with obstructed views, are also at Tiger Stadium. The front row of the upper deck in right over-hangs the field by about 10 feet catching fly balls and turning them into home runs.

—Leigh Montville, SI, July 12, 1999

Fans still maintain the old field as a memorial.

7

AT&T PARK

SAN FRANCISCO

" After making their fans endure blustery Candlestick Park for 40 years, the Giants rewarded supporters with the glory of AT&T Park. With its panoramic views of San Francisco Bay, there are few (if any) better places to witness a baseball game. " —DAVID SABINO

▸ OPENED 2000
▸ CAPACITY: 41,503

Kayakers await home run balls in McCovey Cove.

PHOTOGRAPH BY DEANNE FITZMAURICE

RETRIEVING the first regular-season home run, Joseph Figone nearly got his motorboat broken in two when another one rammed him. "If he'd have hit me two feet back, he'd have sunk me," says Figone. It'd be a lousy thing to have on your tombstone, wouldn't it? WENT DOWN WITH SHIP AND $9 BASEBALL

—Rick Reilly, SI, July 31, 2000

8

POLO GROUNDS

" This strange, misshapen paradise in upper Manhattan is where Bobby Thomson hit his home run in '51 and where Mays made his catch in '54 and where the old New York Giants collected 13 pennants. (The Giants win the pennant!) " —KOSTYA KENNEDY

▸ 1911–1963
▸ CAPACITY: 56,000

THE POLO GROUNDS is shaped like a huge bathtub, narrow, high and long. The distant [centerfield] clubhouse is wonderful for the fan, particularly when a pitcher is knocked from the box. He can't duck off the field to a sub-grandstand shower. Instead he must trudge out across the endless outfield, head down, a curiously touching and unforgettable sight.

—*Sports Illustrated, September 27, 1954*

Deep centerfield was 483 feet from home.
PHOTOGRAPH BY BROWN BROTHERS

DODGER STADIUM

LOS ANGELES

" Opened by owner Walter O'Malley during the Mad Men era, Dodger Stadium embraced the same modernistic ethos: cool, clean, pastel—and it even added bells and whistles such as seats behind the plate at dugout level. A half-century later, it has aged as well as did ever-dashing Dodgers fan Cary Grant. " —DICK FRIEDMAN

▸ OPENED 1962
▸ CAPACITY: 56,000

IT IS well-known that Los Angeles was a formidable frontier until it was civilized by Walter O'Malley. O'Malley was one of those rare pioneers. Where others saw semiarid desert populated by Chumash Indians—Los Angeles was then little more than a bedroom suburb of the Mojave—he saw season attendance of three million and the elimination of rainouts. He planted groves of orange trees, dropped hints among all of his friends about the possibility of a film business, suggested the birth of an aerospace industry (Mr. Northrup to O'Malley in their now-famous meeting: "Aerospace? Explain!") and relocated thousands of pesky, non-revenue-bearing natives so that he could build a baseball park. And thus was Los Angeles colonized.

—Richard Hoffer, SI, May 9, 1994

The stadium sits on the hillside of Chavez Ravine.

PHOTOGRAPH BY ROBERT BECK

BALLPARKS

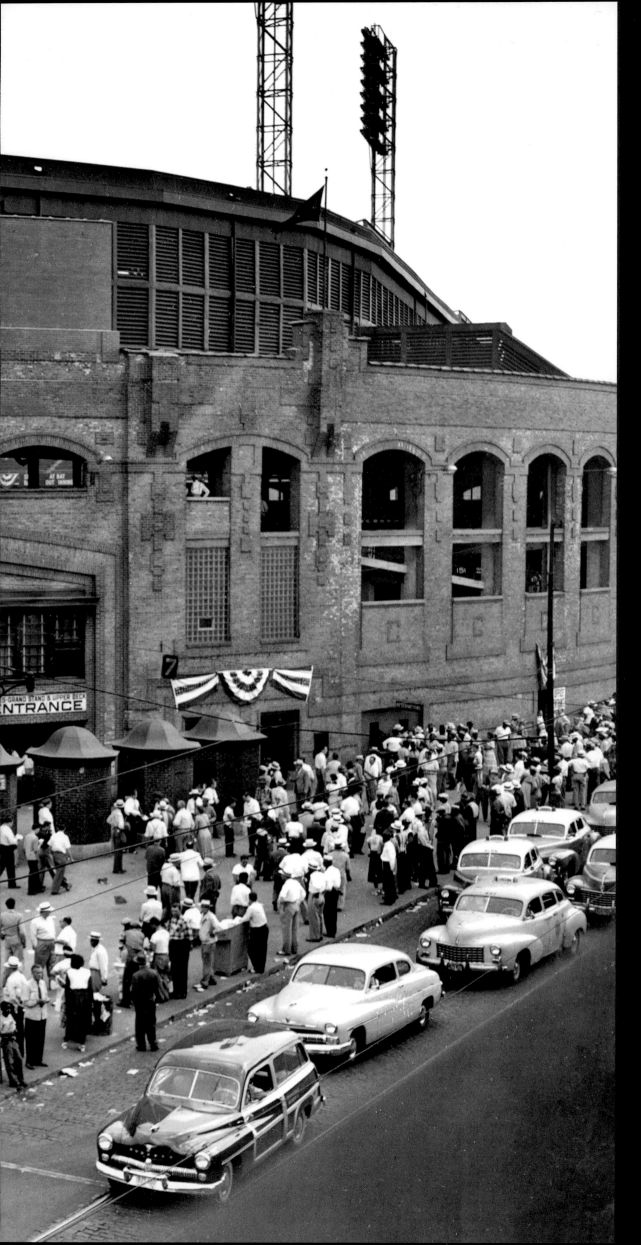

10

COMISKEY PARK

CHICAGO

" When built, it was the envy of all of baseball. Just a few of the more modern charms that kept it special: Bill Veeck's exploding scoreboard, Harry Caray (pre-Cubs) in the booth, Disco Demolition Night—and the Beatles playing there. " —DAVID BAUER

▸ 1910–1990
▸ CAPACITY: 43,951 AT CLOSE

COMISKEY IS WHERE, on June 22, 1937, Joe Louis knocked out James J. Braddock to win the heavyweight championship of the world. Twenty-five years later, Sonny Liston won the same title there by flattening Floyd Patterson at 2:05 of the first round. Comiskey is also where, on a tundra frozen so hard that the players had to wear sneakers, the Chicago Cardinals whipped the Philadelphia Eagles 28–21 to win the 1947 NFL championship. Frank Sinatra and Michael Jackson sang there. Bill Veeck, who twice owned and operated the White Sox, installed an outdoor shower for fans in the sun-baked centerfield bleachers, hired a barber to give free haircuts and regularly made the rounds to sit in all corners of the ballpark, cheerily talking to his customers while putting out cigarettes in the ashtray installed in his peg leg.

—William Nack, SI, August 20, 1990

Comiskey was the site of baseball's first All-Star Game.

10 THE

Best Franchises

OF ALL THE BOOK'S CATEGORIES ON WHICH OUR PANEL VOTED, SIX OF THEM HAD A UNANIMOUS NO. 1 PICK. HOW UNUSUAL IS THIS? WHEN SI PUBLISHED FOOTBALL'S GREATEST IN 2012, NOT A SINGLE ONE OF THAT PANEL'S TOP PICKS WAS UNANIMOUS. JIM BROWN, JERRY RICE, LAWRENCE TAYLOR, VINCE LOMBARDI—NONE OF THOSE GREATS INSPIRED A CONSENSUS.

BUT HERE ALL OUR PANELISTS AGREED THAT IN THEIR RESPECTIVE CATEGORIES, LOU GEHRIG, BABE RUTH (BOTH AS RIGHTFIELDER AND SLUGGER), WALTER JOHNSON AND MARIANO RIVERA WERE THE BEST THERE'S EVER BEEN. ALSO, THEY ALL CHOSE THE SAME FRANCHISE AS NO. 1, AND THE PRECEDING NAMES STRONGLY HINT AS TO WHICH THAT WOULD BE, GIVEN THAT GEHRIG, RIVERA AND RUTH ALL PLAYED FOR THE NEW YORK YANKEES.

GIVEN THE SUCCESS OF THE YANKEES—PERHAPS YOU'VE HEARD ABOUT THEIR 27 WORLD SERIES CHAMPIONSHIPS—IT'S EXPECTED THAT THE TEAM WOULD DOMINATE THIS CATEGORY AND THIS BOOK IN GENERAL. IN FACT ONLY ONE CATEGORY WAS COMPLETELY DEVOID OF PLAYERS WHO HAD EVER DONNED THE PINSTRIPES. THAT WAS SECOND BASE. THE ONLY YANKEE TO EVEN GARNER A VOTE AT THAT POSITION WAS JOE GORDON, WHO WAS THE AL MVP OF 1942 AND APPEARED ON ONE BALLOT, IN SIXTH PLACE. AH WELL. MAYBE THIS GIVES THE YANKEES SOMETHING TO PLAY FOR.

1

THE YANKEES

FOUNDED 1901

"There are no names on the back of their uniforms, and there never will be. Simply saying you're a Yankee has always spoken loudly enough." —KOSTYA KENNEDY

▸ 27 WORLD SERIES TITLES
▸ 23 HALL OF FAMERS

NO SPORTS TEAM in the world takes its mystique and aura as seriously as the New York Yankees. The Yankees have won so many championships and had so many legendary players that they don't need to tell you how good they have been. But . . . they do anyway. It's the Yankee Way. This is unmistakable when you go to Yankee Stadium for any game, and exponentially so for a playoff game. Here's the wind-through-the-trees voice of Bob Sheppard, still introducing (by way of recording) "Nuhm-buhr 2, Deh-rick JEET-uh." Up on the new video board in centerfield, there is the crackling black-and-white footage of Babe Ruth's ferocious swing, Lou Gehrig considering himself the luckiest man on the face of the earth, Yogi Berra jumping into the arms of Don Larsen, Reggie Jackson reaching down and bashing his third straight World Series home run, Derek Jeter running the bases with his right arm pumping in triumph and, finally, Mariano Rivera closing the montage by throwing one more cutter for strike three.

—Joe Posnanski, SI, October 26, 2009

Ruth (left) began a long parade of Yankee winners.

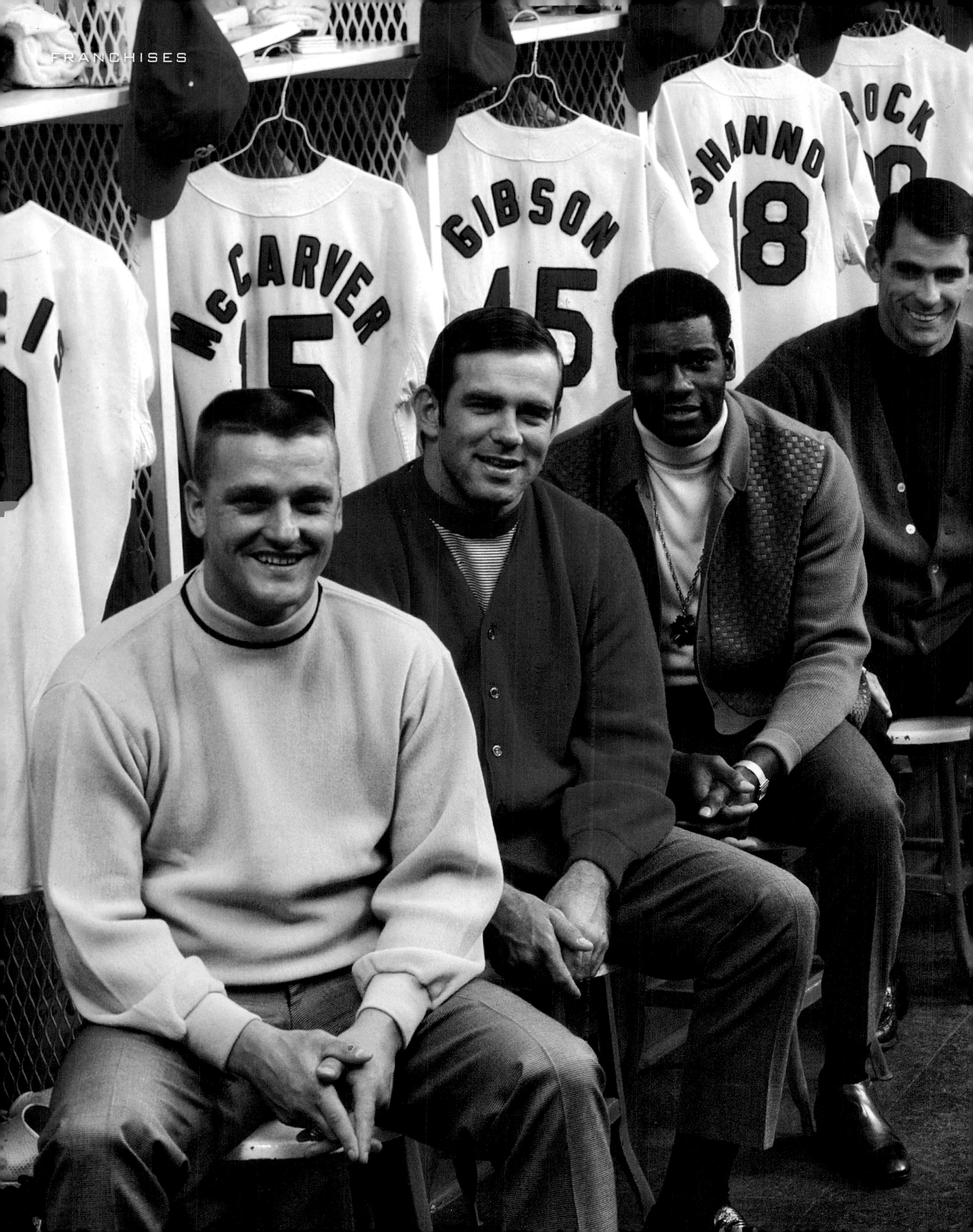
McCARVER
GIBSON
18

THE
CARDINALS

FOUNDED 1882

"The franchise is second only to the Yankees in championships and has produced as many immortals as any other team, from Stan the Man to Bob Gibson to Albert Pujols. But the heartbeat of the Cardinals has always been Redbird Nation, the best fans in baseball." —ALBERT CHEN

‣ 11 WORLD SERIES TITLES
‣ 16 HALL OF FAMERS

BUSCH STADIUM in St. Louis was just what Mudville would have been like if Casey had not struck out. People poured from the stands, horns blew, confetti filled the air. The Cardinals, who had been six games out of the NL lead with only 13 games remaining, were the champions of the baseball world. . . . Moments after the Cardinals had won their championship, most of them were in a room off the clubhouse that has a large picture window overlooking Spring Avenue, already packed with fans pouring out of the stadium. While a record called "Our Old Home Team" played continuously in the background, the players and fans toasted each other in beer and champagne. The Cardinals stayed at the window until every fan had left. "This," said Ken Boyer, "is one hell of a baseball town. God bless 'em all, even the ones who boo."

—William Leggett, SI, October 26, 1964

Manager Red Schoendienst posed with his team in 1968.

PHOTOGRAPH BY NEIL LEIFER

THE GIANTS

FOUNDED 1883

" The Giants can claim more history of success than any other franchise. They have won the most games in baseball history, won the most National League pennants (22) and produced the most Hall of Famers. " —TOM VERDUCCI

▸ SEVEN WORLD SERIES TITLES
▸ 25 HALL OF FAMERS

IT ISN'T important that the Giants finish first or a close second; and it won't hurt too much if they subside quietly into the second division. The important thing is: The Giants have won. They've solidified their beachhead in San Francisco, broadened it, taken a firm grasp on the future. Their striking early success on the field saved baseball's move to California from turning into something of a sordid fiasco. Remember that the Giants, who had finished sixth the past two seasons, were not supposed to do much better than that this year. The expectation was that Los Angeles' Dodgers would give California a pennant pretender for at least another year or two and that maybe then the Giants would start moving up. But the Dodgers have been a colossal flop. If the Giants had turned out as poorly as anticipated, California might well have been completely soured on major league baseball.

—*Robert W. Creamer, SI, June 16, 1958*

Willie Mays (left) and Tim Lincecum each felt title glory.

PHOTOGRAPHS BY HY PESKIN (LEFT) AND DAMIAN STROHMEYER

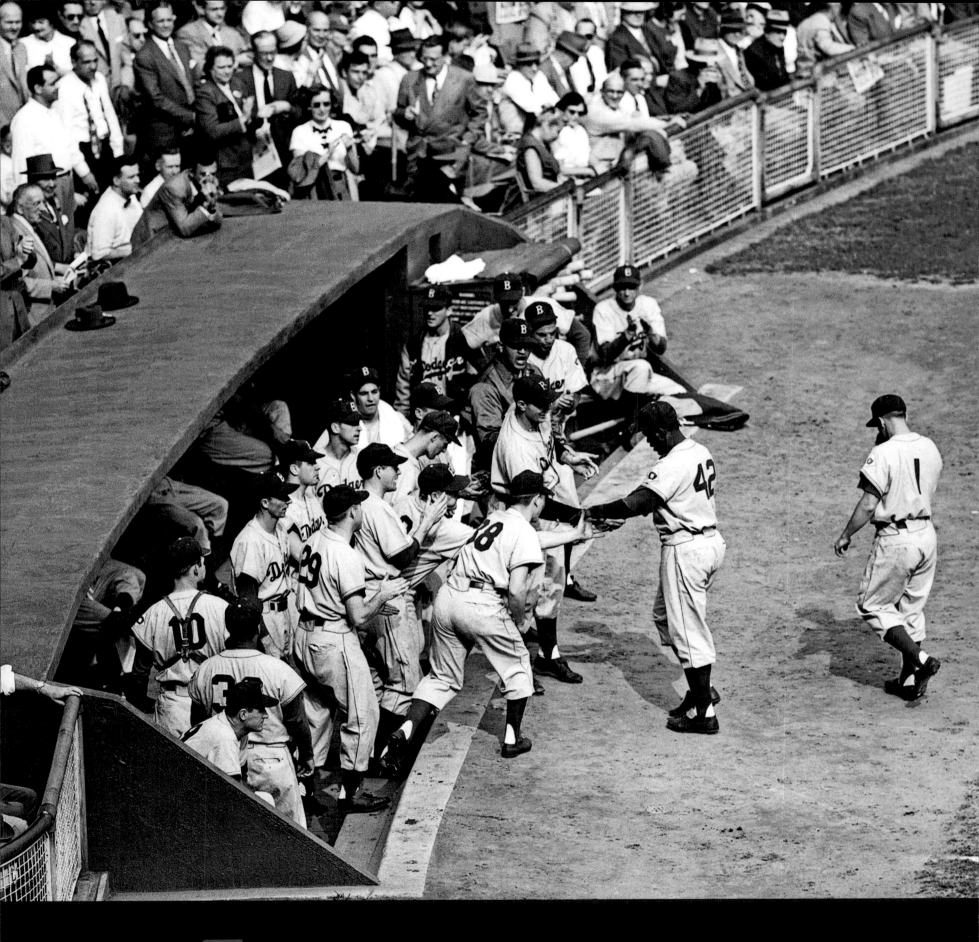

FOUNDED 1884

4

THE DODGERS

" First as "Dem Bums" of Brooklyn, then as the progressive club that broke the sport's color line and finally as one of two teams (with the Giants) to tap the West Coast market, the Dodgers offer a panorama of American life in the 20th century. " —DICK FRIEDMAN

▸ SIX WORLD SERIES TITLES
▸ 15 HALL OF FAMERS

FOR ROY CAMPANELLA, the Dodgertown facilities and Branch Rickey's emphasis on fundamentals were exhilarating. "I never knew what a sliding pit was," he says. "To learn how to slide?" It was no wonder the Dodgers became known for producing the most fundamentally sound players in the game.

—*William Nack, SI, March 14, 1983*

IN VIN VERITAS

Six decades of Dodgers history have been given humble voice by Vin Scully, who became an institution in both a sport that loves its past and a city that resists it

BY RICHARD HOFFER

W *HEN I WAS A LITTLE boy, we lived in a fifth-floor walkup apartment in New York, and we had a big old radio on four legs, and there was a crosspiece to hold the legs together, and I was about eight or nine, and I would crawl under there with a pillow . . .*

The memory is worn smooth in the retelling, wrought perfect after all this time. How much time, 75 years? A little less. . . . a*nd my head would be directly underneath the loudspeaker, and it didn't make any difference, the sporting event. In those days there was only football really, no baseball, but I could be listening to Georgia–North Carolina, Texas-Alabama, and here's this kid in New York curled under a radio and somebody would score a touchdown. . . .*

The delivery is run-on, of course, the broadcaster's trick for building drama, capturing the immediacy of the event. Punctuation is avoided, as if the slightest pause would give the listener enough excuse to tune away. . . . a*nd the crowd would go bananas and the roar would come down and it would just engulf me. It was like water out of a showerhead.*"

The timbre remains refreshingly thin, though not fragile, the syrupy tenor as rich as ever, the cadences doing as much of the work as the actual vocabulary. How many generations have gone to sleep to that sugary soundtrack? Almost 60 years in a Dodgers radio booth, the last 50 in Los Angeles, starting in the Coliseum, but mostly in Chavez Ravine. Speaking of the Coliseum: Back in '58, when the Dodgers moved to Los Angeles and had to play in that converted football stadium, anyone sitting 80, maybe 90 rows from the field couldn't tell the difference between a squeeze bunt and a grand slam. The transistor radio had just been invented, so fans could summon that soothing voice, and it would issue from thousands of little speakers, aisle to aisle, foul pole to foul pole, an odd and reverberating ambience that became a given. Just part of living in the Southland, like the sound of surf, or something.

In a city that is predicated on transience, that celebrates change so famously, there is little room for local institutions. Who would want to do something, the same one thing, for half a century? Somebody without ambition, that's who. Or without the talent to skip town altogether and go national. There is no patience for the parochial, the small-time, the stay-in-place, not in Los Angeles.

But here's Vin Scully, age 80, as suspiciously carrot-topped as the day in 1949 that Red Barber discovered him ("Red Skelton just called," Vin's somewhat excitable Irish mom told him), still calling games (most of them, anyway), not just a comforting presence or a relic but a professional reassurance, always finding the lyric to the singsong music of the night. It's gotten to the point, the man having stitched together all those seasons, all by himself, that when you say *Dodgers*, you really mean *Vin Scully*. Who else? Gary Sheffield? Not even Sandy Koufax.

How do you explain this endurance, this identification? He can't, won't. "I haven't done anything," he says, drawing the distinction (which many of his colleagues ignore) between the principals and himself. "I'm just sitting there." He's gotten this far without so much as a catchphrase; often he has disappeared from the action entirely. His first big call was Game 7 of the 1955 World Series, lefty Johnny Podres beating the New York Yankees. "Reese throwing to Hodges," he intoned. "Ladies and gentlemen, the Brooklyn Dodgers are the champions of the world." A long silence followed, lest he break down crying on air. (He was young then, and these boys were his boys.) Subsequent silences, for which he has become well-known, have been more purposeful, less emotional. "To this day," he says, "what I've always tried to do is call the play as quickly as I can, and then shut up, not only for the benefit of the listener but for my own joy of hearing the crowd roar."

Someone was smart enough to transcribe Scully's ninth-inning call of Koufax's perfect game in 1965—just an example—in all its press-box poetry. Every paragraph is seeded with drama ("A lot of people in the ballpark are starting to see the pitches with their hearts"), bringing you to the edge of your seat. ("He is one out away from the promised land, and Harvey Kuenn is coming up.") It was literature, all right, miraculously appropriate to the moment. ("Swung on and missed, strike two! It is 9:46 p.m.") Someone clocked him, too; he remained silent for 38 seconds after Kuenn fanned for the final out.

Of course, that wasn't the only humdinger. There was Kirk Gibson's shambling pinch-hit appearance in the opener of the 1988 World Series, set up when Scully ordered the NBC cameras to pan the Dodgers' dugout before the bottom of the ninth. ("Well, the man who's been there for the Dodgers all season, Kirk Gibson, is not in the dugout and will not be there for them tonight.") Gibson, iced up in the clubhouse, suddenly inflamed, and you know what happens next. After the game, Scully went down to then owner Peter O'Malley's box and realized all he could do was pace, goose-bumped.

Scully has made a life for himself, and for some millions of listeners, exploring the tension between the mundane and the heroic, maintaining a dignified presence all the while, no rooting for him, knowing just what to say and when to shut up. It's his voice alone that's been floating out over this impossible sprawl, 50 years, gathering everyone under the net, a couple of hours a night, enforcing a community of shared excitement, or puzzlement, or disappointment, Azusa to Temecula. ∎

5

THE RED SOX

FOUNDED 1901

❝The trade of Babe Ruth after the 1919 season plunged them, at least metaphorically, into an accursed 86-year purgatory. A championship in 2004, followed by a consolidating one in '07, however, were the hallmarks of a modern era of reformation in which the Red Sox, the erstwhile little Old Towne team, grew into a powerful national brand known as Red Sox Nation.❞ —TOM VERDUCCI

▸ SEVEN WORLD SERIES TITLES
▸ 10 HALL OF FAMERS

THE MOST emotionally powerful words in the English language are monosyllabic: love, hate, born, live, die, sex, kill, laugh, cry, want, need, give, take, Sawx. The Red Sox are, of course, a civic religion in New England. As grounds crew workers tended to the Fenway Park field last summer after a night game, one of them found a white plastic bottle of holy water in the outfield grass. There was a handwritten message on the side: GO SOX. The team's 2003 highlight film, punctuated by the crescendo of the walk-off home run by the Yankees' Aaron Boone in ALCS Game 7, was christened, *Still, We Believe*. "We took the wording straight out of the Catholic canon," club president Larry Lucchino says. "It's not, *We Still Believe*. Our working slogan for next year is *It's more than baseball. It's the Red Sox*."

—Tom Verducci, SI, December 6, 2004

Manny Ramirez bats in 2001, Fenway's 90th season.

FOUNDED 1882

Pete Rose, Joe Morgan and Johnny Bench won two titles.

" They've played in the same city for 132 seasons and they've had virtually the same logo since 1913. There's a lot to be said for constancy. Not to mention their world titles, the Big Red Machine—and Ted Kluszewski. " —DAVID BAUER

EVERYONE FROM Joe DiMaggio to Joe Garagiola had been asked to compare the Reds to the memorable teams of the past. . . . A team should be measured by what it accomplishes in its own time. The 1976 Reds will never play the '27 Yankees, but they sure knocked the starch out of the '76 Yankees.

—Ron Fimrite, SI, November 1, 1976

THE REDS

► FIVE WORLD SERIES TITLES, 10 NL PENNANTS
► 10 HALL OF FAMERS

THE TIGERS

FOUNDED 1901

" The team, which forged its identity with the hot intensity of Ty Cobb and solidified it with the cool brilliance of Hank Greenberg, has won 11 total pennants (fourth in the American League). Detroit has produced some of the game's most exceptional feats: Denny McLain's 31 wins in 1968 (the Tigers won it all that year) and their astounding 35–5 start to the '84 season (when they won it all again). " —KOSTYA KENNEDY

▸ FOUR WORLD SERIES TITLES
▸ 10 HALL OF FAMERS

AT THE END of last season General Motors decided it could no longer afford to sponsor the fountain over the centerfield fence at Comerica Park, which shoots great plumes into the air whenever a Tiger hits a home run. The fountain is the most valuable piece of advertising space in the stadium, and two corporations quickly expressed interest in taking GM's place. One offered to pay $1.5 million for three years. Mike Ilitch, the Tigers' owner, considered the offer seriously. Then he rejected it in favor of a deal that would pay him nothing at all. Ilitch kept the General Motors name where it was, free of charge, and added the Ford and Chrysler logos on each flank, over the message: THE DETROIT TIGERS SUPPORT OUR AUTOMAKERS.

—*Lee Jenkins, SI, September 28, 2009*

No pitcher has won 30 in a season since McLain.

PHOTOGRAPH BY WALTER IOOSS JR.

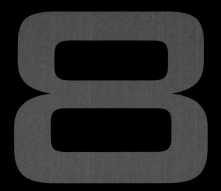

THE CUBS

FOUNDED 1876

❝ "No franchise has suffered more—the Lovable Losers have endured black cats, the Billy Goat, and Steve Bartman—but how many franchises have more tradition and lore? ❞ —ALBERT CHEN

▸ 16 PENNANTS, TWO WORLD SERIES WINS
▸ 14 HALL OF FAMERS

WILLIAM PETERSEN, the Chicago-born star of the TV show *CSI*, is a Chicago sports fan of such intensity that he once left the film set of *Manhunter* in Atlanta and flew to Washington, D.C., just so he could watch the Bears play on TV. He is a Cubs fan and is on the April cover of *Men's Journal*, sitting at a bar with other rabid Cubs nuts. "It's all about Fergie Jenkins and Ernie and Ron Santo," Petersen says. "A tie to your childhood." And of course dislocation makes the tie grow stronger. "I sit here in Los Angeles," says Petersen, "and it's just a wasteland. In Chicago you have elements to contend with. Here it's 76 degrees, it's perfect. And you know what? It sucks." That's a Chicago sentiment. That's where the empathy for the '69 Cubs comes from. Hey, folks, we know how scrawny Don Kessinger suffered in that September heat. Hey, I once lost my car in a snowdrift. Kessinger was nearly a skeleton by Labor Day.

—*Rick Telander, SI, April 7, 2003*

Wrigley and Ernie Banks (near right) are Cubs treasures.

PHOTOGRAPHS BY WILLIAM R. SMITH (LEFT) AND HY PESKIN

9

THE BRAVES

" The Braves are one of two surviving charter members of the National League (with the Cubs) and the only franchise to win the World Series while representing three cities—Boston, Milwaukee and Atlanta. "—DAVID SABINO

▸ 17 PENNANTS, THREE WORLD SERIES WINS
▸ 11 HALL OF FAMERS

THE BRAVES were what almost every company aspires to be—a hugely successful enterprise that maintained a Mom & Pop feel (even though for a time Pop was Ted Turner and Mom was Jane Fonda). Their games were beamed across the nation on TBS, but they still fit right in with the reruns of *The Andy Griffith Show*.

—*Phil Taylor, SI, January 26, 2009*

Hank Aaron and Eddie Mathews went south in 1966.

FOUNDED 1882

The "We Are Family" team enjoyed its 1979 Series win.

PHOTOGRAPH BY AP

10

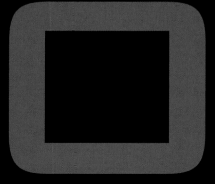

THE PIRATES

"The current streak of losing seasons makes it easy to forget the team's rich history: Pittsburgh played in the first World Series, and is home to icons spanning the game's history—from Wagner to Mazeroski to Clemente to Stargell." —STEPHEN CANNELLA

▸ FIVE WORLD SERIES TITLES
▸ 13 HALL OF FAMERS

PITTSBURGH traditionally has the loosest, most uproarious dressing room in baseball. "Brotherly love is so much bull," says infielder Phi Garner. "You get 25 guys together . . . are you going to tell me they will all love each other? But this team gets it out into the open and brings everybody into it."

—Roy Blount Jr., SI, April 9, 1979

10 THE

BEST DESIGNATED HITTERS, SLUGGERS, BASE RUNNERS AND DEFENSIVE PLAYERS

IN 1969 SI REPORTED ON AN EXPERIMENT TAKING PLACE IN THE INTERNATIONAL LEAGUE WITH A NEW POSITION CALLED THE DESIGNATED HITTER. ONE OF THE TEAMS PARTICIPATING WAS THE ROCHESTER RED WINGS, AN ORIOLES FARM TEAM MANAGED BY CAL RIPKEN SR. (THEN JUST KNOWN AS CAL RIPKEN). THE TEAM'S DH WAS 26-YEAR-OLD DAVE CAMPBELL, WHO LIKED THE NEW POSITION. AFTER STRIKING OUT, HE COULD SIT ON THE BENCH AND THINK ABOUT WHY HE STRUCK OUT, INSTEAD OF HAVING TO GO FIELD. "BEING THE DESIGNATED HITTER," CAMPBELL OBSERVED, "MADE ME START TO THINK A LITTLE MORE ABOUT HITTING."

THE OPPORTUNITY TO SPECIALIZE, CAMPBELL SEEMED TO REALIZE, WAS A RARE LUXURY IN THE GAME OF BASEBALL. IT GOES TO THE CLOSER, THE LATE-INNING DEFENSIVE OR BASE-RUNNING REPLACEMENT, BUT TO FEW OTHERS.

IN COMPOSING OUR LISTS OF THE BEST AT VARIOUS ASPECTS OF BASEBALL—SLUGGING, BASERUNNING, DEFENSE, AS WELL AS THE DH—WE FOUND THAT THE TRULY GREAT AT ONE SKILL WERE USUALLY VOTED TO BE AMONG THE BEST EVER AT THEIR POSITIONS. EVEN PLAYERS WHO ONLY APPEAR IN THIS SECTION—LUIS APARICIO, FOR EXAMPLE, OR SLIDIN' BILLY HAMILTON—EARNED VOTES AT THEIR POSITION LISTS. IT'S NICE TO BE ABLE TO DO ONE THING, BUT IT'S BETTER WHEN YOU CAN DO IT ALL.

10 THE

BEST DESIGNATED HITTERS

1 | ### EDGAR MARTINEZ
Martinez was a power threat and a two-time batting
champion whose .356 average in 1995 was the highest
for an AL righty in 56 years. —KOSTYA KENNEDY

2 | ## FRANK THOMAS
The 6' 5" "Big Hurt" is one of only nine players with both a .300 career average (.301) and more than 500 career home runs (521). —TOM VERDUCCI

3 | ## DAVID ORTIZ
Discarded by the Twins after six seasons as an oft-injured first baseman, Ortiz found a home anchoring a formidable Boston lineup at DH. —DAVID SABINO

4 | ## PAUL MOLITOR
Molitor is one of just four players to have at least 3,000 hits, a lifetime .300 batting average and 500 stolen bases. —DICK FRIEDMAN

5 | ## DON BAYLOR
No MVP winner has played as many games at DH as the 65 that Baylor appeared in during his 36-home run, 139-RBI MVP season of 1979. —KOSTYA KENNEDY

HAROLD BAINES

The quiet slugger was an RBI machine with a flair for the dramatic: He's tied for seventh alltime in walkoff home runs, with 10. —ALBERT CHEN

7 | JIM THOME
The mighty-haunched Thome has slammed 612 homers (seventh alltime) and is fifth in taters per at bat (one every 13.76). —DICK FRIEDMAN

8 | HAL MCRAE
In many ways he was the original DH, but he was no prototype: McRae was a small, crafty hitter with power who earned the position some respect. —DAVID BAUER

9 | CHILI DAVIS
Only four switch-hitters surpassed Davis's total of 350 home runs. And his calming clubhouse influence was as valuable to teams as his bat. —STEPHEN CANNELLA

10 | TRAVIS HAFNER
The ideal DH: lefty bat, no natural position, but a pure hitter and a born slugger. And he has the perfect nickname—Pronk. —DAVID BAUER

10 THE
BEST SLUGGERS

1 | BABE RUTH
Babe's career .690 slugging percentage (dwarfing Ted Williams, second at .634) provides statistical verification for the quintessential slugger. —KOSTYA KENNEDY

2 | TED WILLIAMS
Teddy Ballgame might have topped the Bambino's 714 dingers had he not lost nearly five prime years to military service. —DICK FRIEDMAN

3 | HANK AARON
Six foot, 180 pounds: tiny by slugger standards. Instead of brawn, Aaron did it with an uncanny instinct for outthinking the pitcher. —DAVID BAUER

4 | JIMMIE FOXX
In his 58 home run season, he lost two long balls to rainouts and five more were reportedly kept in play by a screen in St. Louis's Sportsman Park. —DAVID SABINO

5 | LOU GEHRIG
Gehrig had 400 total bases in a season five times (no one else did so even four times) and slugged .632 for his career (behind only Ruth and Williams). —TOM VERDUCCI

6 | WILLIE MAYS

Mays missed the better part of two seasons serving in the Army early in his career, and he still amassed 660 home runs. —ALBERT CHEN

7 | ## BARRY BONDS
Nearly half (49%) of his hits were for extra bases; no one else with at least 2,900 hits has gone for extra bases more than 41% of the time. —STEPHEN CANNELLA

8 | ## MICKEY MANTLE
The most powerful switch-hitter in history hit balls so deep that the Yankees invented the term "tape-measure home run" for him. —ALBERT CHEN

9 | ## ALBERT PUJOLS
The most feared righthanded hitter of his generation set a Fall Classic standard with his three-homer, six RBI night in the 2011 World Series. —ALBERT CHEN

10 | ## HANK GREENBERG
An imposing, 6' 4" strongman with a roundhouse swing who slugged .605 for his career, the seventh best percentage of all time. —TOM VERDUCCI

10 THE

BEST BASE RUNNERS

1 | RICKEY HENDERSON

Rickey Henderson put himself in his own league by swiping 49.9% more career bases than the man in second place, Lou Brock. —DAVID SABINO

266

2 | TY COBB

With no fear of risk and with sharpened spikes, Cobb made baserunning a true offensive weapon in a way that it isn't any more. —DAVID BAUER

3 | TIM RAINES

The Rock was blindingly fast, but his greatest trait was his smarts on the bases. He had an 84.6% success rate on steals for his career. —ALBERT CHEN

4 | LOU BROCK

He led the National League in steals eight times, including in 1974, when he swiped 118 bases, topping Maury Wills's old standard of 104. —DAVID SABINO

5 | WILLIE WILSON

In addition to his 668 steals, Wilson ran the bases aggressively enough to rattle defenses and smartly enough to avoid making outs. —STEPHEN CANNELLA

6

JACKIE ROBINSON
Jackie was safe on better than 86% of his steal attempts and he did his most powerful work coming down the third-base line. —KOSTYA KENNEDY

7 | WILLIE MAYS

Mays used his smarts to take extra bases even after the edge came off his speed. At age 40 he stole 23 bases while being caught just three times. —KOSTYA KENNEDY

8 | BILLY HAMILTON

"Sliding Billy" is one of three players with more runs than games, still holds the record for runs in a season (198) and ranks third alltime in steals (914). —TOM VERDUCCI

9 | COOL PAPA BELL

The Negro leaguer traveled the bases like wildfire, and with a daring recalled in tales of him scoring from first on a bunt. —DICK FRIEDMAN

10 | VINCE COLEMAN

Coleman had 110 swipes as a rookie in 1985, then stole 100 bases his next two seasons. No one since has reached the century mark. —ALBERT CHEN

1 | OZZIE SMITH
Acrobatic and with boundless range, the Wizard would create outs on balls that other shortstops couldn't fathom reaching. —DAVID SABINO

10 THE

BEST DEFENSIVE
PLAYERS

2 | ## BROOKS ROBINSON
Reds manager Sparky Anderson said of the third baseman, "If I dropped this paper plate, he'd pick it up on one hop and throw me out at first." —STEPHEN CANNELLA

3 | ## WILLIE MAYS
We all know the over-the-shoulder catch, but usually Mays glided to fly balls, cradling the easier ones and making difficult chances look easy. —DAVID SABINO

4 | ## JOHNNY BENCH
He won 10 Gold Gloves, and no wonder: Bench seemed born to play catcher, right down to the size of his massive hands. —STEPHEN CANNELLA

5 | ## ROBERTO CLEMENTE
He regularly fired bazookalike throws that made going from first to third a kamikaze mission. His 254 career assists lead all rightfielders. —DICK FRIEDMAN

271

6 | Omar Vizquel

The alltime leader in games played at shortstop has the highest career fielding percentage with at least 1,000 games played. —ALBERT CHEN

7 | JOE DiMAGGIO

He covered the vast meadow of the Yankee Stadium outfield with long, easy strides, improbably rendering the uncatchable caught. —KOSTYA KENNEDY

8 | KEN GRIFFEY JR.

The boyish enthusiasm of "the Kid" was never more apparent than when he reached over the outfield wall to deny a home run. —TOM VERDUCCI

9 | LUIS APARICIO

Little Louie made defense fun to watch. Was there a more memorable double-play combo than Aparicio and Nellie Fox? —DAVID BAUER

10 | MIKE SCHMIDT

Schmidt was amazingly quick and agile at 6' 2", giving him immense range. He won 10 Gold Gloves, including nine in a row. —DAVID BAUER

THE 10

Best Uniforms, Characters, Rivalries, Movies, Quotes, Records, SI Covers and the Full Results

IN PRESIDENTIAL ELECTIONS THE ARGUMENT AGAINST VOTING FOR A CANDIDATE WHO IS NEITHER DEMOCRAT NOR REPUBLICAN IS, "WHY WASTE YOUR VOTE?" YOU MIGHT BELIEVE DEEPLY THAT THE PERSON BEST EQUIPPED TO RUN THE COUNTRY IS, OH, DEREK JETER ("HE'S SO COOL UNDER PRESSURE!"), BUT YOU ALSO KNOW THAT IF YOU WRITE IN THE SHORTSTOP ON YOUR BALLOT, YOU WILL NOT BE VOTING FOR SOMEONE WHO MIGHT ACTUALLY WIN.

FOR THE LISTS IN THIS SECTION, OUR WRITERS KNEW THEIR WHIMS COULD RULE THE DAY, BECAUSE EACH LIST HERE COMES FROM ONE WRITER, AND THE CHOICES REPRESENT HIS OWN IDIOSYNCRATIC VIEWS. THAT'S APPROPRIATE HERE, GIVEN THAT MANY OF THESE TOPICS ARE INHERENTLY SUBJECTIVE. CREDIBLY CHOOSING THE TOP 10 FIRST BASEMEN, FOR EXAMPLE, DEMANDS SOME RECOGNITION OF HOME RUN TOTALS, HALL OF FAME STATUS AND SO FORTH. WHEN CHOOSING BEST MOVIES OR UNIFORMS, THOUGH, THE REASONING NEED NOT GO MUCH DEEPER THAN "I LIKED IT."

THE LIKES OF OUR PANELISTS IN ALL CATEGORIES ARE ACKNOWLEDGED IN OUR RESULTS PAGES AT THE END OF THIS SECTION. THERE YOU CAN SEE EVERY NAME THAT APPEARED ON A BALLOT. THE CATEGORY WITH THE MOST NOMINEES WAS BEST GAMES—WHICH MAKES SENSE. THAT'S THE CATEGORY MOST LIKELY TO BE BASED ON A PERSONAL MEMORY. THAT, REALLY, IS ABOUT WHAT YOU LIKE.

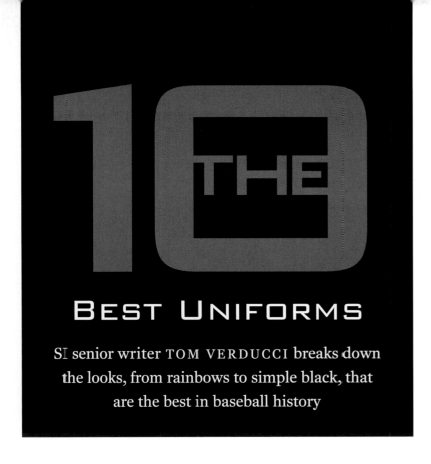

THE 10 BEST UNIFORMS

SI senior writer TOM VERDUCCI breaks down the looks, from rainbows to simple black, that are the best in baseball history

1. 1930 CARDINALS
It's hard to go wrong with any Cardinals jersey since the "birds-on-the-bat" design first appeared in 1922. But the '30 uniforms really nailed it. It was the first time the Cardinals put the "birds-on-the-bat" over "St. Louis" on the road unis. Nicknames are fine at home, but a team should display its city name when it travels. Moreover, the '30 Cardinals used socks with three designs, including a sharp white look at home that was set off by thin red and blue stripes. The hats featured red pinstripes outlining white panels above a red brim. Those cats were stylin'.

2. 1969 EXPOS
Simply beautiful, whether it was the home buttoned-down whites with a splash of piping on the sleeve or the blue-on-baby-blue roads. In its inaugural season the franchise debuted with a fresh take on a classic baseball uniform. The font for "expos" (love the humility with the lower case) seems to be Egizio Condensed, which was created by an Italian designer in the 1950s and is often associated with newspaper headlines.

3. 2012 ATHLETICS
Oakland defines the modern classic, starting with the 1969-71 look (before the beltless pants and pullover tops) in which they wore the "A's" logo on the chest of their cool vests. The Athletics updated the look in 2012 with the addition of the knockout gold jersey with the "A's" on the chest and the elephant mascot on the left sleeve.

4. 1970 PIRATES
For one year only, the Pirates found the sweet spot between classic and modern. In 1957, Pittsburgh adopted the vest for its home and road uniforms, set off by stirrups with gold stripes. It was a sharp look that held through '69. Then in '70, as they moved into Three Rivers Stadium, they retained classic vest look, but also became the first team to wear pullover polyester jerseys and beltless pants. The Pirates also introduced awesome mustard caps with a black brim that year. Alas, the transition was short-lived. The next year the Pirates ditched the belts and the vests to go all-polyester, and by '77 the team look had become a joke, including thick pinstripes and all-gold and all-black uniforms.

5. 1936 YANKEES
Babe Ruth never wore the interlocking "NY" as an active player with the Yankees. The team used the iconic "NY" from 1912 through '16, then ditched it. Ruth wore nothing but undecorated pinstripes at home during his entire Yankee career and road grays that said either "New York" or "Yankees" across the chest. In '36 the Yankees brought back the interlocking "NY" to the left chest, and one of the most famous uniforms in all the world was reborn.

6. 2011 PADRES
The Padres have been wearing military-inspired camouflage jerseys since 2000 (and on home Sundays as well as Memorial Day, Fourth of July and Labor Day since 2008), but they updated the jerseys in '11 with a "digital camouflage" pattern used by the Marines and known as MARPAT, for Marine Pattern. The look is powerful, but even better is the spirit of the uniforms. San Diego goes camo to honor the city's long association with the military.

7. 1919 WHITE SOX
No team has foisted more ugly uniforms upon the paying public than the Chicago White Sox, whose team colors changed from blue to red to black. But the 1919 White Sox, infamous for other reasons, did come up with a clean, classic look after years of messing around with all-blue uniforms, white pinstripes over blue and assorted other uniform daydreams. The logo with the "o" and "x" embedded inside the swirls of the large "S" on the chest first appeared in '12; in '19, without unnecessary embellishment, the logo highlighted the uniform. The White Sox never have looked better. Want to bet?

8. 1983 ROYALS
The Royals went to the power-blue road uniforms in 1973, but in '83 they made two significant upgrades: They ditched the pullover tops and beltless pants for the more traditional buttoned-down jerseys and belted pants, and they replaced the boring block "Kansas City" with the same "Royals" script that always has been featured on the home whites. Sadly, the Royals mothballed the powder blues in '92 in favor of the stock gray road unis.

9. 1952 DODGERS
The Royals cribbed from the classic look of the Dodgers, and why not? No home uniform looks more crisp and just so darn white than the sparkling uniforms of the Dodgers. The famous Dodgers script across the chest is essentially unchanged since 1938. But in '52 the Dodgers added the perfect finishing piece to the look: red numbers below the script on the front of the home uniform. The Dodgers were the first team to put numbers on the front.

10. 1975 ASTROS
Ah, yes, the Rainbow Uniforms. You are likely to find these uniforms on just as many "worst" lists as "best" lists—so daring are they even to this day. This is what happens when you hire an advertising agency, McCann Erickson, to "rebrand" a baseball franchise. Critics howled even in light of the Polyester Pullover Era that was dawning in baseball. But you know what? They are way cool—so cool that the 1975 Astros didn't bother with home and road uniforms. They wore this model, which included the first numbers placed on the pants leg, in the Astrodome and on the road. The look was supposed to mimic the flaming tail of the comet that graced the '65–74 Astros uniforms. It fit Houston's reputation as the cutting edge of space exploration. Though the Astros wore the Rainbows for 12 seasons, they wore the übercool orange hats with them home and away only for the first six of those seasons. And the '75 season was the only one in which the players' number was placed inside a white circle atop the rainbow on the back of the jersey. The '75 Astros uniform defined one of a kind.

1. 1930 CARDINALS

2. 1969 EXPOS

3. 2012 ATHLETICS

4. 1970 PIRATES

5. 1936 YANKEES

6. 2011 PADRES

7. 1919 WHITE SOX

8. 1983 ROYALS

9. 1952 DODGERS

10. 1975 ASTROS

10 THE

BEST CHARACTERS

SI senior editor KOSTYA KENNEDY chooses the men who lived the most strangely wonderful—and wonderfully strange—diamond lives

Fidrych posed with his *Sesame Street* counterpart.

1. MARK FIDRYCH, PITCHER
Big Bird sure carried on out there, grooming the mound, talking to the baseball, going into conniptions after most every pitch. The mania around him (built during his 19–9 rookie season of 1976) was short-lived but anyone who saw the bushy-haired Fidrych exulting after a win, pumping hands with teammates and umpires and cops, won't forget him.

2. MANNY RAMIREZ, OUTFIELDER
The play Ramirez once made in the outfield, catching a line drive, scampering up the wall to high-five a fan, then throwing back in to double up the runner? That's a kind of showman's genius.

3. CASEY STENGEL, OUTFIELDER/MANAGER
Of all the aphorisms produced by Stengelese none was more resonant than this: "The trick is growing up without growing old." Casey did that as well as anyone. When he managed the 1962 Mets at age 72, he reminded those covering the team that he'd "been in the game a hundred years."

4. BRIAN WILSON, RELIEF PITCHER
There was the Mohawk and then the bushy, unfathomably black beard that Giants fans copied in tribute. "Did you dye it?" he was asked. "No, it's tanned from day games," he said. Wilson emits a steady hum of inscrutable and entertaining quips. "I am completely insane," he once explained.

5. BILL LEE, LEFTHANDED PITCHER
"Whatever he want to do he do, whatever he want to say he say," is how former Red Sox teammate Luis Tiant described the Spaceman. Lee's engaging list of unorthodox practices and beliefs includes this explanation of why, during his playing days, he sprinkled marijuana onto his pancakes before going for a five-mile jog: "It made me impervious to gas fumes."

6. LEFTY GOMEZ, LEFTHANDED PITCHER
Once he called the Yankees' rookie shortstop Phil Rizzuto to the mound for no clear reason. "Just stand here," Lefty said. "Just think: Your parents can go home tonight and say that 40,000 people saw their little boy talking to the great Gomez."

7. RICKEY HENDERSON, OUTFIELDER
Rickey admired himself nude in the mirror before games and talked to himself on the field (sample comment: "Rickey, you're the best") and he once framed a $1 million bonus check instead of cashing it. When he homered to become baseball's leader in runs scored, he closed his trot by sliding into home plate.

8. LEO DUROCHER, INFIELDER/MANAGER
Not interested in being a nice guy, nor in finishing last, the Lip made headlines as a manager and also for his dalliance with actress Laraine Day. When they eventually married they once sent out a Christmas card in the form of a last will and testament.

9. BABE RUTH, OUTFIELDER
The furs he wore suited his mojo. The Babe stayed up late and had a spectacular fondness for women. "I like to live as big as I can," he said. For what he did and for the jolly way he did it, everyone loved the Babe.

10. BILL VEECK, OWNER
The man who brought us a midget pinch-hitter and Disco Demolition Night and an exploding scoreboard was ahead of his time. Who but Veeck, a smoker and an injured war veteran, would cut an ashtray into his own wooden leg?

1. YANKEES–RED SOX

Never mind that for most of their joint history, the Yankees have been the dominant team; baseball's Hatfields and McCoys can always find reason to hate each other. The rivalry doesn't just breed passion. It has produced some of the most memorable moments—Bucky Dent, Aaron Boone, Dave Roberts—in baseball history.

2. DODGERS–GIANTS

They've been feuding since the 19th century, when both were based in New York, and their moves to California in 1958 did nothing to bring a laid-back vibe to their meetings. (Juan Marichal and Johnny Roseboro made sure of that.) Throw in a few classic pennant/division races—1951, '62, 2004—and you have a rivalry for the ages.

3. CUBS–CARDINALS

How's this for evenly matched: Going into 2013, the Cubs had scored 10,088 runs in these teams' 2,306 meetings, the Cardinals 10,101. They've shared Rogers Hornsby, Lou Brock and Harry Caray—and a deep hatred for one another since the 1870s.

4. CARDINALS–BREWERS

They battled in the 1982 World Series, but the rivalry really got heated with a spate of beanballs and brawls in the 2000s. If fans in St. Louis and Milwaukee ever tire of debating which town is the true beer capital, baseball will keep their argument going.

5. YANKEES–DODGERS

Bronx vs. Brooklyn, New York vs. L.A.—these franchises could keep a rivalry humming on civic tensions alone. They've met in the World Series 11 times (the Dodgers have won just three) and have produced some of the most memorable moments in October history.

6. MONEYBALL BELIEVERS–NONBELIEVERS

Michael Lewis's 2003 book didn't just give a behind-the-scenes peek at the A's front office. It also sparked a culture war around this question: What's the best way to measure a player, with the eyes or through the numbers? The two sides may never agree.

7. JOE DIMAGGIO–TED WILLIAMS

The Yankees–Red Sox rivalry writ small. Fans measured the two California natives against each other throughout their careers. Their epic MVP battle in 1941—Williams batted .406, DiMaggio hit in 56 straight and walked off with the hardware—was a seasonlong tribute to the joy of watching great players try to one-up each other.

8. METS–YANKEES

It goes beyond their 2000 World Series showdown and even the Subway Series contests of interleague play. The Mets and Yanks battle daily for the hearts and minds of New Yorkers—and the city's back pages.

9. PHILLIES–METS

They've slugged it out in the NL East for decades, but the rivalry is at its most tense in the stands. Phillies-Mets, in September, with a playoff spot on the line is not for the faint of heart.

10. CUBS–WHITE SOX

Each franchise has been hapless for most of its existence, though the White Sox can brag that they beat the Cubbies in the 1906 World Series. But forget their records. The North Side vs. South Side tension feels like the reason interleague play was invented.

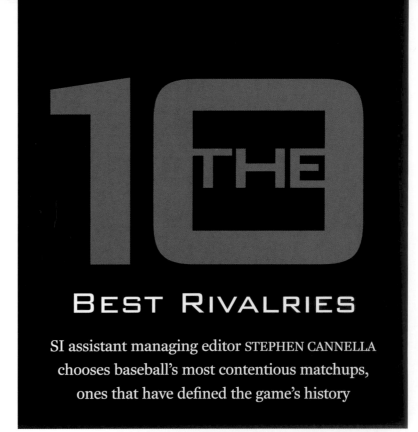

THE 10
BEST RIVALRIES

SI assistant managing editor STEPHEN CANNELLA chooses baseball's most contentious matchups, ones that have defined the game's history

Alex Rodriguez (left) and Jason Varitek lived the No. 1 rivalry in 2004.

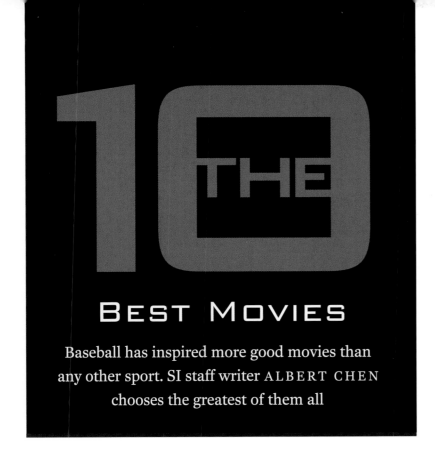

THE 10 BEST MOVIES

Baseball has inspired more good movies than any other sport. SI staff writer ALBERT CHEN chooses the greatest of them all

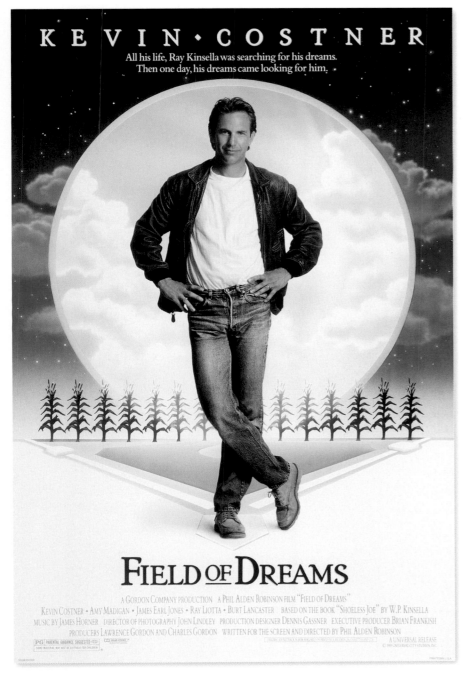

KEVIN · COSTNER

All his life, Ray Kinsella was searching for his dreams.
Then one day, his dreams came looking for him.

FIELD OF DREAMS

A GORDON COMPANY PRODUCTION · A PHIL ALDEN ROBINSON FILM "FIELD OF DREAMS"
KEVIN COSTNER · AMY MADIGAN · JAMES EARL JONES · RAY LIOTTA · BURT LANCASTER · BASED ON THE BOOK "SHOELESS JOE" BY W.P. KINSELLA
MUSIC BY JAMES HORNER · DIRECTOR OF PHOTOGRAPHY JOHN LINDLEY · PRODUCTION DESIGNER DENNIS GASSNER · EXECUTIVE PRODUCER BRIAN FRANKISH
PRODUCERS LAWRENCE GORDON AND CHARLES GORDON · WRITTEN FOR THE SCREEN AND DIRECTED BY PHIL ALDEN ROBINSON · A UNIVERSAL RELEASE

1) FIELD OF DREAMS (1989) — "If you build it, he will come," is the famous whispered line, though the most powerful moment comes when the son asks his dead father, standing before him in that Iowa cornfield, "Want to have a catch?" No film has ever captured why we love baseball so well. It's not perfect: it's a gooey fable that is at times too talky, and sure, it would have been nice if Ray Liotta, playing Shoeless Joe Jackson, could bat lefthanded—but the Best Picture nominee is a timeless celebration of the game in its purest form, the game we fell in love with as children.

2) BANG THE DRUM SLOWLY (1973) — The friendship between an ace pitcher named Henry Wiggen and a sweet, dim-witted catcher, Bruce Pearson, is at the heart of a film that is a slow burn but deepens beautifully, thanks to Robert DeNiro's turn as the dying backstop who has no business being in the big leagues. This is as true a baseball movie as there's ever been, one where the on-field action takes a back seat to rambling conversations in the clubhouse and the bonding that goes on off the field. The film, which Mark Harris adapted from his own novel, has humor and heart, and no movie has better portrayed the often-mundane daily life of a ballplayer. A line from Wiggen (Michael Moriarty) to Pearson at the end of their final summer together—"Everybody knows everybody's dying. That's why people are as good as they are"—breaks your heart.

3) BULL DURHAM (1988) — "The only church that truly feeds the soul, day in and day out, is the church of baseball," says that worshipper of the game, Annie Savoy, in Ron Shelton's sweet paean to minor league baseball, a movie that manages to avoid the clichés as it serves up classic characters: Tim Robbins's Nuke LaLoosh, the righthander with the million dollar arm and the five-cent head; Kevin Costner's Crash Davis, the Susan Sontag–quoting career minor leaguer at the end of the road; and Susan Sarandon's Savoy, the Durham Bulls' most faithful fan. *Bull Durham* is a great comedy with heart, but Shelton, a former Orioles minor leaguer, also gets all the baseball right: the characters, the language, the quirks and the heartbreak.

4) MONEYBALL (2011) — Who knew that a flick about sabermetrics could have so much soul? Who knew that a book about a baseball front office's pursuit of undervalued baseball players could make for such a rollicking drama on the silver screen? Beautifully shot, with a screenplay, by Steven Zaillian and Aaron Sorkin, that sizzles, the tale of baseball in the information age is smart and at times hilarious. What's surprising is that the adaptation of Michael Lewis's 2003 book is also so moving. Credit Oscar nominee Brad Pitt, who nails it as the manic and tortured A's G.M., Billy Beane.

5) SUGAR (2008) — This quiet film gives us a side of the game that's never been shown this convincingly on screen. Every moment we spend with Sugar, from the moment we meet him at a Dominican baseball academy, feels real. Filmmakers Anna Bolden and Ryan Fleck interviewed hundreds of players and former Dominican prospects for the movie, and it shows in the details, from the Dominican players' dorm room banter to their awkwardness when they arrive in the U.S., where ordering food at a diner during spring training is as challenging as facing a 98 mph fastball. The film doesn't follow the arc of the standard sports story, and has very little baseball in the unexpected final third of the movie, but Sugar's journey surely represents that of countless others who have come to a strange land to chase a baseball dream.

6) MAJOR LEAGUE (1989) — "Juuuuust a bit outside," says Mr. Baseball, Bob Uecker, of a wayward pitch from Ricky (Wild Thing) Vaughn, in a comedy that's right down the middle. Full of clichés and shamelessly formulaic, *Major League* is also the most eminently quotable baseball movie ever and the funniest. Writer-director David S. Ward turns the Cleveland Indians into a pack of unforgettable rejects, from the creaky-kneed veteran catcher from the Mexican League, Jake Taylor, to the speedster who can't hit, Willie Mays Hayes, and, of course,

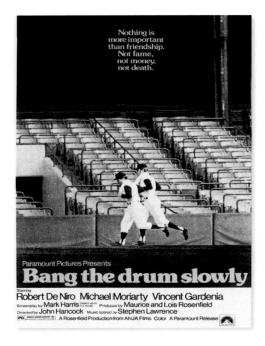

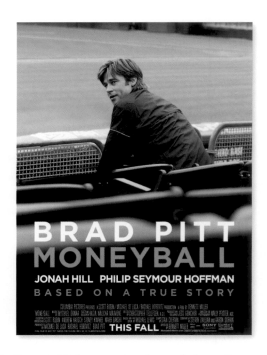

Charlie Sheen's Vaughn. When a packed Municipal Stadium gets and sings "Wild Thing" late in the movie, you just want to get up and join in.

7) THE NATURAL (1984) — It's a scene that's been played over and over on videoboards in just about every ballpark in America: Roy Hobbs bludgeoning the baseball into the lights to win the pennant for the New York Knights, his teammates dancing in a shower of sparks to the strums of Randy Newman's Oscar-nominated score. Hobbs, the farm boy with the magical bat Wonderboy, is one of the great American mythical characters, and Robert Redford slips into the role perfectly, alongside Robert Duvall as the smarmy sportswriter, Wilford Brimley as the weathered manager and Glenn Close as the childhood sweetheart. Barry Levinson's version of Bernard Malamud's dark novel has moments of sap and melodrama, but it effectively captures the romantic spirit of the game.

8) THE BAD NEWS BEARS (1976) — There are loads of big laughs, with Walter Matthau, the beer-swilling, pool-cleaning, former minor leaguer who's been assigned to coach a terrible Little League team, swaying, bleary-eyed and drunk in the dugout with his team down 26–0 in the first inning. But the movie that inspired dreadful sequels and spawned numerous (and mostly bad) kids sports films in the '80s and '90s gets to many truths about America's over-obsession with winning and the beauty of being on the losing side. It's hard not to fall in love with the Bears after they fall short in the final game and

shortstop Tanner Boyle belts out, "Take your trophy and shove it up your ass!" and then the kids celebrate on the field as if they'd just won the World Series.

9) EIGHT MEN OUT (1988) — There's a gritty authenticity to John Sayles's absorbing period drama about the 1919 Black Sox scandal, based on Eliot Asinof's definitive book on the darkest episode in baseball. The baseball is at times wobbly—John Cusack could have used a few more practice swings in the batting cages —but the portrayals of the White Sox, from David Strathairn as tortured pitcher Eddie Cicotte to Cusack as Buck Weaver, the film's tragic hero, are top-notch, and the villains (Clifton James as the greedy team owner Charlie Comiskey; Kevin Tighe as the bookie Joseph (Sport) Sullivan) are deliciously slimy. As historical movies about the national pastime go, this is as good as it gets.

10) A LEAGUE OF THEIR OWN (1992) — It's the reluctant, boozy manager, Jimmy Dugan, played by Tom Hanks, who gave us that famous line, "There's no crying in baseball," but in Penny Marshall's lovely homage to the All-American Girls Professional Baseball League, the heart of the film is the sibling rivalry between Dottie Hinson, the catcher for the Rockford Peaches, and her hurler sister, Kit Keller. Marshall brings to light an important part of baseball history— the formation of a women's league that lasted for 12 seasons—and makes the trip to 1943 a fun ride, thanks to the colorful bit characters played by Rosie O'Donnell, Madonna and Jon Lovitz.

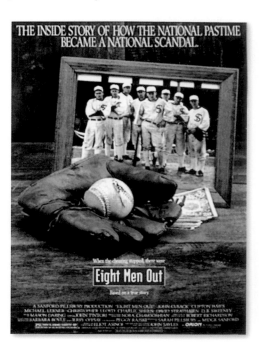

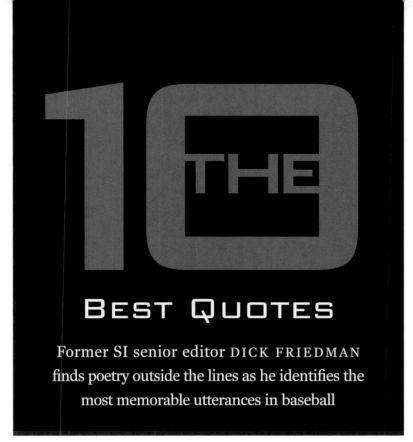

10

THE

BEST QUOTES

Former SI senior editor DICK FRIEDMAN finds poetry outside the lines as he identifies the most memorable utterances in baseball

Pitching great Satchel Paige was also eminently quotable.

1. "IT AIN'T OVER TILL IT'S OVER."
Arguably the most famous of the "Yogi-isms" that may or may not have been uttered by the Yankees Hall of Fame catcher Yogi Berra, it has saturated the culture so thoroughly that it became the title of a song by rocker Lenny Kravitz.

2. "NICE GUYS FINISH LAST."
Then skipper of the Brooklyn Dodgers, Leo Durocher made this Ayn Rand-esque declaration in a 1946 interview concerning the archrival New York Giants and their mild-mannered manager, Mel Ott. For the record, the take-no-prisoners Durocher may not have phrased the line exactly that way originally, but he was happy to claim the revised version. (Also: Ott, who hit 511 career homers, is a Hall of Famer and was a World Series winner as a player in 1933 with the Giants.)

3. "HIT 'EM WHERE THEY AIN'T."
The succinct plate philosophy served Wee Willie Keeler well; in a 19-year career (1892–1910) with four teams, the Hall of Fame rightfielder averaged .341, won two batting titles and had more than 200 hits in eight straight seasons beginning in 1894.

4. "SAY IT AIN'T SO, JOE!"
The anguished cry probably was not hollered at star outfielder Shoeless Joe Jackson in 1920 by a youthful fan when he was leaving the courthouse following grand jury testimony on the World Series–fixing charges involving the '19 Black Sox. Nevertheless, containing poetic truth, it has lived on, and even become the lyrical refrain of a tune by the rock band Weezer.

5. "WHAT THE HELL HAS HOOVER GOT TO DO WITH IT? BESIDES, I HAD A BETTER YEAR THAN HE DID."
Babe Ruth served up this riposte in Depression-ridden 1930 to reporters who noted that his salary of $80,000 was $5,000 higher than President Herbert Hoover's. (Babe's year: .345 with 46 home runs and 154 RBI).

6. "HE WAS SO FAST THAT HE COULD TURN OFF THE LIGHTS AND BE UNDER THE COVERS BEFORE THE ROOM GOT DARK."
This was how Satchel Paige classified the alacrity of centerfielder and base runner extraordinaire—and fellow Negro leagues legend—James (Cool Papa) Bell.

7. "I WOULD IF SHE WAS CROWDING THE PLATE."
The notoriously surly Hall of Fame righthander Early Wynn gave this reply when asked if he would throw at his mom on Mother's Day.

8. "TWO THIRDS OF THE EARTH IS COVERED BY WATER, THE OTHER ONE THIRD IS COVERED BY GARRY MADDOX."
Thusly did Harry Kalas, the longtime Phillies broadcaster, colorfully extol the range of the club's ground-eating centerfielder.

9. "CAN'T ANYBODY HERE PLAY THIS GAME?"
Known for his rambling and near-incomprehensible orations, Casey Stengel was shocked into pithy clarity in 1962 by his inept (40–120) New York Mets. (Managerial runner-up: "I managed good, but boy, did they play bad" was the classic lament of longtime minor league skipper Rocky Bridges.)

10. "YOU CAN'T SIT ON A LEAD AND RUN A FEW PLAYS INTO THE LINE AND JUST KILL THE CLOCK. YOU'VE GOT TO THROW THE BALL OVER THE DAMN PLATE AND GIVE THE OTHER MAN HIS CHANCE. THAT'S WHY BASEBALL IS THE GREATEST GAME OF THEM ALL."
This piece of wisdom was uttered by Orioles manager Earl Weaver, who was not considered infallible by all. His frequent antagonist, O's righthander Jim Palmer, once declared of the man who in his playing days was a career minor leaguer, "The only thing Earl knows about big league pitching is that he couldn't hit it."

1. LONGEST HITTING STREAK: JOE DIMAGGIO, 56

On July 17, 1941, Joltin' Joe's streak was snapped by the Indians, but on July 18 he began a new one, hitting in another 16 consecutive games. Amazingly, the iconic 56 wasn't the longest streak of his professional career; in 1933 he hit in 61 consecutive games for the Pacific Coast League San Francisco Seals.

2. MOST CONSECUTIVE GAMES PLAYED: CAL RIPKEN JR. 2,632

After catching Lou Gehrig at 2,130 games, Ripken went 23.6% farther before finally sitting one out. Accentuating his durability is his unofficial record of 8,243 consecutive innings played from 1982 to '87.

3. MOST GRAND SLAM HOME RUNS HIT IN ONE INNING: FERNANDO TATIS, 2

When the Cardinals third baseman set his mark in on April 23, 1999, the flip side was that Dodgers righthander Chan Ho Park picked up one of the game's most dubious distinctions, and a mark just as unlikely to be broken: Park became the only man in baseball history to allow two grand slams to the same batter in a single inning. Tatis's eight RBIs that day are also a record for a single inning.

4. MOST PITCHING DECISIONS, CAREER: CY YOUNG, 827

He reached this total by also being the owner of two other unbreakable marks: most wins (511) and losses (316). Only 41 pitchers in baseball history have made more appearances than Young had decisions.

5. MOST TIMES ON BASE, CAREER: PETE ROSE, 5,929

During his 24-year career baseball's alltime hits leader (4,256) reached base safely 330 more times than the next man on the list, Barry Bonds. To put Rose's record into perspective, Derek Jeter, the active leader at 4,506 going into the 2013 season, would have to average well over 200 times on base each year until age 45 to tie him.

6. MOST CAREER NO-HITTERS: NOLAN RYAN, 7

Baseball's alltime strikeout king matched Sandy Koufax's old record of four no-no's in the 1970s then proceeded to add one more in the '80s and two in the '90s. His no-hitters spanned 18 years and three teams.

7. MOST STOLEN BASES, CAREER: RICKEY HENDERSON, 1,406

After breaking Lou Brock's career record on May 1, 1991, Henderson went onto play 1,466 more games and steal 468 more bases, a number that by itself would tie him for 43rd alltime.

8. MOST COMPLETE-GAME SHUTOUTS IN ONE DAY: ED REULBACH, 2

What makes Reulbach's 1908 feat even more impressive is that his Cubs were in the thick of a late-September pennant chase with the Giants when he blanked the Superbas 5–0 in the morning and 3–0 in the afternoon at Brooklyn's Washington Park.

9. HIGHEST SINGLE-SEASON PERCENTAGE OF A TEAM'S WINS BY A PITCHER: STEVE CARLTON, 1972 PHILLIES, 45.8%

Wins aren't always the best indicator of a pitcher's prowess, but in this case the statistic is spot-on. Playing for baseball's arguably worst team that year, Carlton won 27 of 37 decisions (.730) for a club that otherwise won 32 of 125 (.256). Remove his 1.97 ERA from the team total and it jumps from 3.66 to 4.22.

10. HIGHEST CAREER BATTING AVERAGE WITH THE BASES LOADED: PAT TABLER, .489

This is an unofficial record, but over 12 seasons from 1981 to '92 the infielder came to the plate with the bases jammed 88 times and hit safely 43 times, driving in 108 runs in the process. His work in the clutch is especially impressive given that his overall .282 batting average ranks 577th alltime among qualifiers.

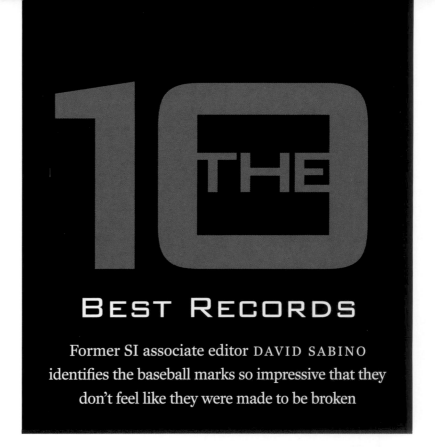

THE 10 BEST RECORDS

Former SI associate editor DAVID SABINO identifies the baseball marks so impressive that they don't feel like they were made to be broken

Ryan threw four of his seven no-hitters for the Angels.

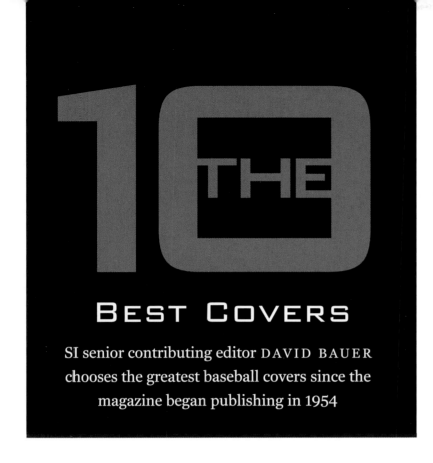

THE 10 BEST COVERS

SI senior contributing editor DAVID BAUER chooses the greatest baseball covers since the magazine began publishing in 1954

1 | JUAN MARICHAL
August 9, 1965

1. LATIN CONQUEST OF THE BIG LEAGUES — This cover turns a rare double play: It's both beautiful and meaningful. Neil Leifer's photo dramatically illustrates the memorable leg kick of Juan Marichal, set against alternating bands of color that give the shot a painterly quality. And Marichal serves to introduce a significant '60s story about the burgeoning impact of Latin players in professional baseball. This cover is very much a personal favorite; as I type, I sit beneath a framed print of this photograph hanging on my office wall.

2. SI DEBUT ISSUE — Yes, SI's first cover is on this list in part for history's sake, but also because it's gorgeous. The majestic scale, the liquid quality of the light, the classic slugger's swing (with the lovable detail of the hugely blurred bat) make for a captivating image by renowned photographer Mark Kauffman. For the 1954 debut of a new U.S. sports magazine it makes perfect sense that the subject be baseball, then the unchallenged king of American games.

3. MANTLE'S DEATH — The cover ran just days after Mickey Mantle died. The photograph, from 1951, shows him as a Yankees rookie in all his youthful innocence—in stark and powerful contrast to his alcohol-ravaged condition at death. The cover, memorably, has no type at all, serving as a kind of tribute to the Mick's iconic stature. This, for me, is the quintessential face of baseball.

4. BOB HOPE — An irresistible choice because of the sheer oddity of it. And you've got to love the deadpan cover line that only adds to the incongruity of the photo. In truth the cover would have been less befuddling to those 1963 baseball fans who knew already that Bob Hope was a part owner of the Indians in his hometown of Cleveland. Not about to joke about his own team, the comedian chose an easier target of the times: "I like the Mets," cracked Hope. "But I like baseball too."

5. 715 — History, simply rendered. The photo of the new home run king, by Neil Leifer, captures the emotional combination of elation, exhaustion and relief as Henry Aaron concluded what had become a grueling and sometimes frightening quest to break Babe Ruth's record. For the caption, the historic number was all that needed to be said.

6. YOGI'S BACK! — A now famous (and often imitated) idea actually came about by accident. Photographer Walter Iooss Jr., was having no success getting a candid shot of Berra, who'd just returned as Yankees manager. "Every time I got near him, he'd get up and move," Iooss later recalled. "I just kept following him around taking pictures, mostly of his back." Proving that design is the residue of luck (with apologies to Branch Rickey), disaster was turned to triumph by its cover line.

7. A LOOK AT LEFTHANDERS — The appeal of this photo is, of course, the spectacular, idiosyncratic windup of Warren Spahn—note the contortions of his glove and his pitching hand. And somehow this man lasted for over 5,000 innings.

8. BASEBALL'S BEST CENTERFIELDER — Baseball pictures don't get much better than this: Curt Flood flying high into the hallowed ivy at Wrigley to make a spectacular catch in one of baseball's best rivalries—and the Cardinals, as usual, getting the better of the Cubs.

9. SEASON OF SURPRISES — A period piece and a great candid photograph. The sideburned, mustachioed Dick Allen (previously known as Richie) provides a fitting image for the swingin' '70s. Never a player to fall in line, Allen uses the dugout to practice his juggling. But the cover is made memorable by the defiant cigarette hanging from his lips.

10. HARDBALL — Randy Johnson was 6' 10", not pretty, threw 100-mph fastballs, and would finish his career tied for fifth alltime in batters hit by a pitch. He also had a nasty habit of glaring over the edge of his glove as he looked in for the catcher's sign. No hitter would admit it but, as this cover illustrated, he was scary.

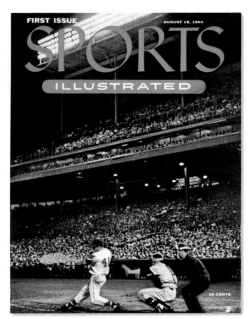

2 | EDDIE MATHEWS
August 16, 1954

3 | MICKEY MANTLE
August 21, 1995

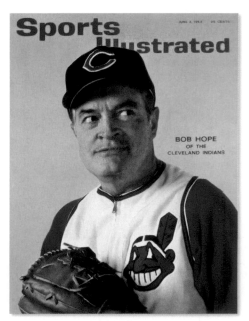

4 | BOB HOPE
June 3, 1963

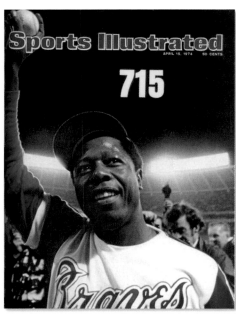

5 | HANK AARON
April 15, 1974

6 | YOGI BERRA
April 2, 1984

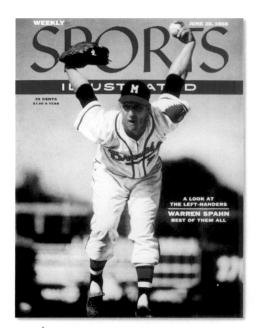

7 | WARREN SPAHN
June 25, 1956

8 | CURT FLOOD
August 19, 1968

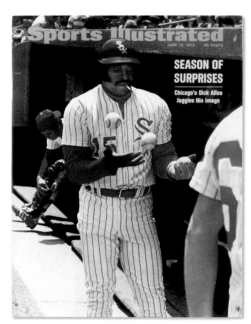

9 | DICK ALLEN
June 12, 1972

10 | RANDY JOHNSON
March 31, 1997

The Full Results

IF THEY WERE LISTED ON A PANELIST'S BALLOT, THEY MAKE IT HERE TOO, IN THIS FULL RANKING OF EVERYONE WHO RECEIVED A VOTE IN EVERY CATEGORY

FIRST BASE

1. LOU GEHRIG
2. ALBERT PUJOLS
3. JIMMIE FOXX
4. HANK GREENBERG
5. HARMON KILLEBREW
6. GEORGE SISLER
7. WILLIE MCCOVEY
8. EDDIE MURRAY
9. JOHNNY MIZE
10. MARK MCGWIRE
11. CAP ANSON
12. PETE ROSE
13. ERNIE BANKS
14. JEFF BAGWELL
15. ROD CAREW
16. BUCK LEONARD
17. ORLANDO CEPEDA
18. FRANK THOMAS

SECOND BASE

1. ROGERS HORNSBY
2. JOE MORGAN
3. EDDIE COLLINS
4. JACKIE ROBINSON
5. NAP LAJOIE
6. CHARLIE GEHRINGER
7. ROBERTO ALOMAR
8. RYNE SANDBERG
9. ROD CAREW
10. FRANKIE FRISCH
11. CRAIG BIGGIO
12. JOE GORDON
13. NELLIE FOX
14. JEFF KENT

THIRD BASE

1. MIKE SCHMIDT
2. GEORGE BRETT
3. EDDIE MATHEWS
4. WADE BOGGS
5. BROOKS ROBINSON
6. CHIPPER JONES
7. HOME RUN BAKER
8. RON SANTO
9. MIGUEL CABRERA
10. PETE ROSE
11. PIE TRAYNOR
12. JIMMY COLLINS
13. PAUL MOLITOR
14. ADRIAN BELTRE
15. RAY DANDRIDGE
16. ALEX RODRIGUEZ
17. SCOTT ROLEN
18. AL ROSEN
19. BUDDY BELL

SHORTSTOP

1. HONUS WAGNER
2. CAL RIPKEN JR.
3. DEREK JETER
4. OZZIE SMITH
5. ERNIE BANKS
6. ARKY VAUGHAN
7. ALEX RODRIGUEZ
8. BARRY LARKIN
9. ROBIN YOUNT
10. JOE CRONIN
11. LUKE APPLING
12. LUIS APARICIO
13. LOU BOUDREAU
14. ALAN TRAMMELL
15. POP LLOYD

CATCHER

1. JOHNNY BENCH
2. YOGI BERRA
3. ROY CAMPANELLA
4. IVAN RODRIGUEZ
5. JOSH GIBSON
6. MICKEY COCHRANE
7. CARLTON FISK
8. BILL DICKEY
9. MIKE PIAZZA
10. GARY CARTER
11. GABBY HARTNETT

LEFTFIELD

1. TED WILLIAMS
2. STAN MUSIAL
3. RICKEY HENDERSON
4. BARRY BONDS
5. AL SIMMONS
6. CARL YASTRZEMSKI
7. JOE JACKSON
8. WILLIE STARGELL
9. LOU BROCK
10. MANNY RAMIREZ
11. GOOSE GOSLIN
12. PETE ROSE
13. ED DELAHANTY
14. TIM RAINES
15. JOE MEDWICK
16. ALBERT BELLE
17. MONTE IRVIN
18. ZACK WHEAT
19. BILLY WILLIAMS

CENTERFIELD

1. WILLIE MAYS
2. TY COBB
3. JOE DIMAGGIO
4. MICKEY MANTLE
5. TRIS SPEAKER
6. KEN GRIFFEY JR.
7. DUKE SNIDER
8. OSCAR CHARLESTON
9. KIRBY PUCKETT
10. COOL PAPA BELL
11. ANDRUW JONES
12. EARL AVERILL
13. HUGH DUFFY
14. BILLY HAMILTON
15. ANDRE DAWSON
16. CARLOS BELTRAN
17. MAX CAREY
18. EDD ROUSH
19. JIMMY WYNN

RIGHTFIELD

1. BABE RUTH
2. HANK AARON
3. FRANK ROBINSON
4. ROBERTO CLEMENTE
5. REGGIE JACKSON
6. MEL OTT
7. PETE ROSE
8. AL KALINE
9. TONY GWYNN
10. PAUL WANER
11. ICHIRO SUZUKI
12. HARRY HEILMANN
13. VLADIMIR GUERRERO
14. SAM CRAWFORD
15. WILLIE KEELER
16. DAVE WINFIELD
17. MARTIN DIHIGO

RIGHTHANDED PITCHER

1. WALTER JOHNSON
2. CHRISTY MATHEWSON
3. CY YOUNG
4. GREG MADDUX
5. TOM SEAVER
6. GROVER CLEVELAND ALEXANDER
7. ROGER CLEMENS
8. PEDRO MARTINEZ
9. BOB FELLER
10. BOB GIBSON
11. SATCHEL PAIGE
12. ROY HALLADAY
13. NOLAN RYAN
14. JUAN MARICHAL
15. JUSTIN VERLANDER
16. KID NICHOLS
17. ED WALSH

LEFTHANDED PITCHER

1. SANDY KOUFAX
2. LEFTY GROVE
3. WARREN SPAHN
4. RANDY JOHNSON
5. WHITEY FORD
6. STEVE CARLTON
7. CARL HUBBELL
8. EDDIE PLANK
9. TOM GLAVINE
10. LEFTY GOMEZ
11. BABE RUTH
12. VIDA BLUE
13. HAL NEWHOUSER
14. RUBE WADDELL

RELIEF PITCHER

1. MARIANO RIVERA
2. DENNIS ECKERSLEY
3. ROLLIE FINGERS
4. RICH GOSSAGE
5. TREVOR HOFFMAN
6. HOYT WILHELM
7. BRUCE SUTTER
8. DAN QUISENBERRY
9. LEE SMITH
10. BILLY WAGNER
11. JOHN FRANCO
12. JOE PAGE
13. JOHN SMOLTZ
14. TUG MCGRAW
15. TROY PERCIVAL
16. TOM HENKE

17. FIRPO MARBERRY

18. ROY FACE

MANAGER

1. JOHN MCGRAW
2. JOE MCCARTHY
3. CASEY STENGEL
4. TONY LA RUSSA
5. EARL WEAVER
6. SPARKY ANDERSON
7. CONNIE MACK
8. BOBBY COX
9. JOE TORRE
10. WALTER ALSTON
11. MILLER HUGGINS
12. BILL MCKECHNIE
13. JIM LEYLAND
14. LEO DUROCHER
15. NED HANLON

GAME

1. 1975 WORLD SERIES, GAME 6 (FISK HOME RUN)
2. 1986 WORLD SERIES, GAME 6 (BUCKNER ERROR)
3. 1991 WORLD SERIES, GAME 7 (MORRIS-SMOLTZ DUEL)
4. 2011 WORLD SERIES, GAME 6 (FREESE HOME RUN)
5. 1960 WORLD SERIES, GAME 7 (MAZEROSKI HOME RUN)
6. 1986 NLCS, GAME 6 (16 INNINGS)
7. 1951 NL PENANT SERIES (THOMSON HOME RUN)
8. 2001 WORLD SERIES, GAME 7 (GONZALEZ HIT)
9. 1956 WORLD SERIES, GAME 5 (LARSEN PERFECT GAME)
10. 2003 NLCS, GAME 6 (BARTMAN GAME)
11. 1947, APRIL 15, JACKIE ROBINSON'S DEBUT
12. 1978 AL EAST TIE-BREAKER (RED SOX-YANKEES)
13. 1988 WORLD SERIES, GAME 1 (DODGERS-A'S)
14. 2003 ALCS, GAME 7 (RED SOX-YANKEES)
15. 1992 NLCS, GAME 7 (PIRATES-BRAVES)
16. 1985, JULY 4 (BRAVES-METS, 19 INNINGS)
17. 2004 ALCS, GAME 4 (RED SOX-YANKEES)
18. 1924 WORLD SERIES, GAME 7 (SENATORS-GIANTS)
19. 1959, MAY 26, HARVEY HADDIX 12 PERFECT INNINGS
20. 1963, JULY 2, GIANTS-BRAVES (SPAHN-MARICHAL DUEL)
21. 1986 ALCS, GAME 5 (RED SOX-ANGELS)
22. 1908, SEPT. 23, MERKLE'S BONER (GIANTS-CUBS)

23. 1999 NLCS, GAME 5 (METS-BRAVES)
24. 1997 WORLD SERIES, GAME 7 (MARLINS-INDIANS)
25. 1933, JULY 2, GIANTS-CARDINALS DOUBLE-HEADER (DUAL 1-0 SHUTOUTS)
26. 1995 ALDS, GAME 5 (YANKEES-MARINERS)
27. 1979, MAY 17 PHILLIES-CUBS (PHILS WIN 23-22)

BALLPARK

1. FENWAY PARK
2. WRIGLEY FIELD
3. YANKEE STADIUM
4. EBBETS FIELD
5. ORIOLE PARK AT CAMDEN YARDS
6. TIGER STADIUM
7. AT&T PARK
8. POLO GROUNDS
9. DODGER STADIUM
10. COMISKEY PARK
11. ASTRODOME
12. CROSLEY FIELD
13. PNC PARK
14. SHIBE PARK
15. FORBES FIELD
16. SAFECO FIELD

FRANCHISE

1. YANKEES
2. CARDINALS
3. GIANTS
4. DODGERS
5. RED SOX
6. REDS
7. TIGERS
8. CUBS
9. BRAVES
10. PIRATES
11. ORIOLES
12. A'S
13. PHILLIES
14. TWINS
15. INDIANS
16. MONARCHS
17. GRAYS
18. METS
19. WHITE SOX

DESIGNATED HITTER

1. EDGAR MARTINEZ
2. FRANK THOMAS
3. DAVID ORTIZ
4. PAUL MOLITOR
5. DON BAYLOR
6. HAROLD BAINES
7. JIM THOME
8. HAL MCRAE
9. CHILI DAVIS
10. TRAVIS HAFNER

Ichiro Suzuki received votes in three categories.

11. DAVE WINFIELD
12. BILLY BUTLER
13. JOSE CANSECO
14. CLIFF JOHNSON
15. RAFAEL PALMEIRO
16. ANDRE THORNTON
17. BRIAN DOWNING

SLUGGER

1. BABE RUTH
2. TED WILLIAMS
3. HANK AARON
4. JIMMIE FOXX
5. LOU GEHRIG
6. WILLIE MAYS
7. BARRY BONDS
8. MICKEY MANTLE
9. ALBERT PUJOLS
10. HANK GREENBERG
11. JOSH GIBSON
12. HARMON KILLEBREW
13. JOE DIMAGGIO
14. KEN GRIFFEY JR.
15. MARK MCGWIRE
16. JOHNNY MIZE
17. MIKE SCHMIDT
18. RALPH KINER
19. MANNY RAMIREZ
20. STAN MUSIAL
21. REGGIE JACKSON
22. JIM THOME

BASE RUNNER

1. RICKEY HENDERSON
2. TY COBB
3. TIM RAINES
4. LOU BROCK
5. WILLIE WILSON
6. JACKIE ROBINSON
7. WILLIE MAYS
8. BILLY HAMILTON

9. COOL PAPA BELL
10. VINCE COLEMAN
11. JOE MORGAN
12. PETE ROSE
13. DAVEY LOPES
14. MAURY WILLS
15. ICHIRO SUZUKI
16. DEREK JETER
17. ROBERTO ALOMAR
18. BO JACKSON
19. MINNIE MINOSO
20. DEION SANDERS
21. CARLOS BELTRAN
22. BARRY LARKIN
23. LUIS APARICIO
24. EDDIE COLLINS
25. CHASE UTLEY
26. HONUS WAGNER

DEFENSIVE PLAYER

1. OZZIE SMITH
2. BROOKS ROBINSON
3. WILLIE MAYS
4. JOHNNY BENCH
5. ROBERTO CLEMENTE
6. OMAR VIZQUEL
7. JOE DIMAGGIO
8. KEN GRIFFEY JR.
9. LUIS APARICIO
10. MIKE SCHMIDT
11. BILL MAZEROSKI
12. IVAN RODRIGUEZ
13. ICHIRO SUZUKI
14. ROBERTO ALOMAR
15. ANDRUW JONES
16. KEITH HERNANDEZ
17. CAL RIPKEN JR.
18. AL KALINE
19. ADRIAN BELTRE
20. GREG MADDUX
21. GRAIG NETTLES

Our fifth-ranked rightfielder signed for the Oakland Coliseum fans in 1969.

THIS BOOK DRAWS FROM THE EFFORTS of a legion of SPORTS ILLUSTRATED writers, reporters and photographers who have covered the major leagues since the magazine's inception in 1954; BASEBALL'S GREATEST would not have been possible without them. Special thanks also goes to Don Delliquanti, Nate Gordon, Gabriella Baetti, Karen Carpenter, Prem Kalliat, Joe Felice, George Amores and Will Welt for their generous help; to Geoff Michaud, Dan Larkin and the rest of the SI Imaging group for their tireless work on this project; and to the Baseball Hall of Fame for their valued assistance in all things archival.

TIME HOME ENTERTAINMENT: Jim Childs, PUBLISHER; Steven Sandonato, VICE PRESIDENT, BRAND & DIGITAL STRATEGY; Carol Pittard, EXECUTIVE DIRECTOR, MARKETING SERVICES; Tom Mifsud, EXECUTIVE DIRECTOR, RETAIL & SPECIAL SALES; Joy Butts, EXECUTIVE PUBLISHING DIRECTOR; Laura Adam, DIRECTOR, BOOKAZINE DEVELOPMENT & MARKETING; Glenn Buonocore, FINANCE DIRECTOR; Megan Pearlman, ASSOCIATE PUBLISHING DIRECTOR; Helen Wan, ASSISTANT GENERAL COUNSEL; Ilene Schreider, ASSISTANT DIRECTOR, SPECIAL SALES; Susan Chodakiewicz, SENIOR BOOK PRODUCTION MANAGER; Anne-Michelle Gallero, DESIGN & PREPRESS MANAGER; Michele Bové, BRAND MANAGER; Alex Voznesenskiy, ASSOCIATE PREPRESS MANAGER; Stephanie Braga, ASSISTANT BRAND MANAGER; Stephen Koepp, EDITORIAL DIRECTOR

PHOTO CREDITS

COVER: FRONT (left to right, from top): John G. Zimmerman, Walter Iooss Jr., Bettmann/Corbis, Chuck Solomon, John G. Zimmerman, Jed Jacobsohn, V.J. Lovero, Fred Kaplan, Walter Iooss Jr., James Drake, Ralph Morse/Time Life Pictures/Getty Images, Damian Strohmeyer, John Iacono, John D. Hanlon. **BACK** (left to right, from top): Neil Leifer, John Iacono, Hy Peskin, Neil Leifer, Ronald C. Modra, Ozzie Sweet, Walter Iooss Jr., Neil Leifer, John Kenney, J.B. Forbes, Bettmann/Corbis, Ronald C. Modra, Lennox McLendon/AP, Chuck Solomon. **BACK FLAP:** Mark Kauffman.

SECTION OPENERS: Page 22: David E. Klutho; Page 33: Chuck Solomon; Page 54: John Biever; Page 68: Chuck Solomon; Page 82: Chuck Solomon; Page 98: Neil Leifer; Page 114: Anthony Neste; Page 128: Neil Leifer; Page 144: Lou Capozzola; Page 158: Herb Scharfman; Page 172: V.J. Lovero; Page 186: Lennox McLendon/AP; Page 200: Al Tielemans; Page 220: Warren Wimmer/Icon SMI; Page 238: Milo Stewart/National Baseball Hall of Fame; Page 256: Stephen Green; Page 274: Al Tielemans.

ADDITIONAL CREDITS: Page 7: Bettmann/Corbis; Page 8: Bettmann/Corbis; Page 9: David E. Klutho; Page 258: David Liam Kyle; Page 259: (left to right, from top): David Bergman, Stephen Green, Tom Lynn, John Iacono; Page 260: William R. Smith; Page 261: Dennis Wierzbicki/USA Today Sports, Mickey Pfleger, Scott Halleran/Getty Images, John W. McDonough; Page 262: Mark Rucker/Transcendental Graphics/Getty Images; Page 263 (left to right, from top): John G. Zimmerman, Neil Leifer, Bettmann/Corbis, National Baseball Hall of Fame; Page 264: John G. Zimmerman; Page 265 (left to right, from top): Al Tielemans, Neil Leifer, David E. Klutho, Charles M. Conlon/TSN/Icon SMI; Page 266: Ronald C. Modra; Page 267 (left to right, from top): Charles M. Conlon/Sporting News Archive/Getty Images, Ronald C. Modra, Herb Scharfman, Heinz Kluetmeier; Page 268: Ralph Morse/Time Life Pictures/Getty Images; Page 269 (left to right, from top): Robert Riger/Getty Images, Transcendental Graphics/Getty Images, National Baseball Hall of Fame/MLB Photos/Getty Images, Sportschrome; Page 270: Tony Tomsic; Page 271 (left to right, from top): Tony Triolo, AP, Tony Triolo, Focus on Sport/Getty Images; Page 272: John Biever; Page 273 (left to right, from top): TSN/Icon SMI, John Biever, Bettmann/Corbis, Mickey Pfleger; Page 277 (left to right, from top): AP, John F. Jaqua, Bill Nichols/AP, Walter Iooss Jr., AP, John W. McDonough, Underwood & Underwood/Corbis, Anthony Neste, Hy Peskin, John D. Hanlon; Page 278: Lane Stewart; Page 279: Damian Strohmeyer; Page 280: Universal Pictures/Everett Collection; Page 281 (left to right, from top): Everett Collection, Orion Pictures/Everett Collection, Sony Pictures, Paramount Pictures/Everett Collection, Paramount Pictures/Photofest, Orion Pictures/Everett Collection; Page 282: AF; Page 283: John G. Zimmerman; Page 284: Neil Leifer; Page 285 (left to right, from top): Mark Kauffman, George Silk, Mark Kauffman, Neil Leifer, Walter Iooss Jr., Marvin E. Newman, Herb Scharfman, John Iacono, Walter Iooss Jr.; Page 287: Darren Carroll; Page 288: AP.

ENDPAPER BACKGROUNDS: FRONT AND BACK SPREADS: John W. McDonough; **FRONT SINGLE:** Gary Bogdon; **BACK SINGLE:** John Biever.

It's one of the greatest pitching performances in Series history: Twins warhorse Jack Morris took the ball to start Game 7 against the Braves, looking like he could pitch forever. He almost did. Ten innings later he got Atlanta's Terry Pendleton to ground out to shortstop, the final out he needed before pinch hitter Gene Larkin singled home the game's only run in the bottom of the 10th to give Minnesota a world title. In the championship bedlam, Verducci didn't even get a chance to record Larkin's name and hit on his scorecard.

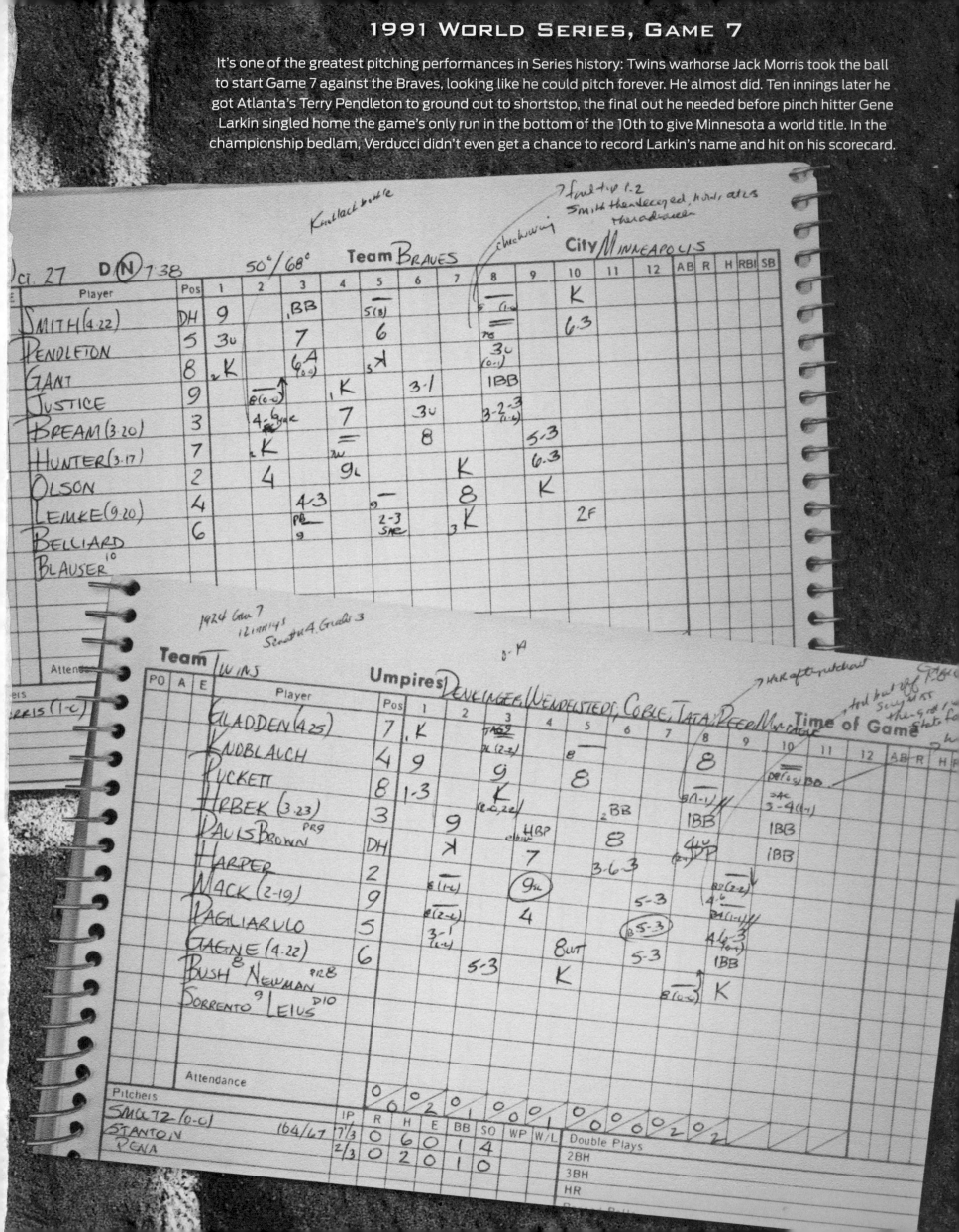

Team Mets

Date Oct. 22 D (N) 8:05   49°

Attendance 56,059

A	E	Player	Pos	1	2	3	4	5	6	7	8	9	10	11
		Perez	9	K		3U			E1		6-3	7		
		Alfonzo	4	K-3			HBP		8			HR		
		Piazza	2	4-3			3F		7L	7		1-U-2		
		Ventura	5		1-3		K			WP(U) 7		7W		
		Zeile	3		6		6-4				8 K 2	7		
		Agbayani	7		K			6-3			1-3	1-6-2 FC		
		Harris	DH		K			5-3				4-3 HR 3		
		Payton	8			K		5-3		7 K	9 K K			
		Bordick Hamilton	6				6							
		Abbott DG												

	1	2	3	4	5	6	7	8	9	10	11
	0	0	1	0	0	0	0	0	1 0 5	5	
	0	0	1	0	0	0	0				

Pitchers	IP	R	H	E	BB	SO	WP	W/L	Double Plays
Clemens	112	8	0	2	0	0	9		W	2BH
Nelson		0	3	3	3	0	0			3BH
Rivera	18-15	1	2	2	2	0	1			HR
										Passed Balls